I Am My Language

T0163475

I Am My Language

DISCOURSES OF WOMEN & CHILDREN
IN THE BORDERLANDS

Norma González

THE UNIVERSITY OF ARIZONA PRESS
TUCSON

First paperbound printing 2005
The University of Arizona Press
© 2001 The Arizona Board of Regents
All rights reserved

∞ This book is printed on acid-free, archival-quality paper.
Manufactured in the United States of America

06   05   6   5   4   3   2

Library of Congress Cataloging-in-Publication Data
González, Norma.
I am my language : discourses of women and children in the
borderlands
/ Norma González.
p. cm.
Includes bibliographical references and index.
ISBN-13: 978-0-8165-1893-7 (cloth : alk. paper)
ISBN-10: 0-8165-1893-9 (cloth : alk. paper)
ISBN-13: 978-0-8165-2549-2 (pbk: alk. paper)
ISBN-10: 0-8165-2549-8 (pbk: alk. paper)
1. Sociolinguistics—Arizona—Tucson.   2. Mexican American
families—Arizona—Tucson—Language.   3. Mother and child—
Arizona—Tucson—Language.   4. Language and culture—
Arizona—Tucson.   5. Education and state—Arizona—Tucson.
I. Title.
P40.45.U5 G66 2001
306.44'09791'776—dc21   00-012672

Publication of this book is made possible in part by a grant from the
Provost's Author Support Fund of the University of Arizona.

To my mother, Mina Cárdenas,

and the memory of my father, José Manuel Cárdenas

I am my language. Until I can take pride in my language,
I cannot take pride in myself.

—Gloria Anzaldúa,
Borderlands/La frontera: The New Mestiza

Contents

Acknowledgments   xiii

Introduction   xv

1. TUCSON: A PLACE IN THE BORDERLANDS   3
  The Borderlands   6
    The Artificial Line   7
    Hegemony and Resistance   8
    The Ambiguity of "Mexican" Tucson   9
    Borderlands as Metaphor   10
    Borderlands as Analytical Tool   12

2. LAS FAMILIAS   15
  The Discarding of Paradigm   18
  Methods and Participants: The How and the Who   19
    Confidentiality of Data   22
    Escobedo Family   23
    Linares Family   24
    Gallardo Family   24
    Martínez Family   25
    Cisneros Family   26
    Aguilar Family   28
    Salazar Family   28
    Robles Family   29
  The Pilot Study   30
    Gómez Family   30
    Gamboa Family   31
  Interviewing   32

3. When the Facts Won't Stay Put:
Finding Emotion in All the Wrong Places   33

4. The Hearts of the Children: Emotion, Language,
and Identity   45
Emotion as Examinable   45
Pushing Emotion beyond Sociocultural Competence   48
The Emotion of Linguistic Input   52
The Emotion of Minority Status   56
Disambiguation and the Construction of Selfhood   59
A Metaphor for Language Use: The Dialogical Staircase,
an Interactional Double Helix   60
Disambiguation and Self-Authorship   63
Diacritica   64
The Tucson International Mariachi Conference:
Musical Discourse and Performed Identities   67
"Structures of Feeling"   70

5. Negotiating Ideologies across Social Memories   72
Women and Language   72
Iris Gallardo   77
Raquel Salazar   82
Maricela Benavides   86
Gender Ideologies and Bailes Folklóricos   92
Leticia's Dance Studio   92

6. Testimonios of Border Identities:
"Una mujer acomedida donde quiera cabe"   97
Native-born and Immigrant Households   97
Cisneros Family   101
Language and Cross-Border Experiences   102
Personhood in Language Use   103
Testimonios of Immigrant Women   106
Señora Hernández   106
Señora Ortiz   114
The Fracturing of Gender Ideologies   125

7. HOUSEHOLD LANGUAGE USE: THE PUSH AND THE PULL   129
  Centripetal and Centrifugal Forces in Language Use   130
    Household Discourse   132
      Breakfast Table Conversation   133
      The Bent Glasses Story   139
      The Gómez Family   144
    The Ties That Bind   149
    Television and Telenovelas   151
    Homework and Language   153

8. WHERE'S THE CULTURE?   167
  Latinos and Culture   167
  Culture and "Multicultural Awareness"   168
  Processual Approaches to Culture   170
  Culture in the Borderlands   171
  If Not Culture, Then What?   172
  Language and Culture   173
  From "Language and Culture" to Language Ideologies   175
    Contested Language Ideologies within the
    Borderlands   175

9. BEYOND THE "DISUNITING" OF AMERICA:
  IMPLICATIONS FOR SCHOOLING AND PUBLIC POLICY   179
  Implications for Educational Public Policy
  and Schooling   180
  The Dialectics of the Centripetal and the Centrifugal   188
  Weaving the Threads Together   190
    Dialogism within the Sociohistoric   192

Notes   199

References   201

Index   215

Acknowledgments

This is a book about mothers and children, and I would be remiss if I did not begin with an acknowledgment of the mothers and children in my life. My own mother, Guillermina (Mina) Carrasco Cárdenas, has always been the anchor in my life, and her deep love of learning and her passion for reading instilled in me a curiosity about the wide and complicated world, and about how other people thought about these things. As a mother and now a grandmother, she delights in making children laugh and can find meaning in their simplest words. My "other" mother, my mother-in-law, came later into my life. Josefina Valenzuela González passed away in 1994, but her spirit is very much with her children, grandchildren, and great-grandchildren. Many times when I felt overwhelmed by the sheer magnitude of putting this book together, I thought of her as a widow raising thirteen children. The image of her struggling against the adversities that befell her has helped me to put things in perspective.

In many ways, all I have ever learned, I have learned from my children. With them, I have experienced motherhood in many of its forms. I have been a divorced mother, a working mother, a soccer mom, a mother in a nuclear family, a mother in a blended family, a stay-at-home mother, a mother of a child with special needs, a stepmother, and now a mother-in-law. When I married my husband, Rodolfo, I had two children, Eric and Nicole, from a previous marriage. He had two sons, Ruy and Alexis. We soon added our own two daughters, Briana and Nadia, to our family. To my husband and children, I express my deepest appreciation for their unwavering love and support in bringing this book to closure. To my brother and sister-in-law, José Manuel and Alice

Cárdenas, I express my heartfelt thanks for expert computer knowledge and long-standing emotional support.

I am also deeply indebted to my colleagues in the Bureau of Applied Research in Anthropology (BARA) at the University of Arizona. Director Tim Finan has been the epitome of supportive collegiality. I am also grateful for the support of the University of Arizona College of Social and Behavioral Sciences in offering me a sabbatical leave. Also, the University of Arizona Provost's Author Support Fund provided much needed financial assistance.

I owe a special debt to two colleagues who, above all others, have been instrumental in helping me along my professional path. Carlos Vélez-Ibáñez has been a mentor and friend who helped me to define myself as an anthropologist. Luis Moll has, for many years, guided me through the complexities of academia.

I am also grateful to those who have read drafts of this book and given me the benefit of their insightful comments. Richard Ruiz and Jane Hill have given me invaluable suggestions; Jay Rochlin helped me to find my own voice; and René Galindo and Javier Tapia gave me the benefit of careful readings and long conversations. I am especially grateful to Jacqueline Messing for her deep interest in the topics in this book and for her persistence in making sure that this book was written.

I am indebted to Susan Philips for helping me start on the road to studying language socialization and to Ana Celia Zentella for being who she is.

I also owe thanks to Chris Szuter, University of Arizona Press editor and current director, for her patience and confianza.

I am grateful to Arte Público Press of Houston, Texas, for allowing the reprint of the poem "Legal Alien" by Pat Mora. Also, I appreciate Lawrence Erlbaum Associates, Sage Publications, and the American Anthropological Association for allowing the use of previously published material (cited more fully in the notes). I also want to acknowledge Gloria Anzaldúa, whose eloquent words from *Borderlands/La frontera: The New Mestiza* inspired the title of this book.

Last, but certainly not least, I am grateful to the families, women, and children who invited me into their homes and into their lives. It is my humble hope that I have presented their words in a respectful manner.

Introduction

JANUARY EIGHTH

Isabel Allende writes that she always begins her books on the eighth of January. I begin to write on this day hoping for an ineffable connection. Her work resonated with me when I first read *House of the Spirits,* yet I am mystified as to why her images tug at me. My reading of her self-hood is that it was forged as a South American of European descent and of the privileged class. Her world (although couched in terms of genteel poverty) included servants, trips abroad, and prestigious family ties, and is far removed from the arid desert borderland strip of Tucson, Arizona, that is my backdrop. No sociedad here, at least not one to which I am privy. Yet her evocations haunt me. They hint at memories I have never lived, essences at once familiar and strange. Why? What binds Latinos and Latinas as Latinos? What does it mean to be a Latina?

The word *Latino* itself crumbles under its own ambiguity. Adopted as the current most "politically correct" form of reference, it is all-inclusive, and because of this very inclusiveness, it is rendered nearly meaningless. Chosen as an antidote to the government census–sanctioned and Eurocentric term *Hispanic,* it nevertheless collapses raza from the northwest coast of the United States to Tierra del Fuego, blurring fifth-generation Mexican-origin families in California, Salvadoreños, New Yoricans, mestizos, norteños, mulatos, indios, chilangos, etc., etc., etc. With one broad stroke of the pen, the vibrant cauldron of diversity is left to simmer, bereft of bothersome chunks that nuance and separate the lives of the professional and the farm laborer, the citizen and the undocumented, the political refugee and the corporate president. After all, doesn't the legacy of colonialism, neocolonialism, oppression, and marginalization elide contexts of local histories? Aren't we all cut from the same cloth? Why is there an implicit understanding that the "Hispanic community" speaks with one essentialized voice and that internal diversities are just blips on the screen?

This book is a study about mothers and their children. It is rooted in the words of common people in their everyday lives. Because the voices of ordinary women and children have been muted in the academic and public policy discussions of "what it means" to be Latina/o (Mexican, Hispanic, Chicana/o, Americanist, etc.), it is an attempt to hear their words. Despite the perceived "common language and culture" of Latinas/os, the particular and local history of this borderlands area reflects only a glimpse of the multifaceted prism of Latina/o identities. Even here in the beginning of the book, exactly how to refer to the "target population" is at issue. Although in academic parlance this work might be identified as a study of Chicana/o language, the nomenclature is not so unproblematic. Rather than imposing my own rubric on the voices I have recorded, I have chosen the term of the moment, *Mexican origin.* Because I echo Renato Rosaldo's (1989) call for a remapping of social analysis as coming not from academic imposition, but from the people themselves, I respect the self-identification of the women within the community. Preferring the terms *Mexican American, Hispanic, Mexican,* or *Mexicana,* my admittedly small sample produced little affinity for labeling themselves as Chicanas.

This study began as a study of language use. It was to be an attempt to describe the language socialization of Mexican-origin children in their households and to analyze the patterns that parents and other caregivers craft in orienting their children toward an understanding of the world that surrounds them. As the study progressed, it became more a tangled mesh of overlapping, impinging, and interacting weavings that fashioned a continuous epic of a people caught up in the intricacies of rearing their young to adulthood. Although I have used the framework of language socialization, it is not a linguistic study. Instead, I have used language as a window to peer into the complexities of life in the borderlands. I prefer to think in what Ana Celia Zentella (1997) terms an "anthro*political*" approach to language, one that connects language to complex issues of political economy and social identities.

During the course of my anthropological fieldwork, the sting of race his classmates, friends, and family, overwhelmed by grief, tried help-lessly to grasp for answers about where the violence comes from and where it will end. His friend, Gerardo, was quoted in the media: "He shouldn't have died. He was innocent. Bad people are supposed to die" (Pence 1996:1B). What of everyday life, though, as it hums along in neighborhoods? What happens within the walls of homes that is not reported in the "News at 10:00"? How does that everyday life come down the generations? Do Mexican people in Tucson feel like "others"? Or is "otherness" a construct from without, a facile attempt to explain away discontinuities?

The first few chapters of this book chronicle my attempt to come to grips with theory and method in the actual practice of how art and science are combined to create an ethnographic account. I have chosen a narrative format because I believe ethnography tells a story. I am also a character in this story. I am not a disinterested or neutral party. I have tried not to remain invisible in this text, without becoming intrusive. Yet I can offer only a partial perspective because my voice, with its own location, implies the exclusion of other voices. I do not have the whole picture. And yes, I am biased: these children are children of promise. They are not "at risk"; they are not disadvantaged. Their struggle is the struggle of children everywhere—to grow and develop in a world that is sometimes confusing, sometimes harsh, sometimes ambivalent, but within which they are uniquely endowed to grow.

In this book, I try to develop four main themes. The first is that to speak of language is to speak of our "selves." Language is at the heart, literally and metaphorically, of who we are, how we present ourselves, and how others see us. "I am my language," says the poet Gloria An-zaldúa (1987:59). *"El idioma, alma de las culturas"* (language, the soul of cultures) proclaims the theme of a banquet honoring the thirtieth anni-versary of bilingual education in southern Arizona. But what if a person has more than one language? Is there a neat overlay of language on identity, and do we shift our identities as we shift our languages? How do multiple languages interpenetrate and reconstruct multiple identities of women and children? More importantly, what identities do children construct for themselves when they use languages in particular ways? The ineffable link of language to emotion, to the very core of our being, is one of the ties that bind children to a sense of heritage. Access to more than one semiotic system helps children explore the infinite permutations of the inner self and its relationship to the outside world. Language is said to be the light of the mind, and our illumination is magnified by multiple beacons exposing unseen corners. The interweaving of language, emotion, and selfhood is a confluence that I attempt to navigate. To deny children a powerful tool for developing their unexplored potential by failing to expose them to multiple semiotic systems is to truncate their eventual development and derail their limitless possibilities. There is a saying that *"El que habla dos idiomas vale por dos."* (The person who speaks more than one language is worth two people.) Our accretive language abilities can multiply the dimensions of our self.

But what about Latinos who have had their Spanish erased through English-only schooling? Can one be Latina/o without speaking Spanish? How do Mexican-origin English-dominant children foreground a linguistic identity? I suggest that the ties that bind are laced with Spanish inflections, linking social memory to a subaltern counterdiscourse of personhood.

The second theme I explore has to do with the borderlands and with women and children's experiences of hybridity. Borderlands women, for themselves and for their children, must constantly negotiate and redefine the paths they will tread. These parents at the borderlands crossroads draw on multiple "repertoires of identity" (Kroskrity 1993) within which persons can ascribe alternate identities in order to craft new cultural practices. Through the complex dynamics of resistance, incorporation, and accommodation, within the constructs of structure and agency, many of the women in this book have struggled to generate an ethos, at times in direct contradiction to their own upbringing, within which they hope their children will flourish. Past and present mesh to give a new vibrancy and vitality to tradition and ritual. The emblems of this tinkering in the community are evidenced as traditional quinceañeras (the coming-out celebration of a fifteen-year-old young woman) give way to a procession of low-rider cars. It is evident as wax and parchment paper replace corn husks in tamales. It is evident as family clan gatherings are replaced by computer link-ups (Vélez-Ibáñez and Greenberg 1992). Within a poststructuralist subjectivity that is "precarious, contradictory, and in process, constantly being reconstituted in discourse each time we think or speak" (Weedon 1987:33), it is evident as both children and parents alter and modify their linguistic and nonlinguistic environment. Yet, the allegoric border crossers within the borderlands belie the geopolitical reality of two nation-state powers meeting at a recognizable and concrete division. In chapter 1, I argue that the physical presence of the border profoundly influences the practices and ideologies of Mexican-origin women and children.

A third theme surfaces because I am an applied anthropologist who works in the area of anthropology and education, and I hope to write for an audience of educators. It is not enough to provide a theoretical and descriptive account of a topic and not provide some practical implications that derive from the work. Applied anthropology should be an "engaged anthropology" that is not content only to paint the portrait, but seeks to extend the brush strokes out of the picture frame and into the arena of public policy discussions. What can teachers, administrators, and other educators take from this study that can impact everyday classroom practices and public school policies?

I hope to illustrate how diversity within the borderlands can dismantle reductionistic ideas of how households work. But how can this awareness be translated into concrete and realistic pedagogical insights? For example, in chapter 7 where I deal with homework transcripts, it is evident that mothers have appropriated the language of the teacher in their interactions with their children. They have become surrogates for teachers, inverting the tradition of the teacher serving in loco parentis into the parent serving in loco magistro. This pattern illustrates how the traditional conceptualization of "parental involvement" is skewed toward the household's accommodating to the dominant discourses of the school, rather than a true partnership between parents and children. As both a parent and an educator, I found myself guiltily reflected in both the mother's quest for excellence for her children as inscribed in these routines as well as the educator's assumption that conformity is comfortably manageable. Rather than an indictment of either household practices or school practices, we must search for mutually educative processes that draw on the funds of knowledge that both households and schools possess.

The fourth theme is an attempt to push the traditional boundaries of "language and culture" that tend to assume a bounded and integrated system or worldview. It is hardly news to anthropologists that for the last fifteen years or so, there has been writing "against" culture, "beyond" culture (Gupta and Ferguson 1992), "critiquing" culture (Marcus and Fischer 1986), "revisiting" culture (Keesing 1994), putting "culture in motion" (Rosaldo 1989), examining the interstitial space for "locating" culture (Bhabha 1994) as well as the "breakdown" of culture (Fox 1995), and proclaiming the "demise" (Yengoyan 1986) of the culture concept (González 1999). Yet, although anthropologists may bemoan the essentialization and reification of bounded and shared cultural traits, the reality is that academic critical discourses have been slow to penetrate curricular practices in schools. Schools continue to operate on texts that emphasize the norms and customs that shape individual behavior and learning. However, if we focus on the interactions between people (often in unequal circumstances) we can expand our vision of what we have considered "culture" to include issues of power and legitimization, as well as the language practices that constitute these issues. Rather than subscribing to reductionistic ideas about "culture," I have attempted to present language use within a framework of "language ideologies." The term *language ideology* has been defined in numerous ways, but the most encompassing definition is presented by Kathryn Woolard. Language ideology, she writes, consists of "representations, whether explicit or implicit, that construe the intersection of language and human beings in a social world" (1998:3). Within this theoretical posture, language *within* social process is the focus. It goes beyond situating language as an individual construction within the brain of the learner, but predicates language use on historical, social, and political contexts of language learning. The language learner does not just learn only grammar, but also the levels of meanings and histories embodied within language use.

A focus on language ideologies gives us access to both a retrievable database in terms of texts, narratives, transcripts, and discourses, but also incorporates the added dimension of their contested and contesting ideological underpinnings. The narratives and transcripts presented in this book demonstrate the complexities of language and language use in contested territories. The centripetal and centrifugal forces of language use are both in play, and children's fluid use of distinct language domains illustrates the dynamism of children's own language ideologies.

I begin the book by situating the reader within Tucson, Arizona, sixty miles north of the U.S.–Mexican border. Conceptualizing this locale is critical for examining the ideological context of language use. It is said that a child's education begins a hundred years before he or she is born. We must go back a hundred years to begin to understand children's language use now.

I Am My Language

CHAPTER I

Tucson

A PLACE IN THE BORDERLANDS

As border citizens, this is our great challenge: to invent new languages capable of articulating our incredible circumstances.—Guillermo Gómez-Peña, *Border Culture*

I was born in Tucson, of parents who were also born in Tucson, so my roots run deep here. The school my youngest children attended is the same school that my grandmother, Soledad Bengoechea Paul, attended. She used to enjoy recounting how she had enrolled herself at the school by knocking at the school door in 1908 and telling the teachers that she wanted to register. They lived on Main Street, the early Mexican part of Tucson, after their arrival from Santa Barbara, Chihuahua, Mexico, and it was an easy walk to Davis School. She would see the children pass by on their way to school, but for some unexplained reason, her mother and aunts did not enroll her, prompting her to take matters into her own hands. On those days when we rummaged through her mementos, she would always pull out the one class picture she had preserved and would proudly tell me about some of her classmates, early settlers of the then-burgeoning town who later became local pillars of the community. She, in turn, became a laundress and seamstress, supporting three sons alone by washing and ironing other people's laundry. When I listened to her stories as a child, it never occurred to me to wonder why the success stories in her classroom were always Anglo and male. It was just the way things were.

It wasn't until many years later that I came to see that what people assume to be natural divisions in the way people live, work, and survive are actually deeply embedded in the local fabrics of ideologies and relationships of power. In 1983, as a researcher of primary census data, I began to work on the Mexican Heritage Project at the Arizona Historical Society, examining material from the 1900 and 1910 Tucson censuses. The collaborative efforts of several researchers were published in the book *Los Tucsonenses,* authored by Thomas Sheridan (1986). The experience was a turning point for me, for I learned the power of social science to dig beneath the surface of why things are the way they are. In her compelling recollection about the healing power of coming to terms with social theory, bell hooks recalls, "I came to theory desperate, wanting to comprehend—to grasp what was happening around and within me. Most importantly, I wanted to make the hurt go away. I saw in theory then a location for healing" (1994:59). I too found theory to be a salve that attempted to explain the inexplicable. With a simple look at raw numbers, the duality of the experience of living in Tucson at the turn of the century exploded in my face. How you led your life, where you lived, the job that you had spun around one factor: Were you Anglo or Mexican?

As *Los Tucsonenses* documents, even as early as the 1860s, data from census figures pick up the divisions in the occupational structure of Tucson. The proprietorial, white-collar, and skilled laboring classes were composed primarily of Anglos, whereas only 26 percent of all Anglo workers could be classified as unskilled. In contrast, 49 percent of the Mexican workforce earned their living as unskilled workers. By 1900, two clear markers of economic subordination were apparent in Tucson: residential patterns and occupational status revealed that most Mexicans in Tucson lived in a world of segregated barrios and worked at unskilled and blue-collar jobs. Although the 1900 census showed Mexicans constituting a majority of Tucson's inhabitants (54.7 percent), this statistic represented a decrease in the Mexican population from the 1880 census, owing in large measure to the decline of immigration from Mexico. Depressed economic conditions in southern Arizona meant that fewer Mexicanos were choosing to settle in Tucson. As Sheridan notes, although the population of Tucson remained predominantly Mexican until 1910, Tucson was soon overwhelmed by Anglo investors backed by national and international capital. Mexican ranchers were of contestation, and as Martínez notes, these regions "frequently depart from the norms of interior zones and . . . develop institutional patterns and interests quite separate from those of the centers of power. Isolation, weak institutions, lax administration, and a different economic orientation prompt people on the periphery to develop homemade approaches to their problems and unconventional means of carrying on mutually beneficial relationships across an international boundary" (1991:2).

In Tucson, a place in the borderlands, the processes of boundary formation have been central to local experience from the earliest days. When the boundary between the United States and Mexico was negotiated, the interests of Native Americans and Mexicans native to the U.S. border area were seen as inconsequential by their governments (Martínez 1991). Hence, the oft-repeated lament of many long-established families that they did not cross the border; the border crossed them.

The Artificial Line

In 1854, when the Gadsden Purchase officially included Tucson as part of the United States, the Arizona/Sonora ecological zone was defined more by terrain and geography than by political representation. The flow of goods (and perhaps population) throughout the region marked a pattern that was centuries old, as archeological evidence suggests Hohokam exchange with Mesoamerica from 300 B.C. (see Vélez-Ibáñez 1996:22–28 for an elaboration of this theme). The presence of a politically constructed 1,947-kilometer demarcation line between two nation-states did not stop the continuous movement of people, commodities, and exchange relationships. Because of its proximity to the border, the Tucson Mexican-origin population is continually in a state of flux in terms of both in-migration and out-migration. The communities of northern Sonora—for instance, Nogales, Magdalena, Caborca, Ímuris, Santa Ana, Agua Prieta, and Hermosillo—provide a continuous round of transborder exchange relationships. Children in Mexican-origin households in Tucson are presented with an array of relatives and products that emanate from the neighboring Mexican state. Trips to the border city of Nogales, Sonora, are the source of candy and toys for birthday parties and piñatas, galletas María (Mexican cookies), Lucas (a powdered treat), and gold bracelets for girls. Households with relatives in the Sonoran ranchos surrounding the urban centers often send children on weekend or summer breaks to live among the horses, goats, and chickens of a modest ranching lifestyle. In contrast to other Mexican-origin populations in the United States, households in the borderlands are involved in frequent and sustained physical contact within regional networks. Although other transborder communities maintain regular contact with their natal point of origin, the reality of proximity is ever present.

HEGEMONY AND RESISTANCE

Although the geographic frontier functioned in many ways as a balanced unit, there were early signs of differentiation between the United States side and *el otro lado*. As the economic gap between Mexican and Anglo communities widened in early Tucson, the relationships of dominance and subordination did not stand unopposed. Low-paying jobs and discrimination compelled the Mexican community to employ strategies of survival and resistance based on mutual reciprocity, nonmarket exchange, self-sufficiency, and cultural arts that affirmed a positive sense of self-identification. Patricia Preciado Martin (1983), in her highly evocative writings on life in the early barrios, describes the strands of mutual support in which produce from home gardens—chili, squash, watermelon, corn, tomatoes, beans, and wheat—were exchanged. When times were tough and wages low, people survived through pulling together.

Calderón and Saldivar, two scholars known for their work on borderlands, locate the genesis of a "discourse of the borderlands" after the War of 1846, "when Mexican-Americans, Chicanos, or mestizos began to project for themselves a positive, yet also critical, rendering of their bilingual and bicultural experience as a resistive measure against Anglo-American economic domination and ideological hegemony" (1991:4). "Where there is power, there is resistance" Foucault asserts (1978:95). Resistance, however, may not be in the form of armed conflict, and Foucault theorizes on how "power is something that works not just negatively, by denying, restricting, prohibiting, or repressing, but also positively, by producing forms of pleasure, systems of knowledge, goods and discourses" (Abu-Lughod 1990:42). Resistance to economic and ideological domination may take many forms, and in Tucson expressive art emerged as both counterdiscourse and a form of pleasure.

In addition to the strategies of support that evolved in the early barrios, there flourished in Tucson a symbolic resistance in the form of music, art, and theater. The most notable "chanteuse" of early Tucson was the renowned Luisa Espinel, born Luisa Ronstadt, daughter of the Tucson pioneer Federico Ronstadt. Her niece, Linda Ronstadt, reminisces in her music video "Canciones de mi Padre" about the influence that this family delight in music had on her own career. Another notable institution that showed the vitality and resistance of the Tucson Mexican community was the Teatro Carmen:

> To the Mexican elite of Tucson, *Teatro Carmen* was a powerful symbol of self-identity, living proof of the depth, power and beauty of their culture. They were the ones who supported the most vigorous cultural institution in town, a theater whose works were in Spanish, not English. Such an institution destroyed once and for all the image of Tucson as a crude little frontier town. In the face of increasing discrimination, *Teatro Carmen* also reassured these cultivated ranchers, merchants, and professional men and women that they belonged to a society equal or superior to that of their Anglo neighbors. The dramas of Spain's Golden Age or the contemporary works of Mexico's finest playwrights and composers gave lie to the derogatory stereotypes of Mexicans so prevalent in the Southwest. (Sheridan 1986:201)

Miguélez affirms further that "This theater presented the other side of the coin and therefore was appreciated not only for its aesthetic value, but also because it accomplished another task, that of affirming a culture, a set of values and a language constantly denigrated by the majority" (1983, quoted in Sheridan 1986:201). Clearly, musical and theatrical discourse were formative forces in early Tucson's construction of a "Mexican" identity, and women were often the prime movers in these expressive cultural practices.

The Ambiguity of "Mexican" Tucson

The binary oppositions in the history of Tucson since its inception have involved a sometimes deeply ambivalent bid to come to terms with the Mexican patrimony of Tucson. Lawrence W. Cheek, writing in the 1989 *City Magazine,* wryly notes this disjunction:

> We are a city with about 150,000 residents who claim Mexican birth or ancestry. That's about a quarter of us. The city itself has Spanish and then Mexican parentage, a fact that we're forever

trotting out to help prove our cultural superiority over bland, dumb Phoenix. Thanks to a little war followed by a Mexican fire sale in the middle of the last century, we now squat firmly on U.S. soil, but we are only sixty miles from *la frontera*. This proximity has made us connoisseurs. We love to take our guests down to sample the quaint customs and exotic foods of our good neighbor. We all know the Catch-22 beach, someone who's making a shrimp run to Guaymas, or someone who'll rent us a beach house at Rocky Point. Mexico is our playground, our pantry, our fountain of cultural energization.

What Anglo Tucson doesn't want to admit, or even discuss, is that all this seeming familiarity has bred a great deal of contempt. Beneath all the hugs and smooches, we really don't respect Mexico or its ways all that much, and in subtle ways we transfer this disdain to Mexican-American citizens living here. Nor do we understand this culture nearly as well as we think we do. We're eager only to embrace those aspects of it that will help promote Tucson or make us feel good about ourselves. (Cheek 1989:34)

Clearly the physical proximity to la frontera is a substantive force in the way Tucson has developed even into this day.

Borderlands as Metaphor

Scholars from diverse intellectual traditions have appropriated the borderlands as allegory for the crossing and remapping of the interstices between "first and third worlds, between cores and peripheries, centers and margins" (Calderón and Saldívar 1991:7). Rosa Linda Fregoso, writing of "border construction and reconstruction," notes that "From borderlands to border texts, border conflict and border crossings to border writing, border pedagogy and border feminism, the concept of 'border' enjoys wide currency as a 'paradigm of transcultural experience'" (1993:65).[1] Guillermo Gómez-Peña, the master of symbolic imagery, regales our senses with his description of the borderlands:

Few places in the world reflect so vividly the contradictions of two worlds in permanent conflict as does the Mexican American border. The result of these conflicts is a *sui generis* fusion of images, symbols, myths and attitudes in a continuing process of reordering. The contrasts are infinite: mariachis and surfers, cholos and punks, second-hand buses and helicopters, tropical whore houses and video discotheques, Catholic saints and monsters from outer space, shanty houses and steel skyscrapers, bullfights and American football, popular anarchism and cybernetic behaviorism, Anglo Saxon puritanism and Latin hedonism. . . . From the border we observe the clash of waves of the two Americas, Superman against El Santo, Contadora against the White House, Atahualpa Yupanqui against Michael Jackson, Sardino against Rambo; and the synthesis is a "third reality." It is charrock and punk-mariachi. It is post-modern flamenco, post-Columbian art, "rascuache" opera, Spanglish poetry, videocorrido, and multi-media "carpa."

As border citizens, this is our great challenge: to invent new languages capable of articulating our incredible circumstances. (1986:1)

In her widely influential and provocative work *Borderlands/La frontera: The New Mestiza,* Gloria Anzaldúa, another icon of the border experience, attempts to remake the border by crossing the defined boundaries of gender, race, and class, and captures the multidimensionality of life on the literal and metaphorical borderlands as she describes the woman of the borderlands:

The new mestiza copes by developing a tolerance for contradiction, a tolerance for ambiguity. She learns to be Indian in Mexican culture, to be Mexican from an Anglo point of view. She learns to juggle cultures. She has a plural personality, she operates in a pluralistic mode—nothing is thrust out, the good, the bad and the ugly, nothing rejected nothing abandoned. Not only does she sustain contradictions, she turns the ambivalence into something else. . . . Because the future depends on the breaking down of paradigms, it depends on the straddling of two or more cultures. By creating a new mythos—that is a change in the way we perceive reality, the way we see ourselves, and the ways we behave—la mestiza creates a new consciousness. (1987:79–80)

So what does this talk about borders and borderlands have to do with women, children, and language? It means that people lead complicated lives and that there are no simple patterns as to how children are socialized through language. Like Gómez-Peña and Anzaldúa playing with metaphors and images, children in the borderlands are artful crafts-people in blending a pastiche of words and making sense of the array of language forms that come their way. Three short songs illustrate my point: the first, sung by my mother in her generation; the second, part of my folklore; and the last from my daughter's fourth-grade classroom in the 1990s. The following three ditties show how children's playful use of language combines elements of their borderland experience into a view of their world:

1. All around the mulberry bush
   The monkey chased the weasel
   The monkey thought 'twas all in fun . . .
   PA-pas con chorizo.

2. (Sung to the tune of the theme song for the 1950s Disney
   television show *Davy Crockett*)
   Born in the mountains up in Tennessee,
   Killed him a bear when he was only three
   Pancho, Pancho Villa,
   King of the wild frontier.

3. Happy Birthday to you
   Happy Birthday to you
   You look like a chupacabras[2]
   and you smell like one, too.

From a child's point of view, heroes are interchangeable, words and worlds fluid and permeable, and language is another form of play. Children reside in the space and place of literal and metaphorical bor-ders, and the deterritorialized nature of postmodern life is a source of playful manipulation of images.

Borderlands as Analytical Tool

Although I have chosen the idea of the borderlands as a space from which we can begin to try to understand language use in this context, the metaphor is not unproblematic. As I stated before, metaphors can become overly romanticized and the political reality of their existence downplayed. Josiah Heyman calls for a "regional particularist stance" within which "we need to locate some of the bitter realities of border life in the traceable actions and failures of powerholders—to point the finger—rather than simply use the life of the border as intellectual fodder" (1994:46).

The use of the borderland as an image has opened up new ground, but it has also mystified the border. This mystification has often resulted in "a facile idea—at the border, two sides equal one hybrid"—that has replaced analysis (Heyman 1994:47).

Tying the borderlands to an actual and real border is returning to a self-evident proposition, as Wilson and Donnan claim, that

> The deterritorialised nature of post-modernity is only one interpretive slant on politics and power in the contemporary world. On its own, the study of the new politics of space and place, identity and transnationalism is incomplete. The balance must be supplied by a reconfiguring of the perspectives of modernists and traditionalists, many of whom are historians and political scientists, whose work continues to point out the necessity of complementing the seductive discourse of the new politics of person and identity with a renewed commitment to the recognizable and concrete manifestations of government and politics, at local levels and at the level of the state. (1998:1–2)

In calling for an "anthropology of borders," Wilson and Donnan argue that borders are "spatial and temporal records of relationships between local communities and between states" (ibid.:5), and that "nations and states, and their institutions, are composed of people who cannot or should not be reduced to the images which are constructed by the state, the media or of any other groups who wish to represent them" (4).

I am painfully aware that the concrete manifestations of the border and of the nation-state are often tragic and sordid. One has only to pick up a local newspaper to find reports of "border crossers" who have died a hideous death in the parched desert, often abandoned by their heartless guides, or of border crossers who have been nearly asphyxiated in the trunk of a car or who have frozen to death in an unexpected cold spell. The romantic allegory of choice and agency fails to capture the underbelly of the borderlands (cf. Annerino 1999).

Yet the seductive pull of the imagery of the borderlands is too powerful for me to forego completely. Even with its shortcomings, the vision of a borderlands space bubbling over with emergent practices, crossed over by transformations of this and that, casts a compelling shadow. In another sense, we all, whatever our circumstances, live in borderlands of some kind, betwixt and between the multiple aspects of our often compartmentalized lives. Hybridity, the ubiquitous twin sister of the borderlands trope, is sometimes referred to as the "third space"—that is, the place "between." But there is little in our interconnected and global experience that is not hybridized in some form. "Pure" forms of language, cultural practices, and social life have fallen prey to the "McDonaldization" of modern life, as even talking chihuahuas insisting "*yo quiero* Taco Bell" are hybridizations of capitalism and commodification.

Although I do not cast aside the metaphorical borderlands, I do attempt to ground the image in the reality of the border. An essential component of "border identities" is the fact that Tucson is a one-hour drive from another political entity and that people can and do literally cross the border (cf. Wilson and Donnan 1998). The border distinguishes Mexican-origin populations from other Latino groups, and its configuration is indelibly inscribed in these borderlands.

I also adopt a borderlands perspective that accommodates contradiction and ambiguity, and I see women and children interacting in ways that are not fixed or even necessarily coherent. I recognize their diverse and often conflicting ways of giving meaning to the world. I have to admit, though, that I did not come to this perspective merely by adopting a poststructuralist position in which the discursive field is openly negotiated. I came to this insight through the back door: by failing to find the unified patterns of language socialization that, at the outset of the study, I had assumed were out there. I felt that I had not done my anthropological job. The quest for the pattern was my mission. In failing to find the facile resolutions to the questions I was asking, I found something much more valuable: I found that what I knew about complexity and contradiction was not anomalous, but the very core of the borderland experience.

In the following chapters, I present the notion that the complexity inherent in the borderlands in general and in Tucson in particular is a formative factor in the language socialization of Tucson Mexican-origin children. Living in an area that is liminal socially, politically, and ideologically, women and children negotiate between the parameters of CNN English and Univisión Spanish, computers and carne asada, Pokémon and cockfights, and, in the process, construct multiple repertoires of language, identity, and ideology.

CHAPTER 2

Las Familias

The voices of women and children are often muted in discussions of social theory. At a large professional conference that I attended in 1998, a popular session on research on children was remarkable for the absence of men in the audience. The often-conjured images of anthropologist Margaret Mead playing with children somehow implicates research on children as belonging within the province of female researchers and, hence, often marginalized (cf. Behar 1993). Yet it is through the affirmation and accommodation as well as the resistance and opposition of women and children that central anthropological issues of space and place, transformation, and identity can be located.

This study did not start out with a focus on women. However, in the transcription of discourse and in the interviewing process, it became increasingly obvious that women—in their multiple roles as mothers, tías (aunts), nanas (grandmothers), comadres, and madrinas (godmothers)—are the keepers of the keys that unlock child-life. Of course, fathers, fathering, and male role socialization figure in the lives of children, and the life-altering influence of men in the developmental years is undeniable; I do not intend to trivialize this influence. Indeed, I found many men were active participants in the lives of children, shuttling them between activities, coaching soccer and softball, and mentoring musical talent. However, because the voices of Mexican-origin women have been largely absent in telling their own stories, I have chosen to highlight women's narratives of the mothering experience. This study draws on critical feminist theory that challenges images of domestic life wherein the household is "viewed as constituting a site for the stable, unproblematic reproduction of routinized activities and relations, free from social conflict" (Collier and Yanagisako 1989:28). Instead, I adopt a poststructural (cf. Weedon 1987) perspective. I see family life as a discursive field in which the ways women and children interact is not necessarily fixed or even coherent, and I try to recognize their diverse and often conflicting ways of giving meaning to the world. The lives of Mexican-origin women are multiply mediated, by ethnicity and class as well as by gender—to say nothing of mediation by a myriad of other factors, such as immigration status. The diversity of such women's experiences challenges discourses of feminist theory that find only one kind of meaning in women's lives (Baca Zinn and Thornton Dill 1994). The lived experiences of women of color have forced a rethinking of more traditional feminist analysis of gender as a unitary phenomenon. New writings on postcolonial contexts emphasize the importance of diverse positionalities and local histories of subaltern populations.

The initial data for this study were collected in 1988, at a time when the subjects of similarities and discontinuities between classroom talk and community language patterns were highly visible in the research literature. Thus, I am writing with the benefit of hindsight. However, I would like to describe details of the research process because I believe they continue to lie at the heart of ethnographic research by native anthropologists. Because minority scholars are few in number, I felt the weight of discovering the *One Truth* that could help children in their academic achievement and that could have an impact on educational policy. I was not to find it, and now I know why.

At the outset of this study, I anticipated examining the linguistic, metalinguistic, semiotic, and ideological influences to which Tucson Mexican-origin children are exposed within their households. I intended to explore how these influences are deployed. Because children learn to be fully functioning adults within a semiotically charged context, I accepted that the study of language socialization could not be limited solely to grammatical elements at the syntactical, morphological, phonological, and lexical levels, but must take into account the whole range of communicated stimuli. I drew on the corpus of research that focuses on the "rich" interpretation of child language, stressing the contextualization and communicative function of utterances (Bloom 1973, Bruner 1985). I was, however, most influenced by models of language socialization advanced by Ochs and Schieffelin (1984) and by Schieffelin and Ochs (1986a, 1986b). I began this study with an attempt to analyze Mexican-origin child language socialization within this framework.

The socialization of children in general and of Mexican-origin children in particular has been viewed through a series of psychoanalytical, developmental, psychological, and sociological lenses. However, in a then-pivotal statement, Ochs and Schieffelin outlined a new paradigm for the study of language socialization: "The language used both *by* and *to* children in social interactions has rarely been a source of information on socialization. As a consequence, we know little about the role that language plays in the acquisition and transmission of sociocultural knowledge. Neither the forms, the functions, nor the message content of language have been documented and examined for the ways in which they *organize* and *are organized by* culture" (1984:276, emphasis in original).

I adopted this paradigm, although I was unsettled by its focus on teasing out models of culture. First of all, I knew from firsthand experience that getting at unitary forms of "culture" was not as simple as it sounded. Second, because I had some anthropological research experience in the Tucson Mexican-origin community, I was keenly aware of the problematic nature of addressing internal diversity. I had worked as a research graduate assistant on the Tucson Project, through the Bureau of Applied Research in Anthropology, studying networks of nonmarket exchange. This methodology included a random stratified sample of households derived from census data with which an attempt was made to explore the diversity within the community. From this research emerged a picture of complex variations in life histories, residential situations, and household ideologies, all shaped by generational and economic distinctions.

I faced what José Limón refers to as the challenge of "native anthropologists . . . to represent ethnic worlds riven with cultural contradiction in this postmodern moment, while responding critically to a history of flattening stereotypical representations of these worlds" (1991:116). To attempt to capture the sources and content of diversity within the community, I selected households drawn from two locally significant residential categories: *barrio* and *nonbarrio*. I felt that this distinction was justifiable on both subjective and objective grounds because the barrio is recognized not only as a geographical and residential entity, but as a separate and distinct social construct with definitive connotative meanings. Second, in social science terminology, *barrio* has been ascribed to a category of designations that incorporate a measurable set of data. It can be quantified by variables such as median family income and other economic indicators, demographic and census factors such as percentage of Mexican-origin households in the area, and percentage foreign born. Housing tenure, household composition, age distribution, and educational attainment are also indicators of these units. As a postscript, reflecting ten years later on this demarcation, I have to add that local patterns have changed enough so that this label is not as freely applied to particular neighborhoods. The contrastive category *nonbarrio* has a more nebulous meaning, but can be defined in negative terms as being the areas outside those traditionally labeled as barrios. These households are located in areas that can be identified as having a lower proportion of Mexican-origin population.

The Discarding of Paradigm

As I have noted, I began this study with a particular notion of language socialization as described in the literature and effectuated in the everyday give and take of social interaction. I started out with ideas of coding linguistic exchanges with categories focusing on participant structures, child's turns at talk, types of interactions sanctioned, turn taking, child-initiated speech, and so on. I assumed that the prepackaged constructs of barrio and nonbarrio could explicate some of the variability I would encounter. But I was soon brought up short, as I describe in the following chapters, because language practices eluded the prefabricated niches I had molded. For a while, I labored under the assumption that I simply had to search harder, to tinker longer with the scenarios I was presented, and that somehow the refined, orderly, and cohesive picture that other language socialization studies described would emerge. This did not happen. Instead, I was jolted out of the frames that I had complacently embraced. I began to question why studies of the language use of children, a topic so politically charged, seemed to avoid analyses of hegemony and power. Eventually, these questions led me to discard the constructs with which I had come equipped and to adopt an approach that fused perspectives and expanded across disciplines. This abandonment, however, did not come easily.

In the following chapters, I attempt to document the resulting ethno-graphic inquiry process. I argue that language socialization is a multi-vocalic process, involving contexts that cannot be examined only in the household, but must encompass regional, national, and transborder zones. Especially, our understanding of each level must include the political, particularly those lived practical relations of domination and subordination summarized under the term *hegemony*.

Because one of my objectives in undertaking this research had to do with examining congruence between community and classroom language patterns, I soon had to reassess certain assumptions. When we search for patterns of discourse "within the community" with the goal of importing these patterns into classroom pedagogy, we risk reifying patterns of "culture" and "community." Discourse may be neither shared nor unified. The enduring theme of "one language–one culture" continues to plague research into Mexican-origin populations, even though anthropologists Edward Sapir and Franz Boas, as far back as 1915, forcefully argued "about the independence of race, language and culture" and "pointed out that the distribution of particular linguistic forms need not predict the distribution of other social, historical and biological facts" (Irvine 1996:123). The notion of community that I incorporate draws on Benedict Anderson's (1983) metaphor of the "imagined community" and continues to be redefined and revisited, as do the semiotic, discursive, and literary practices that socially construct aspects of a shared commonality (Moll and González 1994). Neither the term *culture* nor the term *community* can be accepted as reflecting an agreed upon normativity in human populations.

Methods and Participants: The How and the Who

I chose to follow the essential methodology laid out in the language so-cialization literature, which involves lengthy ethnographic observations coupled with audiocassette recordings of naturally occurring speech. The households in my sample were supplied with tape recorders and cassettes, and members were asked to record their interactions within the households, especially at mealtime and bedtime and during home-work sessions. I taped in-depth, open-ended interviews with parents—

and, in some cases, grandparents—regarding their own perceptions of child rearing, language habits, and household child-rearing ideologies. I also collected extensive household histories, detailing residential, labor, and family history. And, of course, I also interviewed the children themselves.

I chose twelve households for participation in the original study. Later, I conducted interviews with the women of five additional households. Most households for the barrio segment were selected from the federally funded Parent and Child Education (PACE) program for low-income schools of the Chapter I (now Title I) division of a local school district. Children who were enrolled in the PACE program at the time of selection for this study were considered eligible for the program on the basis of residence in an economically disadvantaged neighborhood, one or both parents' lack of a high school diploma, and/or poor performance on a developmental test; since that time, the criteria have changed. These children were considered "at risk" for low educational attainment and dropping out before high school graduation. Most children enrolled in the PACE program are four to five years old because it is a pre-kindergarten program. I secured permission from the PACE director and from the school district for the selection of these children. In order to protect the privacy and confidentiality of the participants, neither the school nor the neighborhoods are explicitly identified in this book. I informally asked teachers in the PACE program to screen possible participants and perhaps suggest households. The teacher made my initial introduction to the families. I used five households from the PACE sample, four originally categorized as barrio, one as nonbarrio. Through personal contacts, I selected three other households from a nonbarrio neighborhood. These nonbarrio families were unknown to me before the study and were recommended by friends as families with children in the four- to seven-year age group. Because I had personal contact with at least one other person familiar with the family, this selection had the additional advantage of pinpointing the family within a certain network of social relationships.

As a preliminary test of the fieldwork methodology, I also conducted a pilot study with four households, two from barrio locations and two from nonbarrio locations. These households are also included in the totality of data analysis.

Eight families form the core of the data collection, and they were first contacted in 1988. I made my last visits with these core households in 1991. I visited each household for an initial interview in which I explained the study and the families signed the permission forms for taping and interviewing. During the first interview, I elicited a household and labor history, and took a language-use survey. I often found that by asking a few questions about where the parents or grandparents were from and what they did for a living opened the door to establishing a lengthy household and labor history. Additionally, questions about the parents' own childhood elicited comparisons with the child-rearing philosophies they adopted in raising their own children. The second interview primarily concentrated on the child, attempting to establish rapport with her or him and exploring language patterns through storytelling and picture books. Through these interactions with the children, during which I asked them to tell me about themselves, I was able to come to a rough idea of competence in English and Spanish. I had a questionnaire for each child that touched on his/her own activities and likes/dislikes. In addition to talking to the child, I interviewed mothers about the daily activities of the child and also of the household because they related to children's participation. The third interview focused primarily on topics of child rearing and what I term *household ideology*. This interview included questions on how the women constructed their roles as mother, how they wanted to raise their children, and the challenges and joys of motherhood. I conducted subsequent interviews on an "as needed" basis in order to cover gaps in the data collection. In addition to these more formalized interviews, I often found myself engaged in lengthy telephone dialogues when scheduling appointments. These informal telephone conversations often formed the bases for following up certain topics that emerged as particularly urgent for the family at that time.

Although the methodology as described appears relatively straightforward, the actual implementation was a convoluted and sometimes frustrating process. Because everyday life in our society depends on maintaining a frenetic pace, interviews were sometimes difficult to schedule. The families had numerous everyday demands on their time, and fieldwork was stretched to a period of more than two years. Last-minute rescheduling because of a child's illness, work demands, or other appointments were common. Additionally, some families, for whatever reason, would regularly forget to turn on the recorder, and months would sometimes go by without a cassette forthcoming. I eventually found that a small payment for each cassette tape proved the most effective way of gathering sufficient data in those households.

Confidentiality of Data

One of the thorniest problems in carrying out this research involved working in a place where I had many of my own relational networks. I was keenly aware from the onset that a misspoken word or a careless offhand comment could easily breach privacy. Because the households were quite open in sharing personal and sometimes quite intimate information, I have attempted to go to great lengths to shield identities. I do not pretend to present uniform data for each household. I have chosen, rather, to cull the transcripts and observations selectively for major themes that recur. Because of the unique situational constraints involved, I feel that I cannot provide more detail than what I have supplied. My aim is that only each household itself will be able to recognize and identify its own description. In this chapter, I describe the core households, but not all are mentioned in later chapters. The immigrant households are described in chapter 6. All names of family members are pseudonyms.

Because the lives of women are enmeshed in complex household dynamics, I have attempted to provide thumbnail sketches of these dynamics. All of the women I interviewed had strong and close ties with their mothers and sisters. Although these relationships were not always unproblematic, exchange between households was effectuated primarily through women. Some women had chosen to live in particular neighborhoods in order to be close to their female relatives. Others dropped off their children every day at their mothers' homes. It was rare that more than a few days would lapse without contact between women. Maternal aunts were also important in this panorama. The circles that enveloped each household network provided support, help, comfort, and sometimes problems. Yet the women in these circles of motherhood and sisterhood were tightly knit together with ties that endured over very long periods of time and survived geographic separations.

It is also important to mention that most of the households struggled economically. Caught in a border economy in which wages are low,

these working-class families encountered significant economic insta-
bility. The totality of household survival strategies (Tapia 2000) helps us
to form a context for the ways in which children are raised.

Escobedo Family

Marina and Raul Escobedo were recommended by a PACE teacher as a
household that would be highly cooperative. Marina had frequent and
regular contact with school personnel and had recently been asked by
the principal at the elementary school to head up a parents' committee.
Her husband had worked as an auto mechanic for several years. When I
first met them, they lived in a home owned by Raul's father, which they
were fixing up, and three other households on the same street are close
relatives. Marina and Raul have four sons: Manuel, Sergio, Anthony,
and Richard. Richard was enrolled in the PACE program at their neighborhood school. Marina's parents (mother and stepfather) live on the far
east side of Tucson in the neighborhood where Marina spent her childhood and adolescent years. Her mother worked most of her life as a
cook in a local hospital, and her father's labor history focused primarily
on mining. Raul's parents are divorced, although he remains close to his
father. Raul attended the same elementary school that his children were
attending at the time of the interviews. Both Marina and Raul are
bilingual, although English is the dominant language of the home. At
the time of the first interview, Marina was a homemaker, serving on
several voluntary parent advisory committees and substance abuse pre-
vention organizations. She later began to work part-time for the school.
Unfortunately, the couple divorced during my second year of contact
with them, and Marina began work full-time as an assistant manager in
a local store.

Marina is deeply concerned about the emotional, intellectual, and
moral development of her sons. She has set standards on television
programming, homework time, and household chores for them. The
children have responsibility for picking up dirty clothes, drying spoons,
and making their own breakfast. Also, "there is no cussing, fighting,
hitting, or name-calling allowed." Marina is an outgoing person, quite
outspoken in asking people to conform to certain standards. She even
goes so far as to ask her neighbors not to use profanity in the neighborhood. Richard reported that his favorite activities were Nintendo, playing with Micro Machines, and football with his brothers.

LINARES FAMILY

Ana María and Ramón Linares, both under twenty-five years old, were the youngest parents interviewed. They are the parents of three girls: Priscilla, four years old (PACE child) at the time of the interviews; Paulina, three years old; and Yvette, two years old. The family lived with the maternal grandparents in the house where Ana María grew up. An addition was built on to the house to accommodate the family. Like the Escobedos, two households of Linares family relatives live on the same street. Ana María's father and his family were born in Tucson, and her mother was born in a small town outside of Flagstaff. Ramón's parents are from Mexico. Ana María was enrolled in bilingual programs throughout her schooling and is comfortable in both Spanish and English, as is her husband. The girls code-switch to a much greater degree than the Escobedo boys, possibly because of the influence of the maternal grandparents. At the time of the initial contact, Ana María was primarily a homemaker. During the course of my contact with her, she did, however, take seasonal part-time jobs. Ramón was also employed seasonally in construction. Both parents stress respect to the girls, stating that the most important values that they try to teach are to "respect their older aunts and family members." The girls are given the responsibilities of keeping their room clean and making their beds. Priscilla, the oldest, had just started a ballet class once a week, which the younger girls were anxious to begin also. The girls also expressed a particular affinity for Mexican music, and Priscilla cited "La puerta negra," a tape that her father has, as her favorite song. Their favorite activity was playing house with their cousin who lived two doors down.

GALLARDO FAMILY

Luis and Iris Gallardo lived on the far south side of Tucson in a small, rented home. Iris Gallardo was born in Tucson and attended school on the southside. She dropped out of high school, although she went back to earn her GED. Her father was employed as a miner and later as a foreman for the Parks and Recreation Department, and her mother has been a homemaker. Luis Gallardo is originally from the border mining community of Douglas, Arizona, and came to Tucson during his elementary years, although several relatives remain in Douglas. He is employed as a driver for a local company. Luis and Iris are the parents of two children, Monique, eight years of age at the time of the interviews, and Luis Jr., five years old (PACE child). Financial worries are a dominant concern of this household because even though Luis works long hours and overtime on weekends, they can "barely make it on his income." He often works until 11:00 P.M. on Saturdays, and, said Iris, the "kids miss him a lot. We drop him off at work early in the morning, and he can never be home to spend time with them." When queried about what values are important in raising children, Iris said she wants her children to learn to listen, so that she does not have to repeat the same thing three or four times. She wants them to "learn manners, to say 'excuse me,' and not just butt in, and to learn respect for other people and not just yell 'move.'" Even though the children are given certain chores, Iris stated that "If I need help, I'll ask them, but I don't like to make a thing where they have to do this thing every day." She feels that she spent a good chunk of her own childhood doing domestic chores, washing dishes, making tortillas, and so on, and that she hardly had time to play. She feels that her children are too young to have to help out extensively. She commented about a niece that "they have her like a little slave around the house, and she has to take care of everything, while her mother just sits there." Iris does not want to push her children too much in that area because she feels that by the time she turned seventeen or eighteen, she was already worn out by housework.

MARTÍNEZ FAMILY

The Martínez family was recruited through the PACE teacher, and my initial contact was with the child's (Rosalba) grandmother, Oralia Acosta, who regularly picked her up after her PACE class. Mrs. Acosta lives across the street from the school and at that time cared for Rosalba and her brother, Andrés, before and after school. She also baby-sat a two-year-old grandson, and a ten-year-old granddaughter lived with her. Because of the close relationship between Rosalba and her grandparents, I interviewed the grandparents as well on household histories, child rearing, and language use. Mrs. Acosta's family is originally from Arivaca, a beautiful but isolated town south of Tucson, and trips to Arivaca continue to be a treat for the Acostas' grandchildren. Mrs. Acosta talked at length about the rural upbringing she had, living on the Los Reales ranch, where her father worked. When he was ready to retire, he was given a plot of land on the ranch, which he in turn passed on to his son. Mrs. Acosta discussed the limited educational opportunities of Arivaca, although she insisted that she "always loved to read.

I would read by the moonlight when I was small. I read all the books I could." She continued her love of reading while rearing her own children and stated that "she would lie down with them and read books to them. I buy lots of books."

Mr. Acosta is originally from Nogales, Arizona; he worked as a plumber for several years before retiring in 1985. He would often chronicle his World War II experiences for me during my visits, detailing his training in Oklahoma and in the eastern United States. Mrs. Acosta's emphasis on literacy has borne fruit in several ways, as three of Oralia Acosta's five children have college degrees. Clara Martínez, Rosalba's mother, has a degree in secondary physical education from the University of Arizona, although she has worked as a cashier for a southside grocery store for fifteen years. Rosalba's father, Eddie, works as a carpenter. Rosalba was at that time five years of age and has an older brother, Andrés, then eight years old. A baby sister was born later. Although Rosalba was enrolled in a PACE program at the elementary school across from her grandmother's house, the Martínez family lives on the far southside on a two-acre plot in a largely rural area. Rosalba had a dog, a rooster, and three ducks that she was responsible for feeding. Her grandmother's house also had a large rabbit, which Rosalba often fed. Rosalba's typical day included breakfast at home, after which she was dropped off at her grandmother's house. She attended PACE until 11:30, and Mrs. Acosta picked her up after she ate lunch. She stayed at her grandmother's until 4:30, when her mother picked her up. Rosalba's great-grandmother, Mrs. Acosta's mother, lives across the street from the Acostas, and the children checked on her periodically. During one visit close to Christmas, the front room at the Acostas had been transformed into an altar, with flowers and vases decorating a large picture of Christ and of the Virgin Mary. Rosalba and Andres have chores to do at home, and her mother reported that Rosalba often asked for a mitt to dust with or washed dishes or helped her mother with baking. Both children helped in making dinner. Rosalba enjoyed going shopping and to the movies. She also liked playing with dolls, putting on makeup, combing her waist-length hair, and coloring.

Cisneros Family

The Cisneros are immigrants from Sonora. The mother, María del Carmen de Cisneros, is from Nogales, Sonora, and the father, Abelardo

Cisneros, is from San Ignacio. The family has six children: Samuel, at that time eighteen years old; Socorro, seventeen years old; Daniel, sixteen years old; Maricela, fifteen years old; Juan, eight years old; and Sonia, four years old (PACE child). The family speaks primarily Spanish, although the older children were in bilingual classes and are fairly fluent in English. The family had been here approximately five years and came to Tucson to join three of Mrs. Cisneros's brothers. They had just been able to move their mother to Tucson. Interestingly, her mother was born in Santa Monica, California, although the family returned to Mexico when she was still a child. Mrs. Cisneros works as a cook and has previously worked in hotels doing both laundry and maid service. Mr. Cisneros is a roofer. Mrs. Cisneros leaves for work very early, having to report at 6:00 A.M. to her job. Because she is employed outside the home, the children have had to assume a great deal of responsibility for the functioning of the household. At times, when I went over to talk to Sonia, the older daughter, Socorro, would greet me in place of her mother and would act as hostess, admonishing her younger sister to behave. During the interviews, I noted that the older girls do a great deal of meal preparation, and Mrs. Cisneros related that the girls all help in making breakfast and washing dishes. The sons are given the responsibility for the outside yard work and general maintenance of the house, and both Mr. and Mrs. Cisneros worry that they have not been complying with their responsibilities. Mrs. Cisneros noted that she often has to chide the older sons for not recognizing that she and her husband must work, on Saturdays as well as the weekdays, and that the boys must shoulder their share of the household responsibilities. Because the older children were adolescents and had their own circle of friends, the family did relatively little as a unit, generally only going out to the park or to relatives' homes. Usually the two older girls went out with their friends, to quinceañeras or to dances, and the boys went with their own friends, although the eldest son worked full-time at a furniture store. The two youngest, Sonia and Juan, more regularly accompanied their parents on shopping trips, trips to Nogales, and Sunday paseos (outings). The family appeared to be connected to extensive networks through the children, with a parade of young people coming and going through the house during every interview. The doorbell would ring several times, with someone asking for one of the children. In spite of all the household hubbub, Sonia was a quiet child and often had to be prodded to speak. She loved playing "school" and often took the role of "teacher," with a young neighbor girl being the student. Sonia told me that she wanted to be a teacher when she grows up. During my initial contact with her, Sonia spoke only Spanish. After she started kindergarten and then first grade, she began to incorporate more English in our conversations, although she always spoke only in Spanish to her parents and siblings.

Aguilar Family

The Aguilar family provided by far the largest corpus of data for analysis. The family—Pete and Becky Aguilar and three children, Eric, Lisa, and Louie—was recruited through a personal contact. The family resides in a nonbarrio westside area of Tucson, and the children attended a school that is ethnically balanced. The Aguilar children are fourth-generation Tucsonans, with all grandparents born locally. Mr. Aguilar was born and raised in a large family in what he referred to as Barrio Centro, near a centralized park. His family is highly athletic, and he was able to pursue a degree in education through athletic scholarships, first at a local community college and later at Northern Arizona University. He recalls that most of his childhood was spent playing ball. Sports continue to be central in his life in that all of his children are involved in T-ball or Little League, and he is an active participant in their sports activities. Mrs. Aguilar was also born in Tucson, lived first in the Barrio Hollywood area, and later relocated to a nonbarrio area. Mrs. Aguilar comes from a family that was among the original inhabitants of the Barrio Anita area and that continues to enjoy an extensive kin network in Tucson. She graduated from a local high school and has worked sporadically, currently as a medical assistant in a doctor's office. The maternal grandfather was employed in construction, and the paternal grandfather was an aircraft mechanic; both grandmothers are primarily homemakers. Mr. Aguilar is an educator. In addition to his full-time job, he is a disc jockey for weddings, quinceañeras, dances, and other celebrations of that sort.

Salazar Family

Raquel and Fernando Salazar reside in a new subdivision of tract homes in what counts as a nonbarrio area of Tucson, although it is located in the predominantly Mexican southside. Raquel was raised in what was at the time a middle-class nonbarrio area of Tucson, and Fernando was raised in the heart of one of the older barrios. They have three children: Mark, eight years of age at the time of the interviews; Melissa (target child), four and a half years old; and Damian, eighteen months old. Raquel was one of my niece's schoolmates, and an introduction was made over the phone. Before our first meeting, I had spoken to Raquel on the phone several times and had a general knowledge of the Salazar household. Fernando sells automotive parts and has worked in the same location for more than ten years. Raquel is a homemaker, although she did try working outside the home at one time. It turned out to be a highly demanding job because she was the only female on the crew at the time. She persevered, however, and was given an award for meritorious accomplishment in her work. She wrestled with her decision to go back to work and commented:

> I did the whole thing. I was home for seven years with the kids, I was . . . since day one, since I got married. And each year more and more members of my family started working. My sister started working, my sister-in-law started working, everybody was working! Everywhere I would turn, everybody was working. I was the only one home. I felt like I had no relationship. I felt like an extinct dinosaur. I said, "What's going on here?"—nobody to relate to. So I thought maybe I should do it because everybody else is doing it and everybody was saying, "the kids, you know they'll do fine by themselves."

After working for a year, Raquel found it increasingly difficult to deal with leaving her children. Melissa would cry and hold onto her legs before work, and she went through five baby-sitters in one year. Eventually, when the company cut her salary from seven dollars per hour to five dollars per hour, she decided that working was not worth it and resigned.

ROBLES FAMILY

The Robles family was included in the study because of its wide kinship network. I should add that accessibility also played a role because I am a part of their circle. Even though Mr. and Mrs. Robles do not have children in the four- to seven-year age group, they do have grandchildren, and they possess a wide range of knowledge relating to child rearing. They are fairly young grandparents, both in their late forties at the time of the initial interviews. They are both members of large extended networks: Amelia Robles is one of thirteen brothers and sisters, and Armando is one of twelve siblings. Amelia was born in Chihuahua. Later, her family moved to Agua Prieta, then emigrated to Douglas, Arizona. Armando's family is also from Douglas. Armando and Amelia moved to Tucson immediately after they married and eventually, the majority of their siblings relocated here as well. All but one of Amelia's brothers live in Tucson. Amelia and Armando have three children, all married. Amelia has very strong and definite ideas on how to raise children and is considered by most people to have produced highly successful offspring. Her youngest daughter was a straight-A student and received numerous scholarship offers to several universities, eventually graduating from the University of Arizona. Her eldest daughter was also an outstanding student, as well as being active in cheerleading, and was selected as a City of Tucson Sixteenth of September queen prior to her marriage. Their son is a firefighter and is talented in a number of areas, from mechanics to computers.

Amelia and Armando own their own parts and repair shop. Prior to their purchase of the shop, Amelia worked at home, networking and filling supply orders with the idea of one day opening their own business. Because of this flexibility in work environments, Amelia has been attentively vigilant and completely involved in her children's (and now grandchildren's) activities. When her daughters were involved in cheerleading, she attended cheerleading camps and explored the subject so diligently that the school district hired her as a cheerleading coach. Marveling at Amelia's intense involvement with her children, a former teacher of the eldest daughter recruited Amelia to watch her as-yet-unborn child "because she wanted a good influence on him."

Subsequently, in 1996, I conducted follow-up interviews with their oldest daughter, Maricela, the mother of four children. Maricela lives two blocks from her mother, and her brother lives next door to his mother. Their younger sister lives in the same area.

The Pilot Study

GÓMEZ FAMILY

The Gómez family was part of the original pilot study, although I continued contact with them and conducted follow-up interviews during 1990. Herlinda and Ralph Gómez live on the far south side of Tucson in a working-class neighborhood. Both household heads were raised in southside barrio areas. Herlinda was born in Mexico, the second daughter of a family with three boys and two girls. The family immigrated when Herlinda was two years old, and she attended public schools on the southside, graduating from Pueblo High School and later going on to Pima College. She worked for several years as an administrative assistant and, subsequent to the tapings reported here, returned to school to pursue her teaching credentials. Herlinda's father was a miner in San Manuel, near Tucson, until his retirement, and her mother was exclusively a homemaker. Both of her parents have an extensive kin network in Tucson, with ten paternal siblings, along with their children, residing in Tucson. The maternal grandmother has lived with them for several years. Herlinda is equally proficient in both English and Spanish. Ralph was born in Tucson, and his parents were also born in Arizona. Some segments of his family have roots in Arivaca. He graduated from Pueblo High School also and did not pursue any further education. He was employed as a miner for nine years until he was laid off in 1983 and then began work in a parts store. He claimed not to be quite as fluent in Spanish as his wife, although he does interact with his in-laws in Spanish. Both parents reported the two sons to be quite different. At the time of taping, they were seven and nine years of age. David, the older, was consistently a high-achieving student and active in sports. Ricky, the younger, did not find schoolwork quite as easy and did not like sports as much.

GAMBOA FAMILY

At the time the original data were gathered, the Gamboa family lived in the same general area as the Gómez family, a nonbarrio area in the far south side of Tucson. Since this time, the couple has divorced, and Irene Gamboa has remarried. Irene was born in Tucson, the eldest of seven children, of parents who were also born in Tucson. Her mother did not finish high school, although her father did. Irene attended Catholic elementary schools and went on to public schools from the seventh grade. During Irene's childhood, her family resided with the maternal grandparents for a number of years. Both grandparents were monolingual Spanish speakers. Irene feels more comfortable in English and uses Spanish primarily when asked to deal with Spanish-speaking cus-

tomers on her job. Immediately after high school graduation, she entered the workforce, working first as a secretary and later at a bank. She
married at nineteen and has continued her full-time employment to the
present day. Mark Gamboa graduated from high school and went on to
approximately three years of college. His parents were also born in
Tucson, his father working as a truck driver and his mother as a tax
preparer. He is the middle son of four brothers and two sisters and is
employed as a miner at Magma Copper mine.

Interviewing

Although the native anthropologist may have particular insights into
his or her home community, it is never a transparent overlay. None of us
has lived the lives of our neighbors and friends, and our external similarities may belie wildly divergent orientations. I learned early on in the
fieldwork process that ethnography is transformative: I was deeply affected by the stories I heard, and I believe that the women telling the
stories tapped reservoirs of deeper self-reflection. As I describe in the
following chapters, even the most mundane of topics are laden with
layers of unseen meanings.

CHAPTER 3

When the Facts Won't Stay Put

FINDING EMOTION IN ALL THE WRONG PLACES

Marina Escobedo sat at her small dining room table as she spoke rapidly. Her voice belied her impassioned hope that her children never get involved in drugs.

> I mean, I've seen families where people will go into the home, and a father and a mother, or an aunt or an uncle, will come, will walk in, and will roll up a joint and smoke it, like it's a cigarette, with the kids around. Then the first time they have difficulty with their child, if they catch the teenage kids with it, and they say, "Why are you doing this?" And the kid retaliates by saying, "Look, you do it."... There was a situation recently... there was a family where there were two teenage boys, OK? Aunts and uncles, everybody in the family smoked it. Their parents are both in jail because of it, OK? These kids have grown up with marijuana and drugs as a normal thing in the family life, OK? Normal, completely. I mean they have never passed a day when it was not in their normal everyday activities, where somebody wasn't rolling it, somebody wasn't selling it, somebody wasn't doing something; it was normal.
>
> OK, and they all went out on a picnic. Unfortunately, the kids stole the stuff from a couple of their aunts and went off to the corner... and got caught doing it. And the aunts *angrily,* I mean really indignant, confronted them and asked them, "Well, *why* did you do this?" You know, "Why are you doing this?" And the kids say, "Well, *you* do it." "But you have to have some respect." And the kids go, "Well, you don't." And they get all upset. They came,

and they were talking to their brother, and —— said, "Well, what do you expect from these children? You do it in front of them, you're their role model to them, they look up to you."

I cringe inwardly at the details of the picnic scene because I always feel a pang of distress whenever the subject of kids and drugs surfaces. My intent in doing this study was to provide an ethnographic description of the processes of language use, not to feed stereotypes of drugs, gangs, and violence. It is not the community that I know. The community I know is, no doubt, an "imagined one," but this imagination is of a nurturing web of familial alliances and friendship, of an interweaving of connections from a shared and inherited Mexican Tucson, where the past slips effortlessly into the present as naturally as the Sonoran Desert, from whose soils it has flourished and blossomed. The imagining of community, Anderson claims, requires a conception of a "deep, horizontal comradeship" (1983:16). My imagined community is a community in the true sense of communitas, a fellowship of shared commonalties in an arid and parched ecosystem into which its early Mexican settlers sowed the seeds of compadrazgo (fictive kinship) and confianza (trust) from which their descendants now reap the fruits. The unwelcome intrusion of drugs onto my Panglossian "best of all possible worlds" was both disturbing and irritating. Yet, this theme surfaced surreptitiously on my very first interview in the field.

I listened as Marina described her part-time work in a program designed by the school district to prevent drug abuse in the elementary schools. She was fervently devoted to her work, and she animatedly rehearsed her presentations to elementary school classrooms. Her tiny, easily overlooked home conveyed the struggle of a family to make ends meet. The furnishings were sparse, even Spartan. It was difficult to imagine six people crowded into the little house. The interior was unremarkable except for one thing—books. As I entered the small frame house, I saw an antiquated set of encyclopedias in an aging bookcase. Marina's conversation was punctuated by sporadic dashes to the bookcase, from which she would retrieve some book or other to display eagerly for my perusal.

Marina was unabashedly outspoken. She chatted candidly about her distress in dealing with her oldest child, born with a birth defect. She spoke of her tireless efforts to shield her children from profanity and from alcohol abuse, and of her undeviating involvement in her sons' classrooms and schoolwork. She was extraordinarily astute and articulate. She was an outstanding anthropological "informant," and she intrigued me. But, I wondered, how typical was she of the neighborhood I wanted her to represent?

In spite of the fact that I favor a highly interpretive, subjective anthropology that is suspicious of ideas such as "representative sample," I was unsettled by what I perceived to be Marina's unrepresentativeness. I had chosen to start looking for children in a classroom within a Chapter I school precisely so that I could address the issue of child language socialization within the framework of what in federal nomenclature is considered an "at risk" neighborhood. Marina did not fit what I thought the demographic profile of the neighborhood should be. She lived smack in the middle of it, and her income level was consistent with it, but somehow she didn't fit. She had been raised on the far east (mostly non-Mexican-origin) side of Tucson. She had attended Pima Community College for a year, and she had been in the military and in law enforcement. How many other mothers in the neighborhood liked martial arts and guns?

But I kept listening as Marina rattled off a string of her views on child rearing:

> It's like another situation. I have a nephew who drinks. He's fifteen years old, OK? His uncles tell him, "Look, it's OK, drink when you're with the family." If he had asked me, I would say, "*No, don't. It's illegal. You're not of age. When you turn eighteen, you can make that decision for yourself."* . . . Later, he fell down and hurt his knee. I asked his aunt, and she said, "Well, my husband said he could drink." And I said, "Well, turn it around and pretend your son is fifteen years old. Would you let your husband tell him that? That it's OK for him to drink on social occasions?" She said no. "Then why don't you do something for this child, who needs as much guidance from you and your own family?" This kid doesn't have a father. He's living with his grandmother. She has no husband. *Somebody* has got to tell him it's not acceptable. I'm not afraid to tell him, and you guys put me down for telling him that. I don't care. He has got to know. He's got to grow in a circle of discipline. All children do. As they keep growing, that circle gets

wider and wider and wider, until they're finally responsible for their own. Then they have to put their circles around their children. . . . Look, my children, if they *ever* get into drugs, they will never be able to point an accusing finger at me because I don't do it. I try to set the slate clean. I don't drink, I don't smoke, I don't do drugs. I don't even curse in front of my kids because I don't want to send that kind of role-modeling message. I want them to understand that they have the choices to do that in their life. But I want them to understand what kind of a life they can have without it. That's my . . . where I'm coming from. And when these people come and they cry to me about this, I say, "You have nobody to blame but yourself. I mean, look at what they've got to go by. I mean if *one* of you, just *one* of you could set a good example, then I could understand it." . . . Some people like to point fingers at other people. Like my kids. They say, *"He made me do it."* No. *You* threw the rock; your hand is on it, OK? He didn't make you do it. You did it. You suffer the consequences for your actions.

The whole soliloquy had come in one breath. It sounded like an entire philosophical system laid bare. And yet her terminology alluded to some other, as yet unspoken ideas. "Circle of discipline"? Where did that phrase come from? She had spoken strongly about "consequences for your own actions." Surely these phrases had been honed in discussions with other parents or through her readings, or . . . where?

The answer came in our second interview. As we talked, I became aware of certain clues I should have picked up during my first interview with her, details over which I had glossed. When I had asked her what types of books she liked to read, one of her answers was that she favored books by Dr. James Dobson, especially his then-popular *Dare to Discipline* (1970). Being unfamiliar at the time with the book, I unreflectively jotted down the answer and probed no more. I realize now that this answer was the key that unlocked her views on child rearing. She was an evangelical Christian.

During our subsequent conversations, we talked at length about her spiritual quest. She spoke about her conversion, its permeating influence on her life, and her reliance on Christian self-help books in raising her children. These same themes recurred at each contact I had with her. After a while, I began to doubt that I could effectively utilize

Marina's input in my study. These revelations about her spiritual life made me suspect that she was marginal to mainstream practices of the community I had selected to describe. I reluctantly mentally reviewed our interviews and grimly determined that, absorbing and eloquent as I found her, she could not really illuminate the overarching processes I was looking for. I felt she would be marginal to the study—that is, until I interviewed the mother in the third household, Raquel Salazar.

Raquel was recruited to the study as part of the nonbarrio sample. I did not know her previously, and we were introduced by one of her former classmates whom I had asked to supply me with the names of anyone she might know who had a child of the appropriate age and who resided within the neighborhoods I had designated. My first contact with Raquel was on the phone as I introduced myself and briefly outlined the study. We made an appointment to meet a week later. The day of the interview, she called and asked to reschedule. She explained that she had a cousin who had just been diagnosed with a brain tumor and was undergoing surgery, and that she was watching her cousin's children for the week. We rescheduled, and I made a mental note to record this exchange of children as an aspect of child socialization when there is a network of kin relations in place. After another aborted appointment, we finally met on a Saturday afternoon at her home. Located in a subdivision of new tract homes, her house was spacious and uncluttered, immaculately groomed, both inside and out.

I started out the interview with the household history questionnaire and attempted to interject personal notes of common ground in order to establish some form of rapport. We spoke of the neighborhood where she was born, the neighborhood in which her husband was raised, and her family background. We came to a point in the interview that involved an exploration of the ideological underpinnings of each household's style of child rearing. As she broached this subject, she appeared to undergo a conversational metamorphosis. Polite and reserved during the introductory portion of the interview, she became openly exuberant with a topic shift that allowed her to articulate her spiritual wanderings:

> I've always felt that I had a calling for some kind of ministry or youth ministry, and when I got into the last years of high school, I just kind of lost that part of my life. And then, after I got married, of course things changed. But I still had that yearning . . . I had a

yearning to continue that. And so I wanted to get a youth ministry started at —— parish, for married couples, or mothers at home, self-support kind of stuff, and the priest made it impossible. A lot of red tape, and this and that. It was real difficult to just start anything over there. And I got real frustrated and . . . I just slacked off until one day I went to Son Life, and then I went to ——, and that's where I am now, at —— Chapel. And the minute I walked into that place, I knew that this was it. That was what I wanted to do. I got filled the minute I walked in. I got the feeling that very minute. I was at [a local church] so long, I was a Catholic for twenty-eight years, and I never really got filled.

It was obvious that her religious enthusiasm spilled over into how she was raising her children:

Well, my brother . . . my brother was really involved, and he gave the kids Bibles and was always giving the kids books like Jonah, the story of Jonah, books that are for kids, characters that are for kids. My oldest son, he . . . he's not afraid to express it. And we have a lot of Christian tapes, and we listen to Amy Grant. The kids know all of the verses to the songs, and there's . . . see, their cousins are the same age as mine are, and they listen to Mötley Crüe, you know, and my kid will go up to them and say: "Hey, don't you listen to Christian music?" And his cousins will say: "Christian music? You mean that kind of angel kind of stuff?" And you know, [my son] would say, "No, you should . . . you should listen to it. It's . . . it's really neat, you know?" He's not afraid to *say* that, and the other kids will kind of like be embarrassed, you know, but my brother gives us tapes, and he . . . he's really expressive about it. . . . I mean, you know, I don't want him to grow up to be a priest, but I want him to learn the right morals because of society right now is getting so bad, and the television is . . . I want him to learn the—a right way, you know? . . . And I get them tapes, vcr tapes that are Christian. For Christmas, I was looking at buying the kids something that was more educational for them, and I bought them stuff like cassettes and dictionaries. Stuff like that. But I wanted something that would help them more with their morals—teach them self-confidence that I wasn't taught as a child.

As she talked, I tried to maintain a veneer of professional detachment, but I was inwardly stunned. How could such a minuscule sample of households already contain two households wherein the mother was undergoing such a fundamental religious transformation? The impact for language was astounding. Books, cassette tapes, music, scripture reading, all geared to evangelical Christianity, were suddenly appearing, a none too welcome intrusion on what I already felt was an overly cluttered methodological landscape. I felt that there was little documentation of language practices within what one would consider "traditional" households, and no real baseline, as it were, of uncomplicated cases, so I did not want to interject any more complexity.

Both Marina and Raquel had an almost palpable enthusiasm for discussing their newfound conversion. They avidly solicited my views and opinions on these subjects, as if to validate their own quest. I found myself sharing with them my own private excursion away from the Catholicism of my youth and the significance that exodus had in my own life. I knew firsthand what an arduous course one chooses when attempting to tread a path that deviates from the ethnic unity of traditional Catholicism.

I had reached a juncture in the research process that was unpredictable and even disagreeable to me. I was being furnished with a methodologically discomforting reality: the nonuniformity of the field. The categories that I had tried to identify were in a state of flux. I had tried to capture the heterogeneity of the population by dividing the sample according to some notion of naturally occurring divisions within the community. I had opted for a residential variable—that is, comparing families from barrio settings with families from nonbarrio settings. This division was proving problematic. Marina, originally tied to her barrio street, moved to the eastside home of her parents during the course of my fieldwork. Iris Gallardo moved from her home to her parents' southside home and then again to a northside working-class nonbarrio area. Other factors confounded a neat delineation of the households. Rosalba, chosen for the study based on her enrollment in a PACE classroom, was cared for by her grandmother who lived in the PACE neighborhood, but Rosalba actually lived on an acre of land with ducks, chickens, and rabbits.

Other "deviations" cropped up as well. Rosalba's mother turned out to have a degree from the University of Arizona, even though she worked as a cashier at a small southside grocery store. How could I classify her family? I had also hoped to get a fair number of Spanish-dominant households from the PACE sample. I had only one. The emergence of language patterns within the homes grounded in evangelical Christianity was completely unexpected to me. This data set was not the one that I had hoped for, yet it reflected very real processes in the area in which I was working: the community was by no means monolithic and defied any simplistic two-dimensional analysis based on class, education, or residential pattern. My primary question remained: Are there identifiable processes by which children are socialized through language in Mexican-origin households? The next question that inevitably followed was more discomfiting: How can these processes be elucidated taking into account the smorgasbord of households I was encountering?

As I contemplated the disjointed scenario before me, I attempted to come to grips with what I faced. How could I devise neat theoretical constructs when the continuum of everyday life kept getting in my way? I was unaware at the time that it was precisely because of the fluidity of the field I was observing that I would glean one of my most significant insights.

I began the process of analyzing tapes and observations as soon as I had visited the households. I initiated a preliminary classification of household language use along one of the initial grids outlined by Ochs and Schieffelin: "adapting the child to the situation" versus "adapting the situation to the child" (1984:285). (For a more complete review of child language socialization literature and socialization of Mexican-origin children, see González 1992.) Because this division was somewhat analogous to that found in the literature on social class and language use, which tended to differentiate modes of parental control, I was curious about the patterns that would emerge. The early literature on social class and language use viewed "working"-class families as being more authoritarian, more inflexible, and less elaborate in their speech to children—in short, tending to "adapt the child to the situation." White-collar workers or middle-class families, according to this outlook, would be more likely to explain rules to their child, have less-rigid expectations of the child, and negotiate with the child to a greater extent—in effect, the adapting the situation to the child (see Gecas 1979).

Because I had divided my sample into barrio and nonbarrio samples roughly analogous to the determinants of working-class versus middle-class constructs, this demarcation between child adaptation or situation adaptation households was to be the point of departure for my initial analysis.

According to my very broad categorizations of the eight households on which I had collected initial data, six fell in the category of "adapting the situation to the child," and two fell into the taxonomy of "adapting the child to the situation." I looked at the households that fell into the latter category and tried to extract some rationale for the difference. In one home, the target child's family (mother, father, and siblings) lived in the grandparents' home. In the other, the child spent a good deal of time at the grandparent's home. I tried to formulate other justifications for the division, but had only tentative and preliminary impressions. Then an interesting thing happened.

Because of a change in my husband's employment, it became necessary for my family and me to leave Tucson for a period of time. I visited all of the households before I left, supplied them with blank tapes so that they could continue taping in my absence, but was not able to communicate with them personally for several months. I essentially lost contact with the households for a period of time. I came back to Tucson with the express purpose of reestablishing a connection with the households and contacted them all anew. In my absence, the household moves that I have already mentioned took place: Marina and her children moved into her parents' home, and Iris, her husband, and children moved into her parents' home. As I recontacted these two women, I noticed a subtle shift in their demeanor. They were a bit more reserved, a little more reluctant about the interviewing situation. Most important, I noticed a definite shift in their language patterns toward their children. Whereas both of these households had previously fallen into the "adapting the situation to the child" orientation, I detected a pronounced shift toward the other direction. In fact, if I had to recategorize the households, they would fall well within the parameters of "adapting the child to the situation." Parents increased the use of imperatives and directives with their children and seemed to be more overtly controlling in their behavior. In one instance, the target child, who had previously been allowed to interact freely with me, was now banished into a back bedroom while I undertook a stilted interview with his mother. Whereas other interviews had produced photo albums and lengthy conversations, this one was unelaborated. In the other household, the mother actually confessed that she felt like she had to "be on top of her children" all the time now and felt more constrained because she was not within her own home:

It's been hard, *hard, hard* being here. You know, it's just like they say: you go into your mother's home, and it's like you're a kid again. You know, I would reprimand my children, and no sooner would I reprimand them than my mother would jump in and say, "And if you don't listen to your Mom, then *I'm* going to get you." . . . And then she gets angry over certain things that I find are not so important to me. Like, I have no difficulty with my kids wrestling. They're boys, you know, that's normal everyday wear and tear on them. But, for her, it's wrong, and I have to suppress that energy, and that's very difficult. But I honor her because that's how she feels. Loudness . . . quietness, they have really had to tone down themselves; they can't let loose like when they're with me. . . .

Other things that we may disagree on, well . . . just child-rearing things in general. And it's really funny because I sit here, and I listen to her, and she's got a set of rules for my sister and one for my brother, and she tries to cross the two of them together between me, so things . . . Like, for example, my sister gives her children an allowance for what they do, and my brother does not. I decided to do it, and all of a sudden it was wrong, and I said, "Well, *why?* Because my brother doesn't think it's cool? [My sister] does. Why is it so good for her to do it, but so wrong for me?" . . . I tell my mom: "I don't want to put my responsibilities for my kids on you. I don't like being here. This is your home, and you have your measure of how you like your house to be, and I don't live up to that. You want your house immaculate; I don't live up to that. I don't like every little thing in its place where nobody should touch it. I have [children]; I can't afford that right now. . . . There is no room for kids here. You have to understand what I'm trying to suppress here. It's like taking energy and packing it into a box, and it's fighting to get out, and I'm holding it in, and I'm having trouble holding it in there, and every now and then it leaks out, and something happens, and it's inevitable."

There was no mistaking the indisputable fact that caregiver speech directed toward children had shifted in these households.

The idea that language patterns should vary owing to fluctuations in the social environment was not particularly startling. It is, after all, a basic tenet of sociolinguistics. But it was extremely awkward to discover that the pattern that had appeared to be a robust dichotomy in the literature and on which I had planned to begin to build a preliminary analysis was alterable in a relatively short period of time. I had learned a distressing rule of ethnographic research: that a seemingly accurate observation at one point in time may not be so in the next.

I now had a pattern that could not be overlooked: in all of the households that exhibited the orientation of adapting the child to the situation, the maternal grandparents were a dominant presence. Three of the children were actually co-residential with the grandparents, and the other spent a high percentage of her waking time at her grandparent's house. Although the pattern was clear, the significance of it was not.

The longer I examined this pattern, the more I felt that the conclusion that could be drawn from this chain of events was self-evident. The mothers in this sample were responding *not* to social variables in setting, interlocutors, and other aspects of speech events. They were modifying their linguistic style in response to deeply felt and deeply internalized emotions.

The emotional element of the linguistic environment was a densely woven fabric of familial interactions. I had witnessed exchanges between mother and adult daughter, seen the shifts in gaze, the nonverbal indications of profound emotionally ambivalent intertwinings. These women were reacting to their own legacy of socialization, to their own unresolved sibling rivalries and parent-child cooperation and conflict. I could only guess at the individual permutations of each set of relationships, but one thing was plain to me: in all of the households that I had visited, with the multiplicity of dimensions impinging on discourse, speech directed toward children was infinitely more complex than a categorization of its surface characteristics. "Context" took on an unimaginable magnitude.

If emotion-laden factors could alter the patterns of the language directed toward children at the level at the household, I attempted to consider the impact of affective and emotional domains within a larger context.

The shifts in household patterns had evidenced to me that context was more of a substantive difference than a stylistic difference. It was evident that emotion and affect colored the language directed toward children. It was equally evident that context, at both the micro and macro levels, loomed as the larger issue in this language socialization study.

At first, I was reluctant to take on this topic, even though "affect" was a common thread in much language socialization research—reluctant because I didn't think of feelings and emotions in quite the same way that they were described in the literature (cf. Besnier 1990). For me, the link between emotion and language was intuitive and subjective, understood implicitly, yet unexplored explicitly. I had to swallow hard before I could give myself permission to think of my personal experiences as somehow contributing to an "objective" analysis. The constructs within which I worked had always been framed by others. In my early years of college, it had been exhilarating and validating to learn that there were theoretical terms such as *code-switching* that accounted for the everyday patterns of language use that I experienced. It was a leap of faith to contemplate that I could invert this paradigm and theorize the personal. And so I leaped.

CHAPTER 4

The Hearts of the Children

EMOTION, LANGUAGE, AND IDENTITY

And he shall turn the heart of the fathers to the children,
and the heart of the children to their fathers.
—Malachi 4:6

Emotion as Examinable

Once I had decided that emotion loomed large on the language horizon,
I began to think about the relationship between the two. I knew that the
role of emotion—or, to use the more psychological term *affect*—was not
new to language socialization studies. In a major collection of studies
(Schieffelin and Ochs 1986b), several authors examined the expression
of affect in interactional routines. Miller, in her study of South Baltimore, shows that teasing is a patterned interaction utilized consciously
by mothers to "toughen up" their children for the vagaries of life, to
prepare them for their affective battles with linguistic weapons. In the
same volume, Eisenberg views the teasing sequences in Mexicano (Mexican immigrant) homes in the San Francisco Bay area as encoding
messages about relationships. Schieffelin, examining teasing and sham-
ing with Kaluli children, sees the interactions as a means of conven-
tionalized control. In Clancy's study of Japanese communicative style, a
category for expressing affect had to be created during the coding of the
data because the informants so repeatedly interjected the issue. Taking
this interest one step further, Ochs marks the saliency of emotion in her
observations on Samoan children: "So much of the talk was intensely

emotional. Caregivers and children talked *about* feelings and emotional states a great deal" (1986a:252).

Across time and space, dealing with the young is intensely emotion laden. But what emotions are in play, and what can we understand about the idea of "emotion"?

The role of emotion in social processes has been the locus of an animated debate in psychological, anthropological, linguistic, and neurobiological disciplines. Emotion is now recognized as a legitimate object of study, not to be relegated to the realm of the "inaccessible" or "unscientific." However, there does exist a debate as to the nature of emotions and to the organizing role that they play.

The debate can be reduced essentially to the differences between three opposing camps. The first camp, based fundamentally on a functionalist Darwinian paradigm, holds that emotions are innate biosocial manifestations of adaptive processes and, in some form or other, are ontologically universal. Advocates of this psychobiological emphasis (Ekman, Friesen, and Ellsworth 1982; Frijda 1986; Izard 1977) argue that primary emotions are evident in the neonate and are cross-culturally manifested in adult forms. This universalist view holds that "basic emotions are transcultural and that while they may be nuanced in different ways in different societies, at core they must be biologically determined and always the same" (Leavitt 1996:518). A second position, as reported by Fischer, Shaver, and Carnochan (1990), cites a corpus of research that has grown around the contention that cognitive (thought) processes such as judgment, appraisal, and intentions or goals are also operant in emotional processes. A third approach, with its prime proponents emerging from anthropological perspectives, takes the point of view that emotions can be socially constructed and that the emotions can be placed "squarely in the realm of culture by pointing to the ways local cultural concepts of emotion such as the Ilongot *liget* (anger), and the Pintupi *ngaltu* (compassion) borrow from broader cultural themes and reflect, in their ideological shape, the forms of indigenous social relationships" (Abu-Lughod and Lutz 1990:4). Lutz and White, for example, describe the "culturally constituted self, positioned at the nexus of personal and social worlds. . . . [Thus] emotions emerge as socially shaped and socially shaping in important ways" (1986:417). These constructivist anthropologists have located various degrees of emotional meaning embedded within ideology and social relations, and claim that emotion is one "aspect of cultural meaning" (Lutz and White 1986:408). If we ask ourselves how languages can encode emotions that are socially constructed, we could take linguistic relativity to its extreme and claim, as does Wierzbicka, that there is no common emotion term that is lexicalized in all languages: "Until recently many scholars refused to believe that the categorization of 'emotion' can differ from language to language and insisted that at least some 'emotions' must be linguistically recognized in all languages. There can no longer be any doubt, however, that this is not the case" (1999:24).

In this chapter, I argue that there can exist emotions, particularly the "emotion of minority status," that are *sociohistorically* constituted. An example by John Leavitt conveys this message:

> Affective or felt associations, like semantic ones, are collective as well as individual; they operate through common or similar experience among members of a group living in similar circumstances, through cultural stereotyping of experience, and through shared expectations, memories, and fantasies. A major festival like Christmas among English speaking North Americans is accompanied by a stereotypical set of emotions. Certainly we do not all actually feel these emotions: for many, Christmas is primarily lived, according to self-reports and actions, in a mode of disgust at overindulgence or in a heightened sense of loneliness. But this does not mean that Christmas evokes feelings at random, or that one's feelings about Christmas depend exclusively on factors that will change entirely from person to person. They depend, rather, on personal elements that to a large degree are common to those who share common experiences and a common exposure to stories, songs, images, and ritual practices—all features that reinforce a message of comfort and joy, homeyness [*sic*], and familial good cheer. (1996:527)

As Leavitt postulates, the emotion of "Christmas cheer" may not be one that has been universally experienced across human time and space, yet particular groups can identify it as a "feeling." In this chapter, I make the same contention about the "emotion of minority status." This connection, however, begs a fundamental question: Can human social structures impact the workings of our brain? I would contend that the answer is yes, although I claim that it is a dialectical relationship. I would like to highlight here the work of Joseph LeDoux (1996) in neuropsychology, where he has problematized the relationship between the amygdala, the part of the brain that registers emotion, and the neocortex, the "rational part" of the brain, and I extend some implications of his research. LeDoux states:

> The bottom line is this. Human consciousness is the way it is because of the way our brain is. . . .
>
> Emotional feelings result when we become consciously aware that an emotion system of the brain is active. Any organism that has consciousness also has feelings. However, feelings will be different in a brain that can classify the world linguistically and categorize experiences in words than in a brain that cannot. The difference between fear, anxiety, terror, apprehension, and the like would not be possible without language. At the same time, none of these words would have any point if it were not for the existence of an underlying emotion system that generates the brain states and bodily expressions to which these words apply. . . . The brain states and bodily responses are the fundamental facts of an emotion, and the conscious feelings are the frills that have added icing to the emotional cake. (1996: 302)

So, if we could not categorize an emotion linguistically, does it mean it does not exist? Could we "feel" the difference between terror and apprehension if English did not happen to encode these two words? I argue in this chapter that different languages encode different emotional dimensions within the same semantic referent. Does this mean that the neural systems of speakers of different languages are different? No. But it does mean that socially constituted emotional states derived from human social structures must have a place in our neural activities, and I contend that language mediates this process.

Pushing Emotion beyond Sociocultural Competence

Although language studies have been concerned with the role of affect in language socialization, it seemed to me that emotion was being subsumed under a strategy for studying interactional "routines." For instance, one way that emotions were placed in the realm of sociocultural competence was to identify linkages between affect and linguistic structures:

An important component of sociocultural competence every child must acquire is the ability to recognize and express feelings in context. Every society has ways of viewing moods, dispositions, and emotions, including how they are to be displayed verbally and nonverbally and the social conditions in which it is preferable or appropriate to display them. . . . When children are exposed to language in use, and begin to use language with older members of society, they are presented with an array of affective structures, a set of contexts, a set of relations linking the two (e.g., markedness of affective forms vis-à-vis social identity of speaker/audience, social setting, activity, etc.). (Ochs 1986b:8)

In consideration of how I had seen the role of emotion playing out in the households I was studying and my own awareness of the role that emotion has in speaking a particular language, this stance toward affect did not resonate. The assumption that something as intangible and transcendent as emotions could be demarcated and isolated as one of a number of linguistic variables to which the child is exposed in learning "to become a member of a society" and that emotions could somehow be "contextualized" seemed to relegate them to the sidelines. Emotion was just one more social construct, like status and rank, that language encoded. I, on the other hand, began to see emotion as the infrastructure for child language socialization, a processual and dynamic locus for constructing meaning and identity. Emotion to the child is ubiquitous. Language does more than index prefabricated affective structures, and emotion does not have to be contextualized.

Why do I make this claim? Admittedly, it springs from my own reflections on the use of language in the borderlands. I was not "taught" about language. It was simply there. "Nothing worth learning can be taught," Oscar Wilde once observed. My own lack of consciousness about language in my childhood is illustrated by an offhand remark I overheard referring to the fact that my great-grandmother, Yaya, could not speak English. "Well, of course she speaks English," I insisted. "I understand her, and she talks to me, and *I* understand English." I was convinced that what was intelligible to me was intelligible to her because somehow we understood and communicated. Languages had blurred, and it was difficult to disentangle where one left off and another began. There was no boundedness to language, no readily identifiable edges that could be marked off. There was only communication, however and whenever it took place. How often have I heard of Latino adults who as children were admonished to speak only English in the school grounds and their unspoken dread that somehow they would not be able to tell the difference. As languages blur, the contexts that they evoke intermingle and blend.

Although I was aware that language use with Yaya was fraught with the seductive pull of her cuentos (stories) and the sublime narratives of her childhood, I could not fathom that *she did not speak English*. Even in my immature state, I could discern that a person who did not speak English was invisible. He or she did not exist. English was the currency of exchange for securing personhood. Yet my Yaya existed, and the world that she created for me through her crafting of language often bore little resemblance to the world that I then inhabited. I became aware of the legacy of bilingual children everywhere: the arbitrariness of the sign. When she drank cafecito, it was more milk than coffee, sugary and served in a glass. It was not the same as coffee, which was dark and bitter and always in a cup. A *vaso de leche* was milk warmed to just before boiling and was drunk with *pan de huevo*. A *glass of milk*, on the other hand, was cold and drunk with cookies.

I learned that the world was not carved into discrete and knowable chunks that were simply labeled differently in different languages. When Yaya spoke of the sierra, of the smoky campsites of Mexican miners on their treks to mining camps, the images that she conjured could not be mapped onto any English equivalents. Ineffably, I knew that the dimensions of Spanish were far different from the dimensions of English. They did not feel the same, taste the same, or sound the same. Spanish was the language of family, of food, of music, of ritual—in short, of identity. It was the language of endearments to children. It was the language of dressing in white in long processions in dark churches. It was the language of tinkling music on Saturday morning radio. English was for arithmetic, for the doctor's office, for the teacher. English was the newspaper and television. Even though in my family, we mixed languages effortlessly, the underlying symbolism was correspondingly parallel: home and hearth were woven with Spanish; "out there" was constructed with English.

So I will throw caution to the winds and speculate how language and emotion come to be intricately intertwined for children. First of all, the neonate, as it is thrust out into its nonaquatic, light-filled environment, is extraordinarily perceptive to extralinguistic, affective signals. Pure communication to the newborn, unfettered by linguistic structure, is conveyed in its essential form of raw emotion. This is the infant's first exposure to human communication, an awareness that there is a method whereby messages from another being can be received. Her first exposure to the transmittal of messages is based on raw emotion.

I would argue that as the infant is exposed to human language, a reliance on intuition and subjectivity continues to play a pivotal role. As the child grows, she is receptive not only to acoustic properties, but to the affective dimensions contained within the parameters of the words. In this sense, words are instruments the child disassembles in order to extract the emotional essences being transmitted to her. Although words may be identical phonetically, they may carry distinct affective properties, varying from speaker to speaker and from situation to situation. Words are symbolically examined, in much the same way that the child will come to manipulate objects in the environment. The emotional impact that words have on a child exercises a creative force. Language and its attendant subjectivities orient the child not only as "a member of a culture," but as a member of the human species who happens to live within a human group. The approach that says that linguistic features key affect and that these features are used as a basis for constructing the feelings of others (Ochs and Schieffelin 1989) does not take into account children's emotional reactions in the absence or ambiguity of social referencing. The monitoring of others' affective displays may not convey a unified cue to the child, and contradictions or multiple perspectives are not taken into account.

Early routines with infants and children take a variety of forms, as documented in the various literatures. I think we can safely say that all societies in all times and all places have incorporated some notion of infant/child interaction with adults. An anecdotal tidbit of negative evidence for this generalization can be found in the misguided experiment performed in the thirteenth century by Frederick II, emperor of the Holy Roman Empire. He had a perverse interest in learning what language children would speak if no language were directed toward them from birth. He chose fifty unfortunate infants to serve as subjects for his "experiment" and placed them with a caregiver who was to bathe and feed them, but was forbidden from talking, caressing, or otherwise interacting with the infants. Frederick never learned the results of his dismal research because all fifty of the infants died. There appears to be a species-specific tendency to engage infants and children in some type of emotional stimuli in order for the young to survive. Medical and psychological literature amply documents the "failure to thrive" syndrome of infants deprived of meaningful human contact. When we study language and children, we must not neglect the affirmation of the emotional intensity of bonding with children. What is conveyed to the child through this process, I believe, is a sense of personhood. Interactional routines, at this point, can take on a primordial importance. Their magnitude, however, can be reconstrued as being meaningful not only at the social level, but in transmitting to an emergent being her unique and particular existence as a defined human entity. Routines define the fact that the child exists and has an inherent worth: she matters and is being taken care of. Routines, in this view, orient the child to her own nascent emotional tableau. She is questioned, teased, shamed, praised, and otherwise engaged in order to convey a range of human emotion. The child is introduced into personhood by experiencing the parameters of the inner self.

The Emotion of Linguistic Input

At some point, each child will embark on a highly individualized process of evaluating language. She will react to the emotional pull of language in a unique, specialized manner. We know from language acquisition studies that no two-year-old learns language in exactly the same way as her peers. Language learning appears in the absence of "motherese" and may be delayed even with the most conscientious adult modeling. A newspaper article about Katherine Nelson, a psychologist interested in child language, reported that some children have a "strong inclination toward naming objects, while others tend toward more 'expressive' speech, using 'socially useful' phrases like 'leave me alone' or 'that's mine' or 'I want it.' In her studies of videotapes of fifty-two children, she demonstrates that the mother can shape the child's speech patterns, but that the innate inclinations of children exert a powerful, and in some cases, decisive force. . . . 'You can't just point to an object and get the kid to learn,' . . . 'It's what the child is interested in' " (Berger 1988:11D). Each child has, for whatever reason, her own agenda for accepting certain social elements of language and for discarding others.

Parental guidance does not guarantee immediate understanding on the child's part or a willingness to participate as intended by others. These tendencies place the children within an affective universe, choosing from the constellations before them their own particular socio-affective linguistic strategies. This notion draws on Goodenough's early construction of the "ideolect," in which he underscores the fact that no two individuals experience language identically: "There are as many versions of a language as there are speakers of it" (1971:14). If we add to this mix the use of two languages, the affective dimensions become even more complex. Wierzbicka, a linguist drawing on her own experience as a bilingual and bicultural person, obliquely alludes to the possibility of language *creating* particular emotions:

> I would say that I tend to perceive my daily emotions in terms of lexical categories provided by Polish [my native language]. . . . None of the categories [in these examples] . . . has exact equivalents in English, and the sentences themselves cannot be adequately translated into English.
>
> However, within an English-speaking context, I often talk— and sometimes think—about my daily subjective experience in terms of the lexical categories of the English language, such as *upset, frustrated, resentful, annoyed, disgusted, happy,* and so on. None of these categories has exact equivalents in Polish, and they suggest a different interpretation of emotional experience. I think that this different interpretation cannot be separated from the subjective experience itself. (1994:135)

Eva Hoffman, in the quintessential essay on emotive aspects of differential linguistic domains, describes her experience thus:

> For a long time, it was difficult to speak those most intimate phrases, hard to make English—that language of will and abstraction—shape itself into the tonalities of love. In Polish, the words for "boy," and "girl" embodied within them the wind and crackle of boyishness, the breeze and grace of girlhood: the words summoned that evanescent movement and melody and musk that are the interior inflections of gender itself. In English, "man" and "woman" were empty signs; terms of endearment came out as formal and foursquare as other words. (1989:245)

Barbara Myerhoff makes a similar point in her study of elderly Jews in Venice, California: "All the elderly Jews in the neighborhood are Eastern European in origin. All are multilingual. Hebrew is brought out for punctuating debates with definitive learned points, usually by the men. Russian or Polish are more used for songs, stories, poems and reminiscences. But Yiddish binds these diverse people together, the beloved *mama-loshen* (Mother tongue) of their childhood. It is Yiddish that is used for the most emotional discussions" (1978:5).

Cannot minority group status involve a powerful evocative dimension? Yet the evocative dimensions of race/class and minority status have been absent in language studies of children. The developmental impact of growing within a racialized climate, indexed by language, must be foregrounded.

Markus and Kitayama address both the issue of the construction of selfhood and the influence of emotion on this process. They claim that the

> concept of a self as the particularized locus of various socio-cultural influences prevents an oversocialized conception of the person and helps to explain why two people, even those in similar sociocultural circumstances (e.g., twins in the same family) are unlikely to feel exactly the same way in a given set of circumstances. . . . The "I" who then feels an affective state of emotion has, as its referent, a particular configuration of self-representations and conceptions that reflect the individual's unique construction of experience. However, there are still ways of feeling that can be linked systematically to particular cultural frameworks, even though a given emotional state cannot be completely explained from these perspectives. (1994:92)

Thus, even though individual agency inheres in language socialization, there are social referents that cannot be ignored. For the Mexican-origin child, the issue of language and linguistic input is complicated by hegemonic structures that inhere in minority status. Language is not simply a vehicle for communication, but the site of a highly politicized and vitriolic debate concerning the nature of who speaks what language where and under what circumstances. No homogenous, nonambiguous system of social or linguistic knowledge is transmitted to children, and there are affective dimensions to differential linguistic domains. Steven

Krashen, the well-known expert in children's second-language acquisition, has long referenced an "affective filter" that impacts language
learning within the classroom (1981). The U.S.–dwelling child of Mexican descent is heir to varying amounts of interplay between English and
Spanish. Each household has its own particular history of dealing with
the intangibles of race, class, and minority status, which have very
tangible lived experiences behind them. Children must deal with the
linguistic legacies of their forebears. Words, in both English and Spanish, have a generative force—are charged with the aggregate of their
semiotic history. Bakhtin, in his essay "Discourse in the Novel," notes
that there is no single way (even in one language) that words relate to
their object:

> Between the word and the speaking subject, there exists an elastic
> environment of other, alien words about the same object, the same
> theme, and this is an environment that is often difficult to pene-
> trate. It is precisely in the process of living interaction with this
> specific environment that the word may be individualized and
> given stylistic shape. . . . The word, directed towards its object,
> enters a dialogically agitated and tension-filled environment of
> alien words, value judgments and accents, weaves in and out of
> complex inter-relationships, merges with some, recoils from oth-
> ers, intersects with yet a third group. (1981:276)

If we add the complexity of a dual lexicon, the interrelationships become even more "ideologically saturated." Although referentially identical, words may generate contradictory impacts. A process of dialogism, Bakhtin claims, is the basis for our multilayered interpretations of
words: "The word is born in a dialogue as a living rejoinder within it;
the word is shaped in dialogic interaction with an alien word that is
already in the object. A word forms a concept of its own object in a
dialogic way" (1981:279).

A child with a dual lexicon may pronounce and use both systems, but
the emotional load may vary differentially. Words, then, can pack a more
powerful "punch" in either one language or another. Utterances in English, Spanish, or both are charged with the aggregate of their semiotic
history. The linguistic evidence for affection is one area where endearments represent a rich example of these "complex inter-relationships"
that Bakhtin mentions. Children are regularly addressed with a wide

range of affective markers. Whether referred to as *niños, chamacos, angelitos, muchachitos lepecitos, criaturas, bukis, mocosos, pedacitos, rey, reina, amorcitos, huercos,* etc., etc., they are well aware of the evocative dimensions of the terms. *Mijo,* a shortened version of "my son" *(mi hijo),* evokes a multifaceted prism of meaning in Spanish. It links speaker and hearer with an almost palpable bond. When spoken by father to son, it forges a link in a paternalistic chain that extends into historical antecedents we can only guess at. When spoken from mother to son, the consummate metaphors of Mexican motherhood rest on it. When spoken by a nonparent to a child, it cements a kinship that may or may not be genetic. The Mexican-origin child may have receptive and/or productive capacities in both languages, but the polysemic potential of the discrete units varies contextually. This verbo-ideological system evokes differential affective dimensions with the child.

In *The Labyrinth of Solitude* (1961), Octavio Paz confronts these subliminal connections and recounts his conversation with a Mexican friend on the loveliness of Berkeley. Commenting on the beauty of the area, she reflects,

> Yes, it's very lovely, but I don't belong here. Even the birds speak English. How can I enjoy a flower if I don't know its right name, its English name, the name that has fused with its colors and petals, the name that's the same thing as the flower? If I say *bugambilia* to you, you think of the bougainvillea vines you've seen in your own village, with their purple liturgical flowers, climbing around an ash tree or hanging from a wall in the afternoon sunlight. They are a part of your being, your culture. They're what you remember long after you've seemed to forget them. It's very lovely here, but it isn't mine. (18)

Ineffably, the evocative dimensions of Spanish and English are not the same. The symbolic content of the linguistic product, as well as its form, emerges as formative force within the child's language socialization.

THE EMOTION OF MINORITY STATUS

The legacy of Mexican-origin populations in the United States is one of flux. The historical junctures that have given rise to the status of Tucson neighborhoods include war, revolution, immigration, and the constant movement of peoples. The collective consciousness of the borderlands area has been affected profoundly by deportation actions, repatriation, and other immigration legalese, from the forced relocations of the 1930s to Operation Wetback of the 1950s to the Simpson-Rodino Immigration Reform Act of the 1980s and to the anti-immigrant and anti-bilingual-education initiatives of the 1990s in California. A clear message of foreignness and "otherness" is sent to the Mexican-origin community through legislative enactments and hypermedia manipulations. Although long-established households may not have felt their direct impact, even their indirect impacts are not easily obliterated. On children, the effects are incalculable. Children do not discern a uniform, undifferentiated national ideology whose mores are transmitted unequivocally across the board. Instead, they detect whisperings of an "English-only movement." They hear veiled references to "wetback labor." News reports speak of armed citizen border patrols that aim to sever the flow of Mexican nationals into the United States. They glean that blond and blue-eyed is esteemed as the standard of beauty. They can intuit that somehow they don't fit.

Yet, as is endemic in human symbolic systems, the cultural legacy of the area is fraught with ambiguities. Although overt negative forces are pervasive, there have existed in the borderlands area romanticized and idyllic versions of Mexican-ness, as the mystique of señoritas in black lace mantillas has long enchanted local writers and artists. This ambiguity toward Mexican-ness is part and parcel of the local children's patrimony. They see the Mexican-inspired artifacts at the malls, offered for the de rigeur touch of the Southwest, along with the red chili strings on the Santa Fe–style homes of the upwardly mobile. They hear the plaintive strains of Linda Ronstadt, surrounded by mariachis, serenading the Muppets on Sesame Street with "Andale." Nine o'clock mass on Sunday at the cathedral is a celebration of mariachi and popular songs blended into a melange of the sacred and the profane. They hear Tucson touted as the "Mexican Food Capital of the West," its ethnic diversity applauded in Chamber of Commerce brochures and in the festival formerly referred to as Tucson Meet Yourself. Spanish interlaces the allure of Tucson the Old Pueblo, its Fiesta de los Vaqueros Rodeo, and the romantic-sounding names of its upscale resorts, La Paloma, El Conquistador, and of course the names of its downtown streets, Granada and Alameda. Yet beneath these surface nods to Tucson's Spanish-language heritage lurk other veiled processes that Jane Hill has identified as a racializing discourse, which she terms "Mock Spanish" (1993a, 1993b, 1995). In the Spanish of Tucson, particularly evident in public symbols such as street names and billboards, appear grammatical aberrations that do not take into account basic elements of syntax and noun-adjective agreement. Hill documents numerous instances. For many years, we had a well-known street dubbed Camino del Tierra until some enlightened souls were able to change it to its more grammatical Camino de *la* Tierra. She cites the names of streets—for instance, San Anna, which should be Santa Ana—and names of housing communities—for example, Rancho Sin Vacas (Cowless Ranch), which boasts the street Calle sin Envidia (Street without Envy)—that seem to be random collections of elegant-sounding Spanish names, but that have no real meaning. Calle de Albondigas may sound wonderfully romantic, but Meatball Street may not be where we would want to live.

This disregard for phonetic, morphological, and syntactic rules of Spanish marginalizes the language as not being worthy of grammatical accuracy and sends the message that non–Spanish speakers need not attend to rules that are not considered to make much difference in a nonprestige language. The trivializing of these structures conveys to children that grammatical accuracy is a privilege reserved for English. This kind of semantic derogation—the affixation of Spanish grammatical elements (for example, "no problemo") to transform meanings into a pejorative or jocular connotation—as well as a strategy of hyperanglicization accomplish the "elevation of whiteness" (Hill 1999). "In order to 'make sense' of Mock Spanish, interlocutors require access to very negative racializing representations of Chicanos and Latinos as stupid, politically corrupt, sexually loose, lazy, dirty, and disorderly" (Hill 1999:683).

Again, on the other side of the coin, however, Mexican ranchers' intimate connection with the earth, the allure of warm, supportive, extended families, the seductive pull of Catholic holy communions and posadas have played on the stage of public newspapers, novels, and media. In an article that appeared in the *Arizona Daily Star,* after having first appeared in the *New York Times* (1990), Christine Wald-Hopkins chronicled the narrative of a seventeen-year-old Anglo-German Tucson High School student who lamented her seeming lack of identification. She wanted only one thing:

"To be Mexican. All my friends are Mexican. I like only Mexican boys. I like only Mexican music. When I was little I prayed God every night, 'Please let me wake up Mexican.'" . . . So why does Carrie want to be Mexican-American, anyway? For something the culture offers that hers lacks? For the inviolability of the Mexican family, which drifts well past the nuclear unit to as far as a net is needed? For the inextricability of the secular and the sacred— saints and the Virgin peopling their houses; candles and incense and mysterious chants and recited prayers—the seductiveness of sensual Catholic service to the plank-pew and empty-cross-raised Protestant girl; romance of the bride gown First Communion? For the unequivocal, piquant quality of being part of La Raza: immediate, first glance cultural identification? . . . She's "just white," in a small ill-fitting family removed a generation ago from the Midwest. Vague. She sees it featureless, colorless, without ritual or custom: everything the Mexican-American culture here is *not*. (Wald-Hopkins 1990, A11)

These ambiguities of the borderlands context for language socialization do not reflect a unified consensual ideology that is transmitted to children. Rather, each household and caregiver-child dyad or polyad has the capacity to respond particularly to the affective and evocative dimensions of race/class and minority status.

Disambiguation and the Construction of Selfhood

This chapter takes two points of view: first, ambiguity and contradiction are a backdrop to the study of the language socialization of Mexican-origin children; second, this ambiguity gives rise to an "emotion of minority status" that is socially constituted and embedded within sociohistorical relations, and one that I would refer to as the emotion of "subalternity." For Mexican-origin children, the experience of being "minority group" members has an impact that in many ways overshadows other social and familial variables and that creates a particularistic, socially constituted emotion that is identifiable to those people with a nondominant status within a pluralistic environment. It is an emotion that juxtaposes assimilation and alienation, and combines centripetal and centrifugal forces of language. One small vignette from

Enrique Hank López effectively represents the paradoxes of border-lands experiences:

> During this phase of my childhood the cultural tug of war known as "Americanization" almost pulled me apart. There were moments when I would identify completely with the gringo world (what could have been more American than my earnest high-voiced portrayal of George Washington, however ridiculous the cotton wig my mother had fashioned for me?); then quite suddenly I would feel so acutely Mexican that I would stammer over the simplest English phrase. I was so ready to take offense at the slightest slur against Mexicans that I would imagine prejudice where none existed. But on other occasions, in full confidence of my belonging, I would venture forth into social areas that I should have realized were clearly forbidden to little chicanos from Curtis Park. The inevitable rebuffs would leave me floundering in self-pity. (1971:265)

This slice of child-life evocatively outlines the contours of a process that jerks children in competing directions. On the one hand, such children evince a deep and fierce loyalty to the emotions that being Latino engenders. On the other, there is a desperate bid to belong to a totality that is greater than they, powerful and alluring in its domination of their lives.

A Metaphor for Language Use:
The Dialogical Staircase, an Interactional Double Helix

How does emotion intersect with the dialogism of interaction within a sociohistorical context? First of all, we must relate both language and emotion as both "in the brain" and yet inherently social in nature.

Steven Pinker, in his much praised book *The Language Instinct* (1995), claims that "Language is not a cultural artifact that we learn the way we learn to tell time, or how the federal government works. Instead, it is a distinct piece of the biological makeup of our brains" (18). By regarding language as an instinct, we can begin to look at language "not as the ineffable essence of human uniqueness but as a biological adaptation to communicate information" (1995:19). It is no longer an "insidious shaper of thought . . . but our biological birthright; it is not something that parents teach their children or something that must be elaborated in school" (ibid.). Of course, Pinker here is dealing with a capacity hard-wired into our brain for learning "Language" writ large. However, if we accept his claims, then the language socialization of children, tied in as it is with their acquisition of language, might be likened to other biological functions. In other words, the relatively short window of critical learning ability is invested in the very young, and "the language acquisition circuitry is not needed once it has been used" (ibid.:294). However, the emotion of the linguistic input, especially at this critical learning stage, I believe can have dramatic effects on interactive patterns later in life, and it as at this point that nature and nurture intersect. In the realm of emotions, again with reference to the work of Joseph LeDoux, an emotional feeling requires certain ingredients to turn an emotional reaction into a conscious emotional experience:

> We've got a specialized emotion system that receives sensory inputs and produces behavioral, autonomic, and hormonal responses. We've got cortical sensory buffers that hold on to information about the currently present stimuli. We've got a working memory executive that keeps track of the short-term buffers, retrieves information from long-term memory, and interprets the contents of the short-term buffers in terms of activated long-term memories. We also have cortical arousal. And finally, we have bodily feedback—somatic and visceral information that returns to the brain during an act of emotional responding. When all of these systems function together, a conscious emotional experience is inevitable. When some components are present and others lacking, emotional experiences may still occur, depending on what's there and what's not. (1996:296)

If both language and emotion are part of our biology, how does the social get woven into the mix?

The metaphor I would invoke draws from our knowledge of molecular biology and involves the double helix—the spiral staircase of the DNA molecule, the mechanism for the transmission of genetic information. My metaphorical image is an interactional double helix: a dialogical staircase of a process of intertwining responses between adults and children, both being touched by and affected by the links between them, transmitting on an individual level the unique and particularistic version of each generation's social memory.

This model draws on a Vygotskian perspective, wherein the child is seen as unfolding through a reciprocal influence with social environment, and whereby the child engages in independent action through the assistance of others. Within a "zone of proximal development" (Vygotsky 1978), the child receives each caregiver's personal rendition of the many macro forces in a society. A sociohistorical perspective is essential to understanding any representation of knowledge transmission. Vygotsky, true to his Marxist roots, draws on the notion that although we may create and fashion our lives, we do not create them exactly as we please. However, no two caregivers will experience societal forces in precisely the same way. Therefore, the multivocality of each child's experiences must be taken into account. Linguistic and nonlinguistic stimuli are charged with a semiotic history apart from their sociohistory. Gender, race, ethnicity, minority status, and hegemonic relations of symbolic domination present a multiplex and heteronomic setting for the processes of language socialization. This polyphony speaks, often unevenly, and children will hear some voices more than others.

Both child and adult are engaged, shaped, and reshaped in an ongoing interplay—a continuous process, a continuum of existence within the everyday world. Both are shaped by mutual actions and reactions, utterances and replies, verbal and nonverbal cues, modifying and being modified at each interactional, affect-laden node.

This metaphor is an attempt to join "Bakhtin's dialogism to Vygotsky's developmentalism" (Holland et al. 1998:184). Within Bakhtin, "escape from being ventriloquated by first one and then another authoritative voice comes through the orchestration of and adoption of stances toward these voices" ibid.:185). For Bakhtin, the word in language is "half someone else's":

> It becomes "one's own" only when the speaker populates it with his own intention, his own accent, when he appropriates the word, adapting it to his own semantic and expressive intention. Prior to this moment, the word does not exist in a neutral and impersonal language (it is not, after all, out of a dictionary that the speaker gets his words!), but rather it exists in other people's mouths, in

other people's contexts, serving other people's intentions: it is from there that one must take the word, and make it one's own. . . . Language is not a neutral medium that passes freely and easily into the private property of the speaker's intentions; it is populated—overpopulated—with the intentions of others. Expropriating it, forcing it to submit to one's own intentions and accents, is a difficult and complicated process. (Bakhtin 1981:293–94)

According to Holland and colleagues, within Vygotsky we find the emphasis on

the ability of humans to use mediating devices, especially symbols, to modify their own mental environment and so direct their own behavior. These devices were generally first taken up in interaction with others, and then only gradually taken into one's self-activity. The resulting complex (device plus behavior—not forgetting context) could eventually become habitual or "fossilized," in Vygotsky's term (1978:68), be moved out of awareness, possibly with no observable trace of the mediating means; "the" act, subsuming its exterior development, became seemingly an essential characteristic of the person. (1998:175)

The double helix metaphor helps us to understand the dialogical emergence of sociohistoric legacies, not in a way that reproduces structures uncritically generation after generation, but that allows a space for everyday practices and interactions to contest, reframe, and author selves and identities. Like our genetic material, meanings can recombine in a variety of ways, creating distinct formations and interactions. Yet these meanings arise within dialogic interactions: "Language lives only in the dialogic interaction of those who make use of it" (Bakhtin 1984:183).

Disambiguation and Self-Authorship

I contend that because mothers of the borderlands are aware of and have endured the ambiguity of borderlands status, the intragenerational transmission of useful knowledge incorporates a quest for "disambiguating" the paradoxes of Latino identity for the child in the United States. It is a search for the construction of self in the muddle of conflict-

ing values, symbols, and nuances. Caught within the pervasive discontinuities and heretofore insoluble antinomies of race, class, ideology, and
ethnicity, Mexican-origin borderlands households are a fertile landscape
for the genesis of forms of the construction of self within southwestern
society. It is one of many strategies adopted in order to disentangle the
structural inconsistencies intrinsic to borderlands status. In the next
chapter, I take up this issue with regard to mothers in the borderlands.
This pursuit of disambiguation can be demonstrated in the language
socialization of children. If parents have struggled with a lack of definition of social categories, expectations, and norms, then, of course,
they have also made an attempt at stabilizing and relieving these social
tensions. For the Mexican-origin households that I studied, there is a
marked and definite tendency to organize activity, linguistic and non-
linguistic, with the sense of "selfhood" for the child.

DIACRITICA

Frederick Barth, in his early work on ethnicity, referred to the existence
of badges of identity, which he dubbed "diacritical features" (1969:14).
As social units continue a long period of interaction, the more such units
become structurally similar and differentiated only by a few clear diacritica. Although the total inventory of cultural difference is no longer
substantial, those differences that remain take on a new magnitude
because of their function as emblems of identification. They become
symbolic. These symbolic emblems "mark off" Mexican-origin households and help to overcome the contradictions inherent in being an
ethnic minority within a larger society. Ethnicity in this way becomes
more a strategic presentation of self than an unwitting reflection of the
authentic self.

In response to subalternity, the emotion of minority status, I contend
that Mexican-origin families selectively and strategically deploy certain cultural traits to differentiate themselves from the "outside" Anglo
world and that these diacritica serve the function of marking off the
household as an identifiable unit within a larger regional context.

The following case study illustrates the interplay of identifying
markers for children.

The Aguilar family (described in chapters 2 and 7) provided me with
a rich supply of naturally occurring household discourse. Upon my
analysis of the tapes of this household, I found very little Spanish

used for functional communication. Additionally, neither parent feels a particularly strong religious inclination, although they do attend a Catholic church together occasionally. Thus, two traditional markers of Mexican-origin identity, use of Spanish and Catholicism, are not evident in the household.

During one of the interviews with the family, the father casually asked if I would be interested in viewing a videotape recently made of the children. The tape was already in place and was played as much for the children's benefit as for mine, as they manifestly exulted in the presentation, embellishing the video with running commentary, making sure that I noticed small details. The tape consisted of the antics of a brother and a sister, seven-year-old twins, whose playful charade the parents noticed and recorded. It showed the twins, garbed in Mexican charro outfits, lip-synching a soulful version of Vicente Fernandez's perennial favorite "Volver, volver, volver." They moved their lips in perfect harmony to the words, and when they came to the fervent crescendo of the refrain, they contorted their faces in mock romantic distress, re-creating a dramaturgical plot of a scorned lover, grieving over his rejection by his beloved.

It was an illuminating segment to me, particularly in light of the context that I had assembled of the household. At the time of the interviews, the children in the family had little productive ability in Spanish, although receptive ability was higher. They were avid consumers of Nintendo and video games, Batman, and rabid fans of the University of Arizona Wildcats. Saturday morning cartoons claimed a much higher portion of their consciousness than any Sixteenth of September celebration. It is more likely that they felt more kinship to Puritan Pilgrim "forbears" than to any association with Benito Juárez, more affinity with Bart Simpson than to the Niños Héroes de Chapultepec. They evidenced a pattern common in second- and third-generation borderlands households with extended family in the area—that is, when addressed in Spanish by grandparents or other Spanish speakers, the children responded in English. Their receptive abilities were more developed. As Mr. Aguilar wryly reported, the children understood more Spanish than he was aware of. At times, in order to disguise the topic of conversation, he and his wife would converse in Spanish, and the children would pick up on the themes discussed. The father, in addition to his everyday job, moonlights as a disc jockey, often spending weekends playing for weddings, quinceañeras, and parties. Several of the tapes revealed the children singing solos in Spanish or singing along with tapes of Mexican music. They did not reveal, however, any sibling interaction in Spanish, and my own conversational efforts to elicit their level of productive and conversational ability in Spanish revealed that the Aguilar children overwhelmingly preferred English. This pattern of Spanish in musical discourse is not uncommon and has even been recognized to a certain extent in the community. As many young people participate in mariachi groups as part of their community activities, they learn a repertoire of classic Mexican songs and pronounce them perfectly in their performance. This apparent fluidity in the language is not evidenced in their everyday conversation, however, and I have heard a snide reference to a successful mariachi singer as suffering from a "Mel Tillis" syndrome: with the productive ability in the language to sing but not to converse.

The Aguilar children, by virtue of their father's avocation, were and are exposed to a notable and significant amount of music in Spanish evocatively tied to another diacritic marker of ethnicity: ritual participation. Thus, they chose to highlight in a broad definition of discourse an element within their language socialization that they actively and strategically manipulated for their own purposes. Spanish for these children is essentially preserved in music and affective relations. It becomes, in Bakhtin's terminology, a type of living heteroglossia: two languages with highly differentiated levels. Spanish is associated with music, with affect, with the diacritica of construction of self. English, as evidenced in the sound tapes of family interactions, is the medium of informational exchange and of functional subsistence within the community. The Aguilar children are tied into a whole cycle of calendrical ritual participation in birthdays, piñatas, baptisms, and quinceañeras, where the affective diacritica define their nascent selfhood. Within the analysis of the transcription of the tapes, elements in Spanish revolve around kinship terms: *nanas* and *tatas, mijo* and *mija, tíos* and *tías;* shared activities of *birria* and *carne asada,* Christmas tamales, Lenten *capirotada,* and *huevo* and *chorizo* burritos for breakfast, *saladitos, raspados,* and the like; personal and intimate articles of clothing: *chones* for *calzones* (underpants); pejorative terms: *loco* in the *cabeza;* affinal nicknames: *primo, chuy, cha cha, yaya,* etc.; and teasing. Teasing is a significant speech activity in the family that involves the parent's switches to Spanish, which the child will attempt, unsuccessfully and ungrammatically, to emulate, and his response then becomes part of the teasing process. In chapter 7, transcripts of dinner table conversations reveal these patterns.

Extending this process to current community settings, a common phenomenon in family and friendship gatherings is readily recognizable to any observer of the Tucson community: conversational discourse during the festivity will evidence a dominance of English. When the guitars are brought out and the mood waxes nostalgic, however, Spanish fills the air. The songs that are often sung at parties and family get-togethers—corridos such as "Juan Charrasqueado," "Gabino Barrera," "Siete leguas," and canciones románticas such as "Perfidia" and "Usted"—are genres of music made popular during the 1940s and 1950s at a time when many of the parents and grandparents of present-day households came from Mexico. Mexican nationals have told me they are often surprised to hear songs being sung here that are considered "quaint" or old-fashioned in Mexico. There has been a time warp, in a sense, in that many of the most well-known songs have been stranded in an anachronistic setting, sung by new generations, who do not always sense the context of the song or the historical processes that gave rise to it.

This living heteroglossia—the connection of one language with the domain of food, relatives, music, and affect—is clearly evident in transcripts of naturally occurring conversation within the Aguilar household. In a related phenomenon, the impetus to advance positive images of self-identification to children is filtered through expressive culture in the form of dance, music, art, theater, and drama. In a continuation of a familial tradition, Linda Ronstadt, grand-niece of Luisa Espinel, has focused on a nostalgic renaissance of the music of early Tucson in her albums *Canciones de mi padre* and *Más canciones.* At a national level, the recognition of the impact of drama, art, and music resonates with artists and children alike. One such showcase is a unique phenomenon of Tucson, the Tucson International Mariachi Conference.

The Tucson International Mariachi Conference: Musical Discourse and Performed Identities

The scene is the Music Hall of the Tucson Community Center. Mariachi Cobre, the Tucson-grown celebrities of Epcot Center, has graciously consented to perform at the Students' Concert for elementary age children. There is standing room only as more than two thousand students cheer the opening bursts of trumpet music. The representative from the local corporate sponsor appears and encourages the students to continue in their education, but reminds them that education is not just tests and books, but includes music, song, dance, and art. She stresses the local origins of the group, reiterating to the children that hard work is behind all success. As the individual members of Mariachi Cobre are introduced, they too note their local roots. Elementary schools Menlo Park, Mission View, and Saints Peter and Paul are cheered as the home schools that some attended.

Mariachi Cobre is the outgrowth of Los Changuitos Feos, a juvenile group formed by a local Catholic priest and a unique Tucson musical tradition. Before they begin their concert, the mariachi group from Davis Bilingual Magnet School,[1] Las Aguilitas, makes its debut. Composed of third to fifth graders, it is one of the youngest school-based mariachi groups in Tucson, a pint-size rendering of the authentic version. The group owes its existence to the tenacity of their music teacher, Mr. Alfredo Valenzuela, who, against all odds, formed it in 1995. Warned that elementary school children were too young to learn the complex mariachi music, he doggedly pressed on in his pursuit. Now these young musicians appear as special guests of the Mariachi Cobre, specifically invited because of their impressive performances. An explosion of applause from the youthful audience follows their rendition of "Los laureles," featuring a vocal soloist, whose opening notes stun the audience with their depth and maturity. It's one thing to hear adults produce exciting sounds, but the chance to see and hear students their own age performing is doubly appreciated. Mariachi Cobre fills the auditorium with its full-bodied sounds, and a local folklórico group performs in full costume. The totality is a glorious panorama of music, song, and dance. One grandmother in the audience comments, "They should have had this kind of thing in the '30s and '40s when I was in school. We never had anything even close to this. *Para sentirnos orgullosos de ser mexicanos* [to feel pride in being Mexican], instead of always knocking us down."

Indeed, the affirmation of positive constructions of identity is one of the foundational premises for the Tucson International Mariachi Conference. Although students attending the conference are primarily local, groups from across the Southwest as well as from Mexico also are registered in the music workshops. Working with master teachers of the different instruments (violin, vihuela, guitar, guitarrón, trumpet) and with expert dancers of folklórico, elementary, middle, and high school students are afforded the opportunity to learn advanced techniques, compositions, and dance steps within a supportive, culturally permeated setting. Instituted in 1983, the conference has evolved into the largest international mariachi conference in the world. Initially a forum for adult groups (and a fund-raiser for a local mental health agency), the emphasis on children's workshops began in 1987, when educators on the conference board recognized the potential for enhancing students' musical and cognitive skills. The conference is a gargantuan effort by several community organizations, volunteers, and corporate sponsors, and it impacts the community at multiple levels. One current board member, Guadalupe Romero, describes her own experience, as both a parent and a professional, with the conference:

The first time my son went to the conference, he came back more Mexican than the Mexicans. . . . He came back *so* proud. There was just so much pride in wanting to hear the music. Before this, he had complained about my registering him at Davis, saying "We don't want to be mariachis. Why are you putting us in that school?" . . . But let me tell you that after that one experience that he had in fourth grade with the Mariachi Conference, he thought he had become an expert in mariachi music. . . . When I had played mariachi music before or I had the radio on the Mexican station, they would complain and say, "Put it in English, put it in English," but after that first encounter with the Mariachi Conference, . . . they wanted to hear other types of music. We get letters from parents telling us about the difference that they see in the kids who have gone to the conference. . . .

Even now, in Mexico, many people still think that mariachi music and corridos are only for the bars [and is a lower class of music]. Here, we in Tucson, are now being called "La Cuna del Mariachi" [the Cradle of the Mariachi], and we are experiencing a rebirth of mariachi music. Some people from Mexico will tell us that in Mexico the students are not involved with mariachi music . . . They might do popular songs, but not the tradition of the mariachi, which is what the Mariachi Cobre represents, the concept of the dignity of the mariachi. For instance, with Mariachi Vargas [from Mexico], when they first came, they played with the

Tucson Symphony Orchestra. At the time, I think we needed people to realize that the Mariachi Vargas were *musicians,* excellent musicians, who could play anywhere and with anyone, and that gave them another status. If you will notice, Vargas will always play classical music, symphony style, classical music from the great composers. Their music is a mixture of the classical, the ranchera, and boleros.

The focus of the conference is *education,* in its broadest sense— we get the kindergartner there for one day, to the eighty year old, who still plays in a mariachi or just wants it for their own benefit. What is a true mariachi? What is the music that comes from the mariachi? How is this music different from any other musician or band? Mariachi Cobre and Mariachi Los Camperos de Nati Cano are the mainstay of the conference. Yet they have two very different styles, and the students are exposed to both, and so we have that blend, and you need both.

The semiotic impact of musical discursive practices is explicitly highlighted in this narrative. As an aftermath of attending the Mariachi Conference, parents and educators note marked changes in behavior and attitude. By providing an evocative dimension within a culturally charged atmosphere, the Mariachi Conference is a community-based system for fomenting popular culture. More importantly, children are connected with a bridge that spans generations, thus turning the hearts of the children and creating a social memory that cements family heritages. One local middle school mariachi teacher, Steven Holmes, commented in a television news interview: "I think that [mariachi music] has bonded families together. It brings family unity, in the sense that students can relate to songs and music that their parents have sung" (KGUN News 1999). Because many of the parents and grandparents of these children were punished for speaking Spanish in schools, this revitalization of cultural practices tugs at many heartstrings, and the audiences at the performances of young mariachis are often in tears.

"STRUCTURES OF FEELING"

Raymond Williams, a cultural theorist who focuses on language use, has coined the term *structures of feeling* to refer to emerging and not yet fully articulated interminglings between feeling and thought. "We are talking about," he states, "characteristic elements of impulse, restraint, and tone; specifically affective elements of consciousness and relationships: not feeling against thought, but thought as felt and feeling as thought: practical consciousness of a present kind, in a living and inter-relating continuity" (1977:132).

For children, social experiences are "in process"; that is, the forms of these experiences are not fully in place. However, it is precisely in childhood that feelings or emotion connects with the ideological dimensions of the social worlds. The interweaving of language ideologies and emotion for children cannot be overemphasized. How language connects with formations of identity and community for children is at the crux of the language wars that rage on. Perhaps Gloria Anzaldúa says it best: "So, if you want to really hurt me, talk badly about my language. Ethnic identity is twin skin to linguistic identity—I am my language" (1987:59). The quote at the beginning of this chapter reflects the idea that it is through language and discourses that the hearts of children are turned toward their fathers (and, of course, their mothers). The ties that bind are formed through language in its multiple forms. Why is this important? Children's ties to a heritage and thus to an identity, whatever it may be, are brought about through the heart and mind, and language is the building block of both.

In the following chapter, I take up the other side of the equation: the mothers. How do women refigure their identities within received structures? How is the subjectivity of the self constructed in relation to the social? And, to reiterate Raymond Williams, how is a "practical consciousness of a present kind, in a living and inter-relating continuity" (1977:132), embodied in how women mediate their lived experiences?

CHAPTER 5

Negotiating Ideologies across Social Memories

One thing evident to me as I thought about language, emotion, and what it means to be a member of a historically constituted minority was that I was trying to connect the dots of nonlinear concepts in a linear design. For one thing, I found that women as mothers and socializers of children had very different takes on how to negotiate larger processes at the level of their own households. It made me aware that theorizing practice —that is, trying to figure out how we can theoretically understand everyday practices at the household level—is key to exploring antiessentialist accounts of identities. These construed practices of women and children are consequential for thinking about diversity not only between groups, but within groups, because women can act as both enforcers of tradition and innovators (Zentella 1987). Although the women in this study were active agents in constructing new discourses within which to frame child rearing, they were still embedded in the larger historical forces that can impact our daily lives. We may resist, accommodate, adapt, and act as active agents, but we do so within sociohistorical parameters that do not contain limitless possibilities.

Women and Language

One area of research that has been instrumental in linking macrolevel processes to the microlevel of the household has been carried out in the study of gender and language. Feminist scholarship, affirming that the "personal is political," has articulated the links between social processes and how we normalize the routines of our daily lives.

The emergence of the women's movement in the United States was clearly the defining moment in the linking of larger issues of power and dominance with language practices in face-to-face interaction. In a comprehensive annotated bibliography, Thorne, Kramarae, and Henley document early research that points to "varied ways in which language aids the defining, deprecating, and excluding of women. . . . Men's extensive labeling of women as parts of body, fruit or animals and as mindless, or like children—labels with no real parallel for men—reflects men's derision of women and helps maintain gender hierarchy and control" (1983:9). In a widely influential book, Robin Lakoff (1975) claimed that women's language is powerless, evidenced in her argument by women's more frequent use of tag questions, empty adjectives, and questioning intonations. These speech patterns, she maintained, are part of the socialization of young women in a deferential style that emphasizes their subordinate status, and they convey uncertainty and excessive politeness. This emphasis on power led to a focus on specific women's speech strategies such as politeness (Brown and Levinson 1978), cross-sex interruptions (West and Zimmerman 1983), and "interaction work" (Fishman 1978) that emphasized the constraints in dealing with the more "powerful" speech of men. The emphasis on power or dominance continued to be a defining paradigm for analyses of language and gender until the work of Deborah Tannen (1990) gained prominence. In a series of wildly popular monographs, Tannen argued that politics can get in the way of analytical models of language and that what had become the dogma of a power/dominance paradigm was in fact a destructive ideology. Rather, she argued for an emphasis on the constitutive nature of language and claimed that cultural patterning can falsely represent that dominance exits. The trope of male/female interaction as cross-cultural communication emerged as an alternative to power/dominance frameworks for analyzing gender and language.

In relation to the language socialization of children, Susan Philips credits the perspective of the ethnography of communication for focusing on the "full range of aspects of linguistic form that can express gender differences—lexical, phonological, morphological and syntactic" (1987:17). With an emphasis on syntactic structure (cf. Philips, Steele, and Tanz 1987), the cross-linguistic comparison of gender variation in language emerged, supplanting a reliance on phonological or morphological aspects of language use. The subject of inquiry was extended to include the language of children: gender differences in children's arguing and dispute tales (Goodwin 1990), in parent-child interaction (Gleason 1987), and in pretend play (Sachs 1987).

Feminist theory continued to inform much of the research on language, incorporating practice theory, postmodern, and poststructuralist perspectives. The feminist critique of language and language use (cf. Cameron 1990) had uncovered the androcentrism in grammar or the he/man debate (Bodine 1975; Martyna 1983), the semantic derogation of women (Schulz 1975), and the silenced voices of women writers and scholars. The incorporation of what has come to be known as practice theory extended the debate from a focus on language to other forms of "symbolic domination" and "symbolic power." Drawing from the work of Pierre Bourdieu (e.g., 1977a, 1977b), feminist analysts began to examine real people doing real things, with a view toward the ideology that informs these actions.

One of the most powerful influences in the analysis of language has been the writings of Michel Foucault, who emphasized the constitutive nature of language and argued that knowledge is not found, but is constructed in and through language (Foucault 1970, 1972). Not only are social meanings constructed through language, but power relations and subjectivities are also negotiated through discursive practices. "Language," Chris Weedon notes, "is the place where actual and possible forms of social organization and their likely social and political consequences are defined and contested. Yet it is also the place where our sense of ourselves, our subjectivity, is constructed" (1987:21). The concept of a "discursive field," as Foucault elucidated it, is an arena wherein competing and contesting definitions of language, power, and self are played out. Weedon, emphasizing the poststructuralist analysis of language, claims that "How we live our lives as conscious thinking subjects and how we give meaning to the material social relations under which we live and which structure our everyday lives, depends on the range and social power of existing discourses" (1987:35). Further, she notes, poststructuralism is a theory that "decenters the rational, selfpresent subject of humanism, seeing subjectivity and consciousness as socially produced in languages, as a site of struggle and potential change. Language is not transparent as in humanist discourse, it is not expressive and does not label a 'real' world. Meanings do not exist prior to their articulation in language and language is not an abstract system, but is always socially and historically located in discourses" (ibid.:41). For

Foucault, knowledge and power are inseparably connected, so much so that power and knowledge become fused into one (Foucault 1980). This fusion of power and knowledge leads to "Discourses" that construct particular "regimes of truth," truths that are intrinsically embedded within fields of power. These "Discourses" are in themselves both constructed and constitutive. They are constructed by discourses (with a lower case *d*) that enable and affirm particular meanings. However, Discourses also construct meanings and identities through their power and stance, as they form their subject.

The previous chapters attempted to illustrate how the dialogic process, ricocheting between the ethos of the Mexican borderlands and household discourse, involves the symbolization of diacritica that mark off certain aspects of behavior as self-representational profiles for children. Yet, discursive practices may not share an agreed upon significance in order to shape and organize experience. Gal notes that "patterns of choice among linguistic variants can be interpreted to reveal aspects of speakers' 'consciousness': how they respond symbolically to class relations and identity within regional economic systems structured around dependency and unequal development" (1987:637).

I argue that Mexican-origin households are caught up in the experience of the discursive construction of subjectivity within a field of power that is the borderlands. The symbolic resistance of an oppositional response to dominant ideologies is evidenced in the actively constructed transmission of identities. Yet, variation and "competing definitions" are ubiquitous. Poyer remarks that in the symbolic construction of identity, "What is significant here are the choices . . . [made] in order to elaborate a theory of ethnic distinction. Why do people select certain pegs on which to hang their identity?" (1988:476). Thus, whereas the indexing of self-reference for the Aguilar household is effectuated largely through music and ritual activities, other households activate this process through the mechanisms of sports, religion, and political activism. The semiotically constituted self-representations invoked in the language socialization process present different faces of the stone from which the constructions of identity can be sculpted. This chapter juxtaposes the case studies of three women to demonstrate the interplay between the dialectic of structure and agency.

For women of Mexican origin, the hybridity of drawing from multiple semiotic systems and negotiating multiple identities is embedded in the continuum of daily life. However, hybridity invokes not only a fusion of two forms, but the genesis of unexplored formations. In her poem "Legal Alien,"[1] Pat Mora voices the contradiction and ambiguities of women caught between discontinuities of language, nation, and ideology:

> Bi-Lingual, Bi-cultural
> Able to slip from "How's life?"
> To *"Me 'stan volviendo loca,"*
> able to sit in a paneled office
> drafting memos in smooth English,
> able to order in fluent Spanish
> at a Mexican restaurant,
> American but hyphenated,
> viewed by Anglos as perhaps exotic,
> perhaps inferior, definitely different,
> viewed by Mexicans as alien,
> (their eyes say, "You may speak
> Spanish but you're not like me")
> an American to Mexicans
> a Mexican to Americans
> a handy token
> sliding back and forth
> between the fringes of both worlds
> by smiling
> by masking the discomfort
> of being pre-judged
> Bi-laterally. (1984:52)

In the postmodernist conception of fractured or multiple subjectivities or both, the following excerpts from interview sessions reveal the destabilization of a unified subject, as women confront contradiction not only in terms of ethnic identity, but in other aspects of the dialogical construction of personhood. However, these women are not trapped by the liminality of their status, passively bemoaning their marginality. They are active agents in drawing from multiple resource bases and multiple ideologies in order to ensure their children's success. Like Gloria Anzaldúa's "new mestiza," they operate in a plural mode, casting out what is not useful to them, appending new strategies, and merging received structures with the exigencies of their current lives. These three case studies point to the scaffolding of new forms rising from historical antecedents. They reveal the tinkering with the intergenerational forms bequeathed to posterities to assemble inventive bridges that span the gaps between tradition and practice.

I draw in this chapter from the notion of "identity in practice," as constructed by Dorothy Holland, William Lachicotte Jr., Debra Skinner, and Carole Cain (1998). Using the work of Bakhtin and Vygotsky, these authors locate the space of authoring selves within a practice theory of identity. These "practiced identities" are described by reference to four contexts of activity (Holland et al. 1998:271), and I focus on the first: "The first context of identity is the figured world." By "figured world," the authors mean a "socially and culturally constructed realm of interpretation in which particular characters and actors are recognized, significance is assigned to certain acts, and particular outcomes are valued over others . . . These collective 'as-if' worlds are sociohistoric, contrived interpretations of imaginations that mediate behavior and so, from the perspective of heuristic development, inform participants' outlooks" (ibid.:52). The women in these three case studies "form and reform" (ibid.:270) the sets of actions they organize, and they author and arrange their social fields through the mediation of structure and agency. Although they may author figured worlds, however, they do so within a prism of a social memory, a Discourse that has been constructed around particular fields. These social memories are part of the fabric that has been woven across generations, the shreds and patches of which these women take up and knit together.

Iris Gallardo

My initial contact with Iris Gallardo took place in the PACE classroom where we were introduced by her son Luis Jr.'s teacher. I explained the study to her, and she agreed to participate.

I approached the Gallardo household on the south side of Tucson, hidden off in one of the side streets of the barrio, anticipating my first interview with them. The wide avenue allowed high visibility on all sides, and I could observe clotheslines in many of the yards, a quickly disappearing phenomenon in these days of clothes dryers. It was a serene, older neighborhood, with homes built in the 1940s and 1950s. There were several new constructions in the area, however, indicating an affinity for the "old" neighborhood in the wake of increased economic resources.

Iris, the mother, answered the door in a courteous, but reserved manner. Her home was older, although it still maintained its structural integrity. It was tidy and smelled of Pine-Sol, and it activated childhood memories for me. The front room had no carpet and was meagerly furnished. Family pictures were the only adornment. It conveyed an image of economic struggle. Iris herself was neatly, though simply dressed and devoid of makeup. She had dropped out of high school in the twelfth grade, although she went back to earn her GED. She married at nineteen, had her first child at twenty, the second one two years later, and has been primarily a homemaker since then. She was employed previously, at Dairy Queen and at an army surplus store, but quit because she felt that it was important for her to be home with her children. She and her husband worked different shifts, and they were rarely together as a family. She felt that the baby-sitter did not pay enough attention to the children, and they both "hated to stay with her, and would cry and beg 'let Daddy work, not you.'" Even when she did quit, however, because of her husband's long work hours and Saturday work schedule, they had little family time together. During my two-and-a-half-year contact with the family, this situation changed little. Iris did begin part-time maintenance and janitorial work after a move to a trailer on the north side of town, but she and her husband had different work hours again, and she would leave for work in the late afternoon, and he would arrive home between 7:00 and 7:30. At one point, she was having excessive pain and swelling in her knee from torn cartilage and found it difficult to keep up with her job and the heavy physical labor it entailed. They did not qualify for AHCCCS (the state Medicaid program), although her husband was employed at the time as a skilled laborer, and fell into the notch group that neither has Medicaid nor can afford private medical insurance or services, so she could not have the required surgery performed.

The Gallardo family typify a classic study in contrasts. Luis Gallardo, Iris's husband, was born in Douglas, Arizona, and moved to Tucson in his youth, a characteristic migration pattern for this area. Iris, born and raised on the southside, was raised with only Spanish in her household, but feels more comfortable speaking, reading, and writing English. Her children speak English almost exclusively, and my efforts to elicit their level of Spanish productive proficiency revealed only knowledge of lexical items. Their Spanish comprehension skills were much more developed. Although they lived for a time with their grandparents, I observed that they exhibited the pattern demonstrated by the Aguilars in grandparent/grandchild interaction: an English response to spoken Spanish.

Within this constellation of borderland sociohistorical factors exists an indisputable design to establish a household of middle-American mainstream values for the children. During our first interview, Iris spoke regretfully of her own thwarted childhood visions of her idyllic home. She bemoaned the fact that her mother never baked, her mother never sewed or spent time with her. Instead, when she was ten years old, as the eldest girl, she was recruited to make tortillas, iron her own clothes, iron her brothers' and sisters' clothes, and do the household laundry. Now, with her own children, Iris bakes continuously with her children to help her, and sends empanadas and pies to her father. She is an expert seamstress, having taught herself by trial and error. During a subsequent interview, she showed clothes to me that she had sewn for her daughter and pictures of a wedding dress and bridesmaid dresses she had designed and sewn for a cousin's wedding. Once when I dropped by her house, she was sewing complicated Halloween costumes for her children, and she displayed a "poodle skirt" that she had made for her daughter for a school "fifties" party. She also goes to great lengths to engage both her son and daughter in crafts projects with her. She has an artistic inclination and enjoys going to craft stores and learning how to make various projects. Because of their tight money situation, she will usually find a more economical way to create her project, often just sitting down with a paper and pencil and drawing to illustrate the procedure she is going to follow. She volunteered extensively in her son's PACE classroom, often doing crafts with the class, planting a garden, making stew, or helping the children prepare journals.

When work permits, both parents spend all of their time with their children. Again, because of financial constraints, they will often rent a movie and stay home or engage in some inexpensive recreation. In short, based on the types of activities and child-rearing ideologies of the household, the Gallardo family could be transplanted anywhere in the country and fit into the recurring and accepted patterns of mainstream household behaviors. Iris herself has overtly captured this normative ideology as her model and was truly stunned when she discovered that not all "middle America" lives the idyllic routine she has envisioned as one of her goals. After a move to a non-Hispanic neighborhood, her son suddenly became the only Mexican-origin child in his classroom. Because of her training in PACE and her own inclinations, Iris volunteered extensively in the school and in the classroom. During one interview session with me, she noted her surprise that her considerable involvement was not the norm for the northside school:

> I don't know what's wrong. Maybe all the parents work, I don't know. But there's some kids that . . . well, they tell Junior, "Gee, your Mom is so neat, she does so many things with you," you know. And they would say, "My Mom doesn't do things with us." . . . [Junior then commented that his friends say that they wish they had a Mom like his.] I've noticed that a lot of kids don't get that. . . . Like when they have to make their lunch. They have to take lunch. I show them. I mean, you're not just going to take a sandwich and cookies, or this and that. I tell them to cut carrots and take fruit, things like that. . . . And a little girl went in there with her lunch pail, and she opened it, and I noticed that all she had to eat was *five Twinkies*. And I'm like . . . Gaa, is that all you have? And she says, "Well, I made my own lunch." And I go, "Didn't your Mom make your lunch?" And she says, "Oh, no, I make my own lunch." . . . I guess there's some parents who don't notice what their kids take for lunch . . . or even if they *take* lunch, 'cause I noticed that there was a little boy in there who didn't even take lunch. I saw him there at the end of the line crying because he was not going to eat that day. He was crying that he didn't have lunch or money. And he didn't have no breakfast, and I'm like . . . you know. And I talked to the teacher, and she said that she'd make sure that he got at least a sandwich and milk. . . . And so I don't want my kids to be like that . . . tell them, oohhh, just make whatever you want, you know.

Within the Gallardo family, even the overstretched budget situation is seen as an opportunity for the children to define themselves not by what they have, but by who they are. Iris stressed this point several times, and commented:

I can't give my kids everything they want. I can't. My kids have got to learn that they get what we can afford, not anything they want. I wish I could get them what they wanted. But, you know, I *can't*. I get what I can afford for them. Like they say, "I want this because it's this . . . and this is that." . . . Noooo. You gotta learn to use what you can get. They say, "It's out of style." Well, you gotta learn to use what you have. . . . [Even if I could afford it] I would not buy them everything they want. Because then they grow up to where they want it all the time, and then they grow up, and they're *never* gonna have it. Like my little sister, her husband, . . . his mother gave him *everything* he wanted. She would spend seventy-five dollars for a jacket for him. And now that he's married, he can't have that, and you should see the fights they have because moneywise he wants to get it, and it's very hard on her. . . . That's why my parents . . . I mean, they had eight of us, and they could never give us . . . I mean, we would go the whole year of school with just two or three things; that's all we had to wear the whole year, and one pair of shoes that would last us the whole semester. Nowadays, . . . like I try to get them two tennies and a pair of shoes, but sometimes you can't, and they just do with what they have.

My brothers, they tell me, "You're old-fashioned." Well, maybe I am, but that's the way I think. I tell my Dad, "If I had the money, I'd move away from Tucson. I'd teach my kids how to live on a ranch." I *would*. I'd teach them how to make their own vegetables instead of having to buy them, you know; I would. Get the chickens, with the eggs and everything. *I would*. I would prefer living that way than the way we live now. Oh, I have to go to the store for eggs, I have to go to the store for this . . . nuh-uh. I'd make my own garden and my own ranch. . . . I've always liked it, my Dad, too, and my husband, too, because he grew up on a ranch, outside of Douglas. . . . I don't know, I just don't like living in [the city] anymore. I don't want my kids to be like that. They tell me, "Hey, you want to be *Little House on the Prairie*," and I go, "So what?" I'd enjoy it more than I do this.

I found the allusion to *Little House on the Prairie* to be particularly noteworthy because it is that very type of nostalgia that has been a recurrent theme in "back-to-basics" living. The mass media has an undeniable impact on individual and household ideology, and is one of the current forces that interacts with the historical and political antecedents of a region. In the case of the Gallardos, we have a third-generation Mexican-origin household—linked through its kin network primarily to the southside area of Tucson and to the border town of Douglas, and embedded in this dense kinship network—who lives in borderline poverty, but whose household ideology reflects the images of conservative middle America, of a stay-at-home mother who bakes and sews and does crafts with her children, volunteers extensively in their schools, and a father who is the primary breadwinner and the reserved guardian of the family patrimony. Objects of life are valorized so that children are given sense of self despite economic hardships. It is the ideology, rather than the activities themselves, that is a key component in how this household functions. If one were to decontextualize activities, strip the cultural veneer, one could categorize parental involvement with the Gallardo children as incorporating an extensive array of the transmission of knowledge through the household activities of cooking, sewing, arts and crafts, mechanical and construction repairs, and gardening activities—the "funds of knowledge" of the family. Yet Iris struggles mightily to provide what she sees as a stable upbringing, stressing what she feels she missed as a child. Her "agency" does not spring from nowhere, and she draws from Discourses that in some ways belie her lived experiences.

RAQUEL SALAZAR

In retrospect, my initial encounters with Marina Escobedo and Raquel Salazar should not have been startling. As a former Catholic, I was already familiar with a growing segment of the population who has found their spirituality outside of the Catholic Church. A good portion of my extended family, once staunch and dedicated Catholics, was also beginning to filter into Christian evangelical groups. Religious revival and renewal cross-cut age and gender boundaries in my family. Younger couples were turning increasingly to scripture study and evangelization to help manage personal crises, while the parental cohort, more reluctant to change, were also slowly beginning to seek out alternative spiritual avenues. In my own personal odyssey, the accouterments of Catholicism left indelible imprints on my youth. Because I was a student at a Catholic school for all of my elementary years, my memories are forever inscribed within the icons of Catholicism. Yaya (my great-grandmother) was fervently devoted to San Antonio in recompense for favors she had received from him, and she flooded his statue and altar with flowers on his "day." I have always had a feeling of poignant nostalgia for the heady incense of Holy Week processions, statues enveloped in purple shrouds awaiting Easter Sunday, the teacher nuns of our school, and the smell of fresh flowers as we waited, dressed in white, to ofrecer at the altar in May. These stamps of identity are exceedingly difficult to renounce. They form a connection with a mystical past and social memory that is not easily supplanted. The posadas, procesiones, fiestas, visitas, and sociedades that gave form and function to the Tucson Mexican community of believers for more than two centuries cannot be displaced in the swift and fleeting scramble of the new millennium.

Yet, in the poststructuralist Foucauldian position, there is a qualitative difference between structure and history. In a paradigmatic shift from frozen timeless action to human agency and practice, the case studies of Marina and Raquel point to the scaffolding of new forms rising from historical antecedents. In the dialogization of language socialization efforts, Marina and Raquel actively construct an ethos for their children emerging from their search for other patterns of child rearing, to guide their children through what they perceive to be a hostile environment. Raquel's words echo this process:

RS: I mean, you know, I don't want him to grow up to be a *priest*, but I want him to learn the right morals because of society right now is getting so bad, and the television is . . . I want him to learn the—a right way, you know?

NG: What is it about television that you think is bad?

RS: It's the way they, um, . . . the dancing and the language. And I feel that they are showing children that the more they have, the happier they are going to be—you know, with all the toys and . . . stuff. Now with all these hygiene and—and sexual things on the television, it's harder for parents now to tell them *no,* when they're telling them that it's OK as long as they are careful.

Raquel, in recounting her own childhood experiences, was adamant about actively constructing a scenario for her children that will not leave them floundering. She regrets her own lack of training in a variety of areas and vowed that her children will be better prepared:

My parents did not train us to think ahead, as far as to *do* something. You know, I thought that they had us as females, that we were to get—meet—a man, and he was gonna take care of us. And that we didn't have to go to class. They didn't give us any ambitions to try to educate ourselves and push towards anything else. My sister automatically had to because she's been divorced. She's on her third. And so she had to work and educate herself, to better herself, where I didn't. You know, I just kind of went about my way.

You know, when I was first married, everything I tried to do never seemed to work out, and I found that your background has a lot to do with it. My mother, I never saw my mother. . . . I never really saw my mother or father struggle with finances. They never were talking to me about budgeting or how to shop or—or any of these things. So when I got married, I figured, you know, just go to the groceries and throw whatever I want in the cart, and it was no problem, and budgeting checkbooks and all that, I never really learned that. And in school, I never really paid attention; I felt like I really didn't need to. I didn't have any goals, no desire, so, uh, when I got married, I was real surprised, and I went through a big shock because my husband grew up in the other side of the coin [from] where I grew up. Thank God, I had what I wanted, I ate well, I wasn't rich, but I was in the middle class. I always had plenty; I always had my new dresses, my new dresses for Easter and nice Christmas gifts, nice food. See, my husband grew up on the other side. His father had to work night and day and, uh, . . . there was five of them in the family. They only got *one* thing for Christmas, ummm . . . You know they were struggling, but they were always happy and you know they knew what it was to pinch pennies. So when we got married, my husband started pinching pennies, and I was out blowing it. So it was like two different sides of a coin. We're two totally different lifestyles, so it's been difficult. It's been real difficult and almost having to force ourselves to live how he was brought up because my way wasn't working, obviously; we weren't making the money my father was making when I left the home.

So, uh . . . then again, my husband was so . . . I don't know if you would consider it the typical macho image where they just kinda go to work and come home, and everything else is kinda taken care of—you know, like the bills, and all that—but unfortunately he married a woman that didn't care about that stuff. It's not that I didn't care, but I wasn't aware how important it was, and throughout the years I've had to learn on my own, but yet I didn't like it that way. I didn't like that I had to sit down and have to figure out everything myself. So, you know, I started buying books and went into marriage encounters, and things I've read in the books like the Bible and different books, I've learned that it should be the husband and wife together and that we should make the goals and the decisions for our future. . . . That's why I'm always struggling because I might be figuring everything out for the next month, but something always comes up, and it's like I really wasn't going anywhere. And my husband was happy like that because that's the way he was raised. He was raised just to be where they're at, and if they get more, it's fine, and that's fine, but I want to know that what tomorrow brings us, I want to be able to handle that. And to give my kids the opportunity to go to school if they want, to give them an opportunity, and if I don't set goals for them, then I'm not going to be able to send them to school even if they want to go. Not without me encouraging them to, you know, . . . Uuhhh, it's not that I want them to have a rich life, but I want them to be comfortable and to be able to let them go to school, especially their education. I want to be able to offer them an education.

During my conversation with Raquel, she amplified this theme on many occasions. She forcefully elucidated her quest for a template on which to process her family's lives. The reproduction of the models on which she and her husband were raised are inadequate for her. They do not meet the exigencies of the life that she feels she must now face, nor does she want her children to struggle with the same perceived formlessness. She consciously and actively assembles a framework on which to hang their everyday existence:

What we need is to get a format for our lives and that helps us with our kids and helps them set goals and how to handle their money and how to . . . you know . . . If we're yelling at them all the time, when they get to be our age and have kids, they're going to yell at them, too. And they're going to have the same money problems we have, and they're going to have the same problems we have. If we don't get a format or some kind of a goal, some kind of, ummm, instructions from somewhere, if we don't adopt that right now in our lives, then where are we teaching our kids? We are just teaching them just to get by, just to go to school and to come home, and when you get married, get a job, you raise your kids, and then on and on and on. You know, struggle, struggle, struggle, and they have to know that there is something more to life. . . . I just want more for them . . . something different, and the only way is through the church; that is the only way.

Both Marina and Raquel were set on fabricating a new paradigm for their children. They consciously discarded the reproduction of previously transmitted information. Through the small routines of everyday life, in the music played and the books read in the household, in the daily rituals of existence, a new order was being forged. It was in this domestic domain where action was proceeding not unreflexively, but with the directionality of human praxis.

Maricela Benavides

Maricela Benavides was indirectly part of the original study because I had interviewed her parents, Amelia and Armando Robles, although I conducted my interview with her during follow-up fieldwork in 1996. Maricela is the mother of four children, ages fourteen, twelve, six, and two at the time of the interviews. It is through the extended Robles/Gallego (Amelia's maiden name) family that relationships of reciprocity and support are evident as a nurturing web within which children in this kin network are raised. The clustering of related households, the never-ending calendrical round of birthday parties, quinceañeras, weddings, parties, carne asadas (barbecues), and family get-togethers all function to impress on children their sense of identity as well as a sense of sustenance for meeting the exigencies of the outside world. Maricela's parents live down the street from her; her brother lives next door to their parents; her sister-in-law lives across the street from her, and recently, her mother-in-law has relocated across the street, next to her sister-in-law. These moves were not serendipitous, but well planned with the intention of maintaining close geographical proximity. Her younger sister, Ana María, is always on the look out for houses for sale in the far southwest side neighborhood. Maricela's children, aside from their school and sports friends, have close friendships with their first cousins. Her oldest son, David, has always lived across the street from his age-mate cousin, and they have attended the same schools. Maricela is quite satisfied with this relationship because "he doesn't *have* to look other places for friends." Maricela has consciously followed in her mother's and grandmother's child-rearing ideology of "keeping your children close." She recounted how she remembers her growing up years as involving a weekly ritual of visiting her grandmother in Douglas, together with the children of her twelve tíos and tías:

> Every weekend we went to my nana's house. When my Dad got out of work on Friday night, we packed up and left. When we arrived, my Nana always had a big pot of beans, mashed beans with cheese, tortillas freshly made, papas [potatoes], whatever. It didn't have to be an elegant dinner, but she always had something to eat for us when we got there. . . . And we'd have to sometimes sleep on the floor or under the kitchen table, there were so many of us. That's what *she* did. That's how she gathered her family. I think that that's why my parents have continued the tradition of keeping the family together. We have the family that we have now because my grandmother got us together and had us live together for every weekend. . . . I think that's where it started. And, of course, when my Nana moved here, her daughters and her sons would always be stopping by, and we would get together at her house on Sundays. . . . There's certain things that we just *know* that we're going to do together.

For Maricela, the rituals of family get-togethers were a formative factor in her youth, and she embeds her children in these relations of reciprocity.

To some extent, every child in my sample was involved in a procession of festive rituals throughout the year, and in general I would say that an overwhelming majority of children in Tucson Mexican-origin households (cf. Vélez-Ibáñez 1988, 1996) have been involved in such processions. Birthday parties, up until the child reaches about age five, are usually elaborate affairs, with piñatas, music, food for both adults and children, and have often entailed a trip to the border town of Nogales, Mexico (an hour-long journey from Tucson) to purchase inexpensive candies and small prizes for the children. Most important, they involve a ritualized meeting for the kin network to consolidate its functioning as an entity. The birthday child is thus accorded a place within the kin group, a recognition that she belongs and that there exists a host of relatives and family friends who are concerned with her well-being.

The fear that the community may be losing this "closeness" and familial solidarity as families splinter off was brought to the forefront in my interviews of families who have recently engaged in family reunions. This phenomenon is recent (I think) in Mexican-origin social relations, but was reported by two of the families in my sample as a reason for gathering the geographically dispersed extended clan in a central place. One family reported that they have family reunions every year, alternating between California and Tucson. Families from different segments of the clan will wear different colored clothing to identify them, and sports, food, and a dance are the structured activities of the two-day event. Amelia Robles orchestrates a family tradition of having reunions every ten years in Mexico, where all of the descendants of her grandparents gather in Chihuahua for a four-day festivity entailing meeting the cross-border cousins and, again, food, volleyball and basketball games, as well as an elaborate talent show with songs, skits, music, and dances being performed. Again, an emphasis is on music, and the process of "ethnogenesis" can be identified as underlying the ritual—that is, "a development and public presentation of a self-conscious ethnic group" (Roosens 1989:141). These reunions serve the function not only of renewing family relationships, but, for the second, third, and fourth generation of U.S.–born Mexicans, of creating a nexus for the affirmation of their common heritage. There is in these latter generations a form of revitalization, with a strong impetus to forge identities. It is interesting, however, that identities are tied more to an abstract notion, a social memory, rather than to geographical or physical presences. Armando and Amelia Robles commented on paradoxes and ambivalence their children demonstrate regarding their heritage. On the one hand, their daughters have voiced an active interest in learning about their grandparents and how they lived in Mexico. However, when they travel to Mexico, they both have commented that they feel uncomfortable and out of place, and are always anxious to return home. The

nostalgia for Mexico does not encompass a shedding of the second and
third generations' U.S.–based comfort zone. As Roosens notes, "there is
no turning back for the second generation" (1989:138–39). He asserts
the often overlooked consequence of culture contact: that young adults
can simulate their traditional culture, but they are "never completely at
home again" in the culture of their forebears.

During one interview session, Maricela's father highlighted the symbolization of particular events and rituals as self-representational profiles for children. Armando and Amelia own their own small business,
and both work together every day in the heart of South Tucson. Armando was born in Douglas, Arizona, and his wife, Amelia, was born in
Chihuahua and immigrated to Douglas in her early teens. They moved
to Tucson as a young married couple and through inordinate thrift,
scrimping and saving, managed to open their own shop. They have
prospered in their business, although it remains a family enterprise.
Both Armando and Amelia come from families of thirteen siblings and
are acutely aware of the importance of family networks. At the time of
the interview, Amelia's mother, Soledad, was the widowed matriarch of
a clan that prides itself on being *"una familia muy unida"* (a united
family). Goods and resources are continuously redistributed throughout
the family, with Soledad as the focal point of the exchanges. Clothes,
household products, car repair, help with school projects, household
improvements, transportation needs, and child care are regularly exchanged and recycled under Soledad's watchful and perceptive eye. The
family has prospered through its collective interdependence, and family
members actively acknowledge the pivotal role that family networks
and exchange play in their lives. Consequently, Armando criticized the
fact that the last few birthday parties for his nieces and nephews had
taken place at local pizza parlors, rather than at home. He commented:

> We're getting too Americanized . . . if you want to call it. Here,
> they don't have house parties any more. Now, it's the *pizza place.*
> All the kids. . . . Come on, let's take them to the pizza. They want
> somebody else to entertain them. They don't feel like entertaining
> their kids. They want the kids to be entertained by somebody else.
> They'd rather go pay for it than spend their time taking care of the
> kids. . . . I feel that they think that it's easier for them. . . . People
> today just don't want to take the time and trouble. They'd rather

go and sit them down, they bring them gum, they bring them balloons, they have a clown there, they don't have to raise a hand or nothing. And this is where we're changing. You can see it. So what does this do? Most of the parents . . . go, dump their kids, and go home. . . . The older generations don't do that. Just the new generations.

I think that we're losing it. We're losing the Spanish. . . . I think that we're going to lose a lot of the traditions, a lot of the guitar playing, stuff like that. . . . Like when we used to get together, the first thing we did was get out the guitars and sing some songs. It really means something to you. It's meaningful. It's not just to pass the time. Like, for example, when we first got married . . . [all of our relatives], we were close. On Fridays, we would all get together . . . [and sing and dance]. We didn't have to go to dances; we had our own dances at the house. . . . Now, the families are growing, so all the heads [of households] are splitting up . . . and now it's different. Each one goes with their own family. Nowadays, we say, "Let's go," and the kids say, "Oh, Dad, I don't want to go over there." They want to go someplace else. One wants to pull you one way, and one wants to pull you the other way. . . . I think what eventually is going to happen is that everyone is going to go their own ways. . . . When they [their older children] get together, they don't want to stay home. They want to go out. I mean, I can understand, they're young, and all that. . . . They don't have that yearning to stay home, and say, "Oh, man, my tíos and tías, and we're going to stay, and be with them." They don't want to be there. They'd rather form their own little groups and go out.

For Armando Robles, underlying the rituals of family get-togethers is a form of memory making that had historical significance. Armando's claim that children now are losing the closeness of his generation has both an affective and material basis. He is well aware that the solidarity of the family has resulted in a collective beneficial gain. But more meaningful in his discourse is the claim to the sentiment that binds the households in the kin groups. These ties that bind children to tíos and tías can grow more tenuous with less interaction. The splintering into nuclear households can be counteracted through periodic ritual participation, but the displacement of these rituals to commercial establishments strips the interaction at the familiar hearth. In a borderlands context, neither children nor parents can subscribe to a standardized version of what it means to grow up Mexican on the north side of the border.

Maricela Benavides is, by all accounts, a vitally active participant in all aspects of her children's lives. She is a "soccer mom," shuttling her own as well as neighbors' children to soccer, baseball, and volleyball practices and games. Because she is so well-known to her children's friends, she says, "My kids say to me, 'Gosh, Mom, all my friends know you, and they know our van.'" Her children reported that their friends will come up and talk to Maricela before they talk to them. She said that the same thing happened to her during her own experience as a song leader. Because her mother would actively solicit the conversation of the young, they responded by greeting her with warm welcomes and abrazos (hugs) before talking to their own peers. Maricela was a straight-A student during her high school career, and she expects high academic marks from her children. Bright, articulate, personable, and always immaculately groomed, she would be successful in a number of workplace settings. However, she has chosen to stay home, doing freelance accounting and decorating cakes, to raise her children "because we have so few precious years with them as children."

Because of the marked dominance of female participation in this extended kin network (nine of Amelia's thirteen siblings are female), girls have a number of models for their negotiation of gender ideology, and the attractiveness of women and girls is an implicit ideology of gender. Gold bracelets and earrings adorn even the tiniest newborn girls, and clothing is chosen by its marked femininity. Maricela recounted that during the trips to Douglas, sitting around the dinner table for hours, her aunts would ask her and her cousins about the boys they were seeing and would offer advice about the best way to get a boy interested in them was to "not be too available." Maricela was a crowned beauty queen in the Fiestas Patrias of the Sixteenth of September, and at least six of her cousins have reigned as queens or princesses in various local beauty contests. Her aunt on one occasion remembered being asked, *"¿Qué no hay muchachas feas en tu familia?"* (Aren't there any homely girls in your family?). Interestingly, her mother Amelia was also the Sixteenth of September queen in Douglas, and she displays a portrait in her living room in which both Amelia and Maricela are garbed in their royal robes and crowns, a mother and daughter tribute to tradition and gender identity.

Maricela often alluded to practices that she observed in her mother that she tries to follow. Amelia, her mother was "always at home when we got home from school" even though she had her own business. She is also extraordinarily thrifty and recycles everything from plastic containers to aluminum foil pans. Maricela credited these practices as facilitating the functioning of her household in the absence of an income. Both Maricela and Amelia are financially astute, buying items at bargain prices and selling at a profit. They wring every ounce of use from items, a trait they both credited to Amelia's mother, Soledad. Soledad Gallego, widowed while pregnant with her thirteenth child, is the model from which both Maricela and Amelia carve out their identities. Amplifying and elaborating themes of familial solidarity, investment in children, and frugal living, Maricela and Amelia draw from the past to reach to the future.

Gender Ideologies and Bailes Folklóricos

The negotiation of ideologies is not restricted to the political sphere. Children, in their experiences with multiple Discourses, are also participants in other aspects of expressive cultural practices. For many girls and young women, one aspect of musical discursive practices is inscribed in bailes folklóricos (folkloric dances). The proliferation of folklórico groups is a fairly recent phenomenon, as even in the late 1970s there were few performing troupes, and they consisted of adults. As schools have become sites of multiple pedagogies, many of the elementary, middle, and high schools offer folklórico as an extracurricular activity. Additionally, dance troupes under the direction of experienced dancers and teachers offer dance classes on a fee basis.

Leticia's Dance Studio

Leticia Durazo is an honored maestra (teacher), having dedicated her life to dance and to teaching dance. She began her teaching career in Agua Prieta, Sonora, in 1959 and relocated to Tucson in 1970. Because she has continued to develop her knowledge base, continually enrolling in workshops and diversifying her repertoire, the dance classes that she offers the girls, although firmly planted in Spanish and Mexican bailes (dances), span the entire panorama of dance, from Spanish Sevillanas to boleros to Polish mazurkas. All the girls begin by learning the basic movements of ballet, and she insists on exposing them to a broad range of musical genres, hoping to inspire in them a sense that *"el mundo es muy amplio, y que sepan apreciarlo"* (the world is very wide, and they need to learn to appreciate it).

Leticia feels that mothers enroll their daughters in her studio *"para que no pierdan sus raíces del folklor . . . [para] retener una poca de nostalgia y querer rescatarlo"* (in order not to lose their folkloric roots . . . to retain a bit of the nostalgia and to try to rescue it). Yet the girls, as children will, at times prefer the more popular Selena-type music, the "Macarena," or even "Come on Ride the Train," and she allows them this latitude as long as they learn traditional numbers, also *"para que no pierdan el gusto y el interés del baile"* (so that they do not lose the joy and interest in dance).

Her annual recital in the Tucson Community Center Music Hall spans two days and takes place before a packed audience of enthusiastic parents, grandparents, aunts, uncles, and friends who often present the girls with bouquets of flowers after the show. It is a spectacular production, with the girls performing in stunning costumes that are themselves a testament to the social networks that had to be marshaled in order to produce the apparel and designs. They are bedecked in authentic vestuarios, dazzling leotards, and elaborate headpieces. Trips to Mexico to secure rebozos, shoes, hats, dresses, and hand-painted fans have been orchestrated long before the final performance, and mothers, grandmothers, and seamstresses have labored for months, *"para que puedan lucir"* (so they can shine). Again, the physical presence of the border is an important element of this event because many of these items could not be obtained without the proximity of Mexico. Because most of the girls who enroll with Leticia stay with her throughout their youth, she has choreographed a special number when they turn fifteen, a quinceañera dance with their fathers. This dance produces a tremendous emotional impact on the audience, often moving them to tears, as they view the graceful movements of these girls turned young women waltzing with their fathers, embodying, as Leticia says, *"los lazos tan fuertes que hay de una familia"* (the very strong family ties that exist in families). Because the audience has witnessed the first awkward dance movements of the girls since they were four years old, struggling with "Las muñequitas," the visual impact of their blooming young womanhood within the nostalgia of their cultural herencia (heritage) is powerful. Leticia affirms:

> Yo creo que nosotros los Latinos tenemos la música por dentro, desde que estamos en el vientre, y nos cantan las canciones de cuna, tenemos ese gusto de la música, siempre hay música . . . Yo creo que siente uno la música . . . hasta antes de nacer . . . Es algo que nos llega más al corazón, la inspiración de mucho sentimiento.

> I believe that we, as Latinos, have music within us, even while we are still in the womb, and we are sung songs of the cradle. We have that joy of music, and music is everywhere. I believe that music is felt even before one is born. It is something that touches our hearts, the inspiration of deep feeling.

Through the dances, the girls are exposed to traditional regional music that would not necessarily be familiar to them, again discursively re-creating a social memory that is not part of their everyday lives. They are also exposed to music within its historical context; for example, one number, "Las bicicletas," is the product of Porfirio Díaz's era, when young men riding on bicycles was part of the ritual of courtship. In "Las Adelitas," a number from the Mexican Revolution, the girls are draped with the cananas (leather cartridge belts) of the revolucionarias, the women who followed the soldiers of the revolution, providing the foundation from which the men were able to do battle. Leticia explains:

> Ya nadie escucha la música de "El farolito." Sin embargo las niñas aprenden las palabras de la canción y la cantan. Están conociendo que hay otra música, no solamente "rock." Y es una emoción para las abuelitas, que vivieron esos tiempos [de los '30s], que sus nietas estén bailando esa música.

> No one listens to music like "El farolito" anymore. Yet the girls learn the words to the song, and they sing it. They are learning that there is another kind of music, not just rock. And it is very emotional for their grandmothers, who lived in the times that these songs were popular [in the '30s], that their granddaughters are dancing to that music.

Leticia conducts her classes in English because most of the girls are English dominant, although she mixes in a fair blend of Spanish. Thus, this icon of expressive performance, the epitome of the "cultural," is itself a testament to a "figured world" of borderlands children. They are enveloped in a social memory of a bygone age within English, the discourse of their everyday practice.

Many of the dances themselves are exemplars of the hybridity of the borderlands. One in particular features six-year-olds decked out in country-western attire, complete with boots, cowboy hats, and short skirts, dancing a Mexican version of the folk song "O Susannah."

Leticia credits dance classes with providing a sense of discipline, a sense of self, a sense of presence before an audience, and a sense of performing well at any task. In reflecting on the hundreds of girls who have been her students, she cannot recall any who have dropped out of school, and the majority have gone on to postsecondary education. Several have become elementary school teachers and use bailes folklóricos within their classroom and school pedagogy, and others have established their own dance academies. For the girls in Leticia's Dance Studio, the positive affirmation of self within culturally inscribed practices has led to lifestyle choices that are both productive and resilient. Drawing from the best of multiple worlds, these girls have witnessed firsthand the support of their extended families; the association of their personal growth and maturity within the affective and nurturing cocoon of music, dance, and song; and the sense of identity that comes from long hours of practice and discipline. Musical discourse is a formative force in shaping their nascent sense of identity. In the movie *Selena,* Selena's father, played by Edward James Olmos, tells the young Selena that part of being Mexican American is knowing about John Wayne *and* Pedro Infante, Agustín Lara *and* Frank Sinatra, Oprah *and* Cristina. Like Selena, these girls draw from their multiple musical repertoires, fashioning identities that, although unique, are sociohistorically constituted. Yet, as Leticia notes, when she started out years ago, her young students had only dance as their one activity outside home and school. Now the girls are so busy with other activities that she often bemoans the fact that they don't have the time to practice at home. As market-oriented media propaganda infiltrates children's lives, the rush and push for goods and activities compacts childhood experiences into compartmentalized chunks of time, leaving children reeling from one activity to another. The competition from mass media rules.

The narratives of Iris Gallardo, Raquel Salazar, and Maricela Benavides, as well as the musical discursive practices of Leticia's Dance Studio, illustrate the complex and multiple ideologies from which women draw in crafting their own and their children's identities. The dynamism of socialization practices belies any unilineal characterization of becoming Latinos. In the subjectivities that cut across "figured worlds," the transfiguration of authoring ourselves is agency within a sociohistoric context.

CHAPTER 6

Testimonios of Border Identities

"UNA MUJER ACOMEDIDA DONDE QUIERA CABE"

Native-born and Immigrant Households

Although I had initially constructed residence as a comparative basis for households, it soon became clear that most obvious division centered on a demarcation between "native-born" U.S. households and "immigrant" households, the latter denoting both parents born in Mexico. Several areas of research have identified this segmentation of the population within Latino populations, educational research for many years indicating that students from immigrant families tend to perform better in school than native-born students (Buriel 1975, 1987; Suárez-Orozco 1991; Vigil and Long 1981). There are multiple and contested reasons behind this perceived gap (see Valenzuela 1999). What is clear, however, is that the experiences of Mexican immigrant children are qualitatively different from U.S.–born Mexican-origin children.

One of the most extended controversies in literature on the education of minority children has centered, in an indirect way, on the division between immigrant and native-born minority populations (Ogbu 1978, 1981, 1987; Ogbu and Matute-Bianchi 1986; see Foley 1991 for review of voluntary and involuntary minorities). Because much ink has been spilled on the framework proposed by John Ogbu, I will not belabor the point. However, one of the problems with the taxonomic approach Ogbu espoused is that Mexican-origin populations are characterized globally as "involuntary minorities," obliterating the immigrant experience of first-generation families. Guadalupe Valdés, in her ethnographic portrait of immigrant families (1996), argues that the immigrant experience itself—making the decision to leave, going through the illegal period, "arreglando" (becoming legal), and surviving in a new world—fashions historically and socially situated circumstances that implicate particular consequences for the families. Like the families that Valdés studied, the immigrant families that I encountered did not consider themselves to be "involuntary" minorities. They made a very conscious and developed decision to relocate. However, there does exist a "dual status framework" wherein they make active positive and negative comparisons with what they remember about "back home." Immigrant parents often remark on how Mexican schools expect much more of students and that students must often go into a lower grade in Mexico after schooling in the United States. Indeed, this was the experience of one immigrant mother, who remarked to me:

> La educación que dan aquí a como la que dan en México, es muy baja. . . . Por ejemplo, mi sobrinita ——, la niña de mi hermana, ella sabe leer. Lo que enseñan allá en segundo, en tercero, aquí lo enseñan en sexto. Las divisiones, las multiplicaciones que apenas están viendo, allá ya lo pasó ella. Entonces allá está más avanzado porque, cuando mi cuñada se vino a vivir aquí, ella vivía en Ciudad Juárez, sus hijos entraron a la Tucson High, ¡Uhh! (les premiaron) cenas en "La Paloma," certificados y ésto, porque los chamacos allá eran burros, dice mi cuñada —— y aquí llegaron y yo tenía cenas en "La Paloma" por las calificaciones (tan buenas) de la Tucson High. —— y este, resulta de que cuando se vino mi cuñada, dice, "¡Ay! no cállate, verás re-burros [eran] allá. Ve las boletas de allá," dice, "y ve las de aquí." Y con ella, supe que la educación de allá era más alta que aquí. Aquí es más baja que allá en ese aspecto. Pero, luego ahorita, pues ahorita la computadora es la que hace todo.

> The education that they give here, compared to the one in Mexico, is very low. For example, my niece, my sister's daughter, already knows how to read. What they teach over there in second or third [grade], here they teach in sixth. Division, multiplication tables [that my children] are just now seeing, over there, she's already passed that. So, then, it's more advanced over there because when my sister-in-law came to live here, she used to live in Ciudad Juárez, her children entered Tucson High School, and *ooohh* [they were awarded] dinners at La Paloma,[1] certificates for this and that,

because the kids over there were not too bright, says my sister-in-law, and here they arrived, and I had a dinner at La Paloma because of their good grades at Tucson High. And so when my sister-in-law came, she said, "You won't believe it; they were doing awful in school over there. . . . Look at their report cards from over there, and look at their report cards from here." And from her I found out that the education over there is higher than here. Here it is lower than over there in that aspect. But, now, well, now, computers are what do everything.

On the other side of the coin, Mexican immigrants in Tucson, although noting the academic superiority of schools in Mexico, often point out the more punitive measures evidenced in Mexican schools, as well as the lack of support for the child in health, nutrition, and sports. Within a teachers' study group with which I have worked, teacher-researchers undertook ethnographic work within the households of their (mostly immigrant) students (see González et al. 1995). Because some of the questions asked in this work deal with a comparative perspective of U.S. and Mexican schools, the issue is often raised in teacher study group meetings. One teacher (Floyd-Tenery 1993) asked her immigrant students to draw comparisons between schools in the United States and schools in Mexico. For children, the physical surroundings of the school itself seemed to play a significant role in their perceptions of schools. The children drew pictures of cracks in the walls of classrooms in Mexico, but they portrayed U.S. schools as having a great deal of recreational equipment (swings, slides) and supplies. Another teacher noted that the sixth graders in her classroom often felt displaced within the U.S. schools and longed for the safe familiarity of their "home" school. They voiced the complaint that it was not *their* decision to relocate, but rather that of their parents, and they yearned for the easy familiarity with which they maneuvered in their former environment. They missed their friends, their play areas, and the dog they left behind. One teacher, commenting on her own childhood immigrant experience in Tucson, remarked that while she was in school, she felt that she was just marking time until she could go back to Caborca, her home town in Sonora, where her "real" life was, and that she lived in Tucson only "temporarily."

In stressing the importance of seeing the child's point of view in the social worlds of children, Andrade and Moll report the following statement from Susana, a thirteen-year-old who had lived in South Tucson since the age of seven: *"Yo no me siento a gusto estar aquí con los gringos y no estar con mi gente de allá de México. Me quisiera ir a México con mi propia gente'* (I don't feel comfortable being here with the "gringos" and not with my people from Mexico. I would like to go to Mexico with my own people). When asked if she would return to Mexico when she is older, she replies, *'Sí, yo volveré para mi tierra. Yo no estoy a gusto en tierras ajenas como por ejemplo los Estados Unidos. Yo donde estoy a gusto es en mi linda tierra de México. Y todo el tiempo nomás me sentiré a gusto en mi tierra de México'* (Yes, I will return to my land. I am not comfortable in foreign lands, like for example, the United States. Where I am comfortable is in my beautiful land of Mexico. And I will always only feel comfortable in my land of Mexico)" (1993:110–11).

For many immigrant children, the emotion of displacement in the diaspora of cross-border movements is a factor in the formation of their identities. In his studies of European ethnicity, Roosens notes that the "orientation of first-generation immigrants to their country of origin is expressed most clearly in their insistence that they will one day return there. Social rejection by their hosts, and public commitment to their own culture and to their country of origin, give first generation immigrants little reason to immerse themselves in the language and culture of their host country" (1989:134). This orientation takes on a regional significance in the Arizona-Sonora borderlands because households in southern Arizona are often tied to ritual participation in northern Sonora (Vélez-Ibáñez 1996). It is this "dual status framework" and the literal image of the border that I would contend differentiate the environment of language socialization of children in immigrant and native-born households in Tucson. Children in immigrant households have stronger and more multiplex ties to Mexico, and the child's identification is often connected to Sonora or other regions of Mexico. Previous studies on immigrant households in the Tucson area indicate that the cross-border exchange phenomenon is a salient feature of the population, and Vélez-Ibáñez demonstrates that these households tend to be linked to other household clusters in northern Sonora and "organize their extended kin relations in the United States in a clustered household arrangement of dense bilateral kin and maintain kin ties with their Mexican relatives" (1996:144).

Cisneros Family

This pattern was demonstrated in one immigrant family from the PACE sample. At the time of the interviews, the Cisneros family was a recent arrival to Tucson from Nogales, Sonora, and frequently visited a host of relatives who remained behind. Significantly, Mrs. Cisneros's mother was born in California, although her family returned to Sonora when she was a child. The family has thus "hopscotched" U.S. residence generationally, a term Vélez-Ibáñez uses to describe households "in which one or more members of a given household are born in Mexico and others are born in the United States. Alternately, one generation may be born in the United States, a second in Mexico, and a third in the United States. Such hopscotching has both negative and positive consequences for members of a given household, but in general the phenomenon provides the advantage of legal access to personal or institutional resources on either side of the U.S./Mexico border" (1996:143).

For the Cisneros family, trips to Nogales are a pivotal activity in procuring goods and services, medicine, and provisions for birthday and other family celebrations. For immigrant households in Tucson, multiple and dense networks mesh both economic and social functions. Mrs. Cisneros related several instances that exemplified this process and that involved the activation of her entire kin network. On the occasion of her grandchild's first birthday party, she reported how birria for the event was prepared by her relatives in Nogales, Sonora, the piñata provided by the child's nina (short for *madrina,* or godmother) in Tucson, the child's organdy dress purchased by her own mother in Sonora, and the beer by her husband's family in Tucson. Interestingly, this child was born to her son and his girlfriend, who have not married and do not live together. The child is symbolically recognized through the mobilization of the kin network and is incorporated into the ongoing social life of both parents. On another occasion, a niece's wedding shower, not only did a similar host of relatives supply the party, but female relatives enacted an off-color, bawdy skit detailing the events of the wedding night that the soon-to-be bride would supposedly experience.

Because I had only one PACE family who were immigrants, and two households from the pilot study, I sought out two more immigrant households to expand the sample. In listening to the tapes of the immigrant households, I discovered, not surprisingly, a higher incidence of

Mexican radio stations playing in the background, exposing children to particular musical discourses. In the immigrant families I encountered, and in similar studies in the area (Tapia 1991), there also appeared to be a high premium placed on girls learning to cook, clean, and sew. Many of the mothers have outside occupations that involve traditionally female domestic work in cleaning, sewing, or cooking. In addition, mothers will often augment the family income with periodic tamale, tortilla, or empanada sales. Mrs. Cisneros works in the kitchen of a local school and reported that she comes home tired and expects her older daughters to help out with a great deal of the housework. Because she also works Saturdays, family life revolves around outings on Sunday to the park or to Nogales and around the shared evening Spanish television telenovelas.

Language and Cross-Border Experiences

In analyzing tapes and in studying previous data gathered on immigrant children, I concluded that, owing to the pivotal cross-border experiences of immigrant children—their strong sense of identification with the natal culture—language socialization experiences were configured with a strong connection to the sending community. These frequent, calendrically predictable sojourns into Sonora are of particular significance in the patterns of child language socialization. Children in most immigrant families of the region are exposed to sustained transborder relationships and contexts that form the backdrop for a variant form of socialization than that experienced by native-born second- and third-generation Mexican-origin children. A second factor emerging from the involvement in close ties with the natal culture is the development of confianza. *Confianza,* a construct elaborated by Vélez-Ibáñez (1988, 1996), is characterized by the mutual exchange of economic, social, affective, or occupational support that results in "dense" relationships between related or unrelated households. Vélez-Ibáñez focuses on confianza as a pivotal element in the development of children in U.S. Mexican-origin households and notes that children grow up surrounded by a multitude of kinsmen and fictive kinsmen in the form of compadres and comadres (1996:137–81). He further argues that children begin early to learn the expectation of confianza. It is in this context in which he claims there can be "internalization of many other significant object relations with more persons, and expectation of more relations

with the same people, and expectations of being attentive to and invest-
ing emotionally in a variety of such relations" (1996:164). Although
Vélez-Ibáñez does not distinguish between immigrant and native-born
Mexican-origin children in delineating this construct, I would argue
that dense social relationships, although continuing through third- and
fourth-generation Mexican families, provide more financial and economic support in recent arrivals, but become oriented more toward
social and cultural functions in subsequent generations. The children
associated with the Cisneros family, for instance, reported playing "comadritas," a play situation in which girls pretend to be friends and
comadres, and in which the relationship between the comadres is the
pivotal point of the play activity. There was no evidence in the transcripts that playing comadritas situations was a commonly occurring
activity for native-born children. A strong sense of what confianza
entails in reciprocal relationships is part of Mrs. Cisneros's admonition to
her daughter that *"la señora ya no te va a traer libros"* (the lady won't bring
you books anymore), a veiled allusion that warns the child she will be
defaulting on her end of a reciprocal relationship and that if she did
want to be tape recorded, I would not bring the picture and sticker books
that I had previously supplied.

Personhood in Language Use

Although both native-born and immigrant segments of the population
may be perceived by the outside media and community as constituting
one whole, it is readily apparent when one looks at language data in
general, and at child language socialization in particular, that symbolic
and instrumental language processes are not interchangeable. Although
immigrant children are oriented to the affective dimensions of language
and exhibit creative interlocutory techniques, I would argue that the
sense of identity for children is not so much an identity as an ethnic
group member (which was implicit and assumed), but simply a particular identity as a "child." Language encounters appeared to be arranged
so as to imbue the child with a wonder of the sense of childhood, of
being separate from the world of adults. Language tapes reveal a significant use of the diminutive. Speech takes on the definitive construction of
"adapting the situation to the child." In the following transcriptions,
Mrs. Cisneros and her daughter look at a picture book, and a bulk of the

utterances involve the diminutization of nouns and even of adverbs and adjectives. A world of the child vis-à-vis the adaptation of linguistic resources to a child's eye view is paramount. This excerpt from a more extended transcript exhibits the child friendly adaptations of speech the mother makes to her five-year-old daughter. In it, the mother (MO) and child, Sonia (SO), are doing book work in Spanish, and the mother miniaturizes the conversation to fit a child's world:

1. MO: A ver, ¿qué es éste? (Let's see, what is this?)

2. SO: Un pajarito. (A little bird.)

3. MO: Un conejito. (A little rabbit.)

4. SO: Un conejito. (A little rabbit.)

. . .

23. MO: Un cochito. (A little pig.)

24. SO: Un cochito. Una . . . (A little pig. A . . .)

25. MO: Un gatito. (A kitten.)

. . .

60. MO: Con éste le pintas toda la boquita allí, de toda esta ruedita amarilla, primero, sin salirte de la raya. (With this one, you color the little mouth there, all of this little yellow wheel, first, without going out of the line.)

. . .

75. MO: Andale pues, píntale parejita toda, uno y luego el otro. (Go on, well. Color it evenly, first one and then the other.)

. . .

83. MO: Okay. El gatito lo vas a pintar color negro . . . lo puedes pintar el, el gatito. (Okay. The kitten you're going to color black. You can color it, the kitten.)

84. SO: ¿Cuál? (Which one?)

85. MO: Todo este, y luego a este, este monito colorado. (All this one, and then this one, this little red figure.)

86. SO: ¿Cuál monito colorado? (Which little red figure?)

. . .

91. SO: ¿Qué lo pinto? ¿Un monito? (What do I color it? A little figure?)

92. MO: Uh-huh. Puedes pintarle la cabecita blanca y todo . . . el cabello . . . café . . . todo aquí, despacito, las patitas y todo. Todo esto café. (Uh-huh. You can color the little head white and all . . . the hair . . . brown, everything here, slowly, the little feet, and everything. All this is brown.)

. . .

96. MO: No te pases de la raya. Despacito. (Don't go out of the line. Slowly.)

These transcripts also highlight the most salient limitation in studying the language socialization of Mexican-origin children: the complexity of comparing similar speech events when one is in English and one is in Spanish. I had other homework and dinner table transcripts for the Gómez, Gamboa, Aguilar, and Escobedo families in which the interactions are mostly in English. Apart from the obvious language differentiation, the issue of point of origin in Mexico (southern versus northern, urban versus rural) as well as length of residence in the United States become issues. The children are asked a variety of questions in Spanish, or comments are made with the tag *"¿verdad?"* or *"¿que no?"* or *"¿eh?"* The mother in the Gómez family repeats this pattern in English as the tag "huh?" The Aguilar children additionally employ the tag "¿huh, ma?" in a number of utterances. The use of the endearment *mihijita* is sprinkled throughout tapes with interactions between grandmothers and granddaughters. In the case of the Gómez family, the endearment is changed to *babe* and *honey*. Focusing on these microanalytical points, however, does not give an overarching view of regional patterns. Immigrant children in the borderlands region, because of dense cross-border ties, are bound to a larger regional network that involves sustained and prolonged contact with their country of origin. Parents sometimes remarked that going back to live in Mexico was always an option, which has become more of an issue now that Mexico has allowed its citizens to retain dual citizenship. The child's sense of Mexican-ness is much more firmly cemented on notions of selfhood. The language tapes reveal that the extraordinary use of the diminutive with children indicates a caregiver's concern with the child's sense of childhood as a definable status.

Because of the fewer number of immigrant families in this sample, I do not present an exhaustive evaluative summary. What I do suggest, however, is that an investigation of language patterns within the U.S.–Mexican community must define the issues inherent in an immigrant community versus those in a native-born population.

Testimonios of Immigrant Women

One area that cannot be overlooked is the "dual status framework" under which the women in these households operate. Because they lived a harsher life in Mexico, the benefits of life on this side of the border far outweigh their struggles to make ends meet on *el otro lado*. The following two narratives, or testimonios, offer a raw and unvarnished image of the multiple systems of oppression under which many immigrant women have suffered. However, they are also powerful counterstories of both resistance and accommodation on their own terms.

señora hernández. Señora Hernández, the mother of four daughters, is a woman in her mid-thirties, born in 1963. Her description of her early life on a ranch in Sonora paints an appalling scene of patriarchy at its worst. Because immigrant women's stories of strength and overcoming of obstacles are rarely privileged, their lived experiences are often silenced precisely because of their very pain. Yet these early experiences shaped the resistance that these women enact in refusing to reproduce the structures within which they grew. In the following section of her narrative, Señora Hernández describes the economic progress that her father was able to make, built on the work of his wife and daughters, and the control that he exerted over their everyday life:

> Me acuerdo que no teníamos luz cuando estaba chiquita yo, y usaban lámparas, teníamos dos cuartitos nomás y la cocinita. Mi papá y mamá durmieron todo el tiempo separados y todos nosotros hechos bolas en un sólo cuarto. En catres, en tarimas, porque no se usaban las camas . . . Porque nunca nos dejó mi papá dormir en el suelo. Hubo gente que casi todos dormían en el suelo, hasta las parejas. Me tocó a mí dormir en el suelo. Entonces mi papá siempre se procupó para que no durmieramos en el suelo . . .
>
> De los ocho años me acuerdo [mucho] porque cuando se murió mi hermanita, me acuerdo muy bien—se le murió una niña a mi mamá—me acuerdo muy bien de mi abuelita que estaba sentada en la pura puerta del cuarto, llorando por mi hermanita, yo me acuerdo muy bien.

I remember that we didn't have electricity when I was small, and we used lamps [kerosene], and we had only two rooms and the small kitchen. My father and mother used to sleep separate from us, and the rest of us would be crowded into only one room—in cots, in tarimas [wooden frames] because we didn't use beds. . . . Because my father never let us sleep on the floor. There were people who slept on the floor, even couples. I had occasion to sleep on the floor also. My father always took care that we not sleep on the floor. . . .

When I was eight, I remember very well because my little sister died; I remember very well my little sister died—my mother lost an infant daughter. I remember very well my grandmother was sitting in the doorway of the room, crying for my little sister. I remember very well.

From their marginal economic status, the family began to progress economically. However, it is interesting to note that Señora Hernández views this progress as particular to her father, not as collectively beneficial to the family as a whole:

SH: Me acuerdo muy bien [de todo] de cómo mi papá fue progresando, de que mis hermanas, pero para ésto, mis hermanas empezaron a trabajar, y él con una vaca, se hizo de más ganado y pudo vender para comprar otras cosas. Y cuando ya tuvo ese troque, que [fue cuando] ya le ayudábamos todas. No nada más trabajábamos en la ciudad. También había trabajo en el campo, por ejemplo de ir a deshierbar . . . cuando sembraban trigo, la gente trabaja en deshierbar, en levantar el trigo. . . . Ibamos a piscar escobas nosotros. Es como el maíz, y las poníamos, las levantabamos como el trigo . . . Pero ahí enseguida del rancho de nosotros, en otro lugar que se llama Torobene, ahí había de todo, había limones, habían las hortalizas y ahí vendían. Y comprábamos ahí a veces. Barato, muy barato la verdura, calabacitas. Se economizaba mucho porque compraba las calabazas baratas. . . . Progresó mucho mi papá y se compró ese troque. Hizo mucho dinero porque él era el único que tenía troque en el rancho. Entonces toda la gente se iba a piscar con él. Le pagaban a mi papá por llevar gente a trabajar. Trabajaban sus hijas, trabajaba mi mamá. Pues todo ese dinero que se juntó, mi papá empezó a progresar.

NG: Tu mamá ¿en qué trabajaba?

SH: Igual que las muchachas en piscar algodón, en piscar lo que fuera.

NG: Y las muchachas ¿también piscaban algodón?

SH: Todas, a mí también me tocó piscar algodón. Uy pero le tenía un miedo a las arañas que veía. Me ponía ajo donde quiera, porque dicen que con el ajo se espantan los animales. Pero a mí me gustaba ir porque me iba a comer el lonche. *[Risas]* A comer el lonche, porque pocas veces se hacía tortillas de harina, y para los lonches siempre acostumbraban la tortilla de harina. Y yo para ir a comer tortilla de harina me iba también. *[Risas]* Se ríe mucho mi esposo porque le platico. Yo no iba a pesar y que me pagaran a mí. Lo que yo piscaba de algodón se lo echaba a mi mamá o a mis hermanas. O sea que estaba chiquita. No tenía que andar pesando. Se los echaba a mis hermanas o a mi mamá.

SH: I remember everything very well, for instance how my father began to progress, all my sisters began to work, and he [my father] began with one cow, and he acquired more cattle that he was able to sell and buy other things. And when he had a truck, that was when all of us would help him out. We didn't just work in the city. We also would work in the countryside; for instance, we would go and work weeding. . . . When someone would plant wheat, people would go and work taking up the weed and harvesting the wheat. . . . We would go to pick escobas. It is like corn [a kind of broom corn], and we would harvest them like wheat. . . . But next door to the ranch in another place that was called Torobene, there they had everything; there were lemons, there was produce, and they sold it. And we would buy there sometimes—cheap, the vegetables were very inexpensive, like squash. We would economize because we would buy the squash very . . . My father was able to progress, and he bought himself that truck. He made a lot of money because he was the only one who had a truck on the ranch. Then people would go with him into the fields. They would pay my father to take them to work. All of his daughters worked; my mother worked. So with all that money that he gathered, my father began to progress.

NG: What did your mother work in?

SH: The same as the girls [her daughters], picking cotton.

NG: And the girls, they also picked cotton?

SH: Yes, all of them. I also picked cotton. But I was so afraid of spiders that I saw. I would put garlic all over me because they say that you can scare away animals with garlic. But I liked to go because I liked to eat my lunch. *[Laughter]* I liked to eat lunch [in the field] because flour tortillas were seldom made, and flour tortillas were always served at lunch, and so I, in order to eat the flour tortillas, would also go. *[Laughter]* My husband laughs because I tell him this. I would not weigh my gatherings in order to get paid. What cotton I picked I would give to my mother and my sisters [so that their sack would weigh more]. That is, I was younger, and so I didn't have to weigh in, and so I would give it to my sister and my mother.

In the following section, Señora Hernández relates a description of her father as *muy machista,* elaborating what is embedded in this construct for her: his complete autocratic control of every aspect in their lives, his rigid refusal to allow their interaction with young people, especially males, of their own age, and the beatings that he inflicted on them for their interpreted failure to respond to his immediate commands. Although some dominant writings in anthropology have fetishized the idea of machismo as an explanatory mechanism for all that is wrong in Latino households, the term has been ascribed an internal coherence that is not always analyzed. Señora Hernández resisted the authoritarian dominance of her father, fleeing from the household and finding employment elsewhere in the border community of Nogales, Sonora. Although she and her sisters were geographically distant from their father, he continued to demand payments from them, calculating to the penny what their expenses would be, what they were earning, and what they should have been able to send back to him. Yet in spite of Señora Hernández's overt resistance and rebellion, his influence continued to pull at her as his voice echoes in his refrain that *"una mujer acomedida donde quiera cabe"* (a useful woman will fit everywhere). His own words, however, were reinscribed into a form of resistance against him because it is precisely her meticulous work habits that allowed her to achieve an economic independence that enabled her to escape his control. Señora Hernández transformed a highly gendered ideology into an economic strategy that allowed for her own liberatory potential.

Mi papá nunca piscó porque él era el patrón. El que llevaba a la gente y andaba con los otros señores. Él no piscaba. Mi mamá sí y mis hermanas. Él podía haber piscado como otros señores, pero no. Siempre fue muy machista mi papá. Siempre. Ayer estaba platicando con ———, que su papá es igual que mi papá. Si está sentado en la mesa, [por] un vaso de agua no se levanta. [Por] Lo que se le ofrezca no se levanta. Mi papá es igualito. . . . Siempre fue así. Y él no piscaba. Mi mamá era la que piscaba, mis hermanas. Y por eso fue que mi papá progresó, subió mucho. . . .

Y como le digo, mi papá fue muy machista. Y aunque siempre le ayudamos, mi papá siempre fue estricto con nosotros. Si alguien se estaba peinando, mirándose en el espejo, "¿Qué están muy chulas?" Él era muy grosero, "jija de la acá y allá." No se podía peinar. Hasta la fecha a mi papá no le gusta que estemos en el cuarto encerradas. Quiere que todas estén afuera haciendo quehacer. Que estén barriendo, que estén lavando. Como los lavaderos están afuera, todo quiere que lo hagamos afuera. Hasta a las nueras las regaña. No le gusta que estén adentro. Nunca nos dejó asomarnos por la ventana. Fue un hombre muy estricto. Por eso de tantas hijas que tuvo, nomás dos se le casaron de blanco. . . . Todas se fueron con el novio. Y le dió una vida muy fea a mi mamá. . . . Y sí es cierto, mi papá fue muy estricto y muy exagerado, muy violento con nosotros, siempre nos anduvo maltratando, siempre ¡Uh! ¡todo el tiempo nos andaba jalando las orejas hasta que nos tronaba! Porque hablaba como yo: Muy rápido. Él habla más rápido que yo. A mí ya se me ha quitado. Y fíjese que mi papá a veces nos decía, "Ve a correrle [con] las chivas." Y nosostros corríamos con las vacas. ¡Y como eran las chivas y no las vacas, nos agarraba de las orejas y nos tronaba!

Si él decía en la mañana "levántense" dos veces. Si a las dos veces no nos levantábamos, nos levantaba a manguerazos, a lo que fuera. A mi me tocó, me llegó a pegar nomás como dos veces, porque rápido me levantaba, para que no me pegara. La última vez que me pegó mi papá yo tenía como siete años. Dijo "levántense" y yo bien dormida bien a gusto, y no me levanté, y cuando menos pensé

ya me agarró a manguerazos. . . . ¡Uy! a mi hermana la mayor
estuvo mucho tiempo en cama. Se le hizo una llaga porque le pegó
con la hebilla. Y siempre todas [estábamos] enfermas de mal de
orín porque nos golpeaba mi papá muy salvaje. Éramos nueve
mujeres cuando nació el hombre. De chiquito ya lo quería traer
como grande. Sufrió mucho mi hermano. Pero a los quince años se
fue de la casa. . . .

Veíamos a las muchachas que iban al estadio [donde] jugaban
los muchachos, y mi papá nunca nos dejó ir. Y para ese entonces ya
habían camiones en el rancho, de otros pueblos que iban para la
ciudad, pueblos, si pasaba el camión y estábamos mirando "¡Uh!
¿Qué estás mirando ya al que está manejando? o eso o el otro,"
muy celoso. Nunca nos dejó tener amigos, nunca nos dejó ir a la
escuela enfrente a ver quienes estaban jugando basquetbol. O se
juntaban las muchachas a jugar volibol, nunca nos dejó porque
andaban con los muchachos. Fue muy estricto Y yo como ya estaba
harta de ver todos los golpes de mi mamá . . . Mi mamá sufrió
mucho, mi papá la golpeaba, golpeaba a mis hermanas. Sufrimos
mucho. La golpeaba, le dejaba moretes, y fue muy así. . . . Y este así
pasó el tiempo que él se hizo de cosas y progresó mucho, hizo una
casa muy grande.

My father never worked in the fields, because he was the boss. He
was the one who delivered the people and associated with the other
men. He didn't pick anything. My mother did, as did my sisters.
He could have picked like other men, but no. My father was
always very machista, always. Yesterday I was chatting with [a
friend], whose father is just like my father. If he is sitting at the
table, he won't get up, even for a glass of water or whatever is
needed; he will not get up. My father is just the same. He always
was, and he would not work in the fields. My mother is the one
who picked, and my sisters. That's why my father progressed. He
progressed; he really was able to rise. . . .

As I said, my father was very machista. And although we always
helped him, he was always very strict with us. If somebody was
combing herself, looking at herself in the mirror, [he would say],
"Are you real pretty or what?" He was very abusive. He would use
profanity with us. We couldn't comb ourselves. To this day, my

father doesn't like for us to be inside our rooms. He wants us to be outside busy with something. He wants us to be outside sweeping or washing because the wash tubs are outside. He even scolds his daughters-in-law. He doesn't like for them to be inside. He never let us look out the window. He was a very strict man. That's why of all the daughters that he had, most of them, ran off with their boyfriends. . . . And he gave my mother a very ugly life. And it is true, my father was very strict and very extreme, very violent with us. He always mistreated us, always! He was always pulling our ears, until they popped, because he talked like me, very rapidly. He talks even faster than I do. I have gotten over that [talking fast]. And my father sometimes would tell us, "Go and round up the goats," and we would run to the cows. And because it was the goats and not the cows, he would grab us by the ears until they popped.

If he said in the morning "Get up" twice, and after two times we didn't get up, he would get us up by beating us with a hose or whatever. He hit me only a couple of times because I would get up really fast so that he wouldn't hit me. The last time that my father hit me, I was about seven years old. He said "Get up," and I was fast asleep, very comfortably, and I didn't get up, and before I knew it, he grabbed me and hit me with the hose. . . . My older sister was in bed for a long time because of a wound he inflicted on her because he hit her with the buckle of his belt. We were always suffering from urinary tract infections because he hit us so savagely. There were nine of us girls when the first boy was born. Ever since he was a young child, he [my father] wanted to treat him like a grown person. He suffered a lot, but at age fifteen he left the house. . . .

[Sometimes] I would see the girls who would go to the stadium, where the boys played, and my father never let us go. By then there were buses at the ranch and other pueblos that would go to the city. If the bus passed by, and we were looking, "*Oh,* what are you looking at? . . . Are you looking at the one who's driving?" He was very jealous. He never let us have friends. He never let us go to the school in front to see who was playing basketball. Or when the girls got together to play volleyball, he never let us because they were with boys. He was very strict. And I was fed up with all the beatings that my mother suffered. My mother suffered a lot. My father would beat her and would beat my sisters. We suffered a lot. He would beat her and leave bruises on her. And that's how it was.... And so time passed and he acquired more and got ahead, and he built a big house.

When she finally made the decision to leave her house, Señora Hernández, a resident of the Sonoran borderlands, fled to the border city of Nogales, Sonora. Because she had no money and no job, she would accompany her sister to her job cleaning houses. But in order to be fed lunch, she would make herself useful, helping her sister with the housework, making sure that the patrona, the lady of the house, noticed her work.

Ya me conocían [las patronas] me saludaban, y me veían haciendo quehacer y ya era otra cosa ¿verá? . . . Porque mi papá siempre nos dijo que "¡una mujer acomedida donde quiera cabe; una mujer floja, en ninguna parte cabe!" Entonces, teníamos todo eso en la mente y nos poníamos, para que las señoras, pues se agradaran ¿verdad? y no nos miraran así. Y sí tuve muy buena suerte en ese aspecto, porque todas me querían.

The ladies who owned the houses, they knew me; they would say hello to me, and they would see me doing things around the house, and things were different. Because my father always told us that "a useful woman will fit everywhere, and a lazy woman will fit nowhere," we would have all of that in our minds, so we would try to please the women. And I was very fortunate in that respect because they all liked me.

Señora Hernández's preimmigration experience resonates with the themes of immigrant women. Fleeing abuse, seeking to live in circumstances other than in abject poverty, they actively convey to their daughters that hard work and adapting to circumstances will help them on life's journey. It is evident from Señora Hernández's narrative that she considers herself *"una mujer acomedida,"* a woman who accommodates to her surroundings, who makes herself useful, and who is therefore able to fit in anywhere. In many ways, her narrative echos the sentiments that Valdés presents as descriptive of immigrant women:

I was told that women were simply not like men, that we had our role and our mission. Men were different. Things were not easier for men or harder for women. Things just were, and people lived with what was.

As I think about the women in the study, words come to mind for describing them include spirited, brave, optimistic, determined, loyal and perseverant. These were by no means "wimpy" women. Their spirit and their determination, however, were not directed toward goals such as achieving financial independence or individual distinction, or even developing an egalitarian marriage. They were directed at living out their roles in life as they understood them. They were traditional Mexican working-class women who understood their own success to involve meeting the two goals of helping their husbands to make a living and helping their children to grow into responsible adults. Happiness involved small things, everyday satisfactions, the absence of pain, the possibility of laughter, and always the presence of family. (1996:93)

SEÑORA ORTIZ.   Señora Ortiz is a woman in her mid-sixties, mother to eight children of her own and to five others whom she raised after her sister passed away. Her story is one of resilience, of hope against all odds, and a testimony to the human spirit. However desperate her circumstances, Señora Ortiz found a way to persevere and to carve out a place for herself. Because *"se me prendía el foco"* (literally, the lightbulb would light up), she was able to change and adapt her surroundings so that they were more accommodating. As another example of *una mujer acomedida,* she has scratched out a living, sometimes literally with her bare hands, out of the most meager of resources. In this first part of the narrative, Señora Ortiz articulates her ability to survive even if it meant living off herbs and grasses because her first husband spent his meager salary on drink. Like Señora Hernández, though, she transformed this oppression into an uncanny ability to make do, to adapt, and to move on. Her gut-wrenching narrative slices to the heart of the layered systems of oppression and repression she has lived.

[C]omo mi vida ha sido, es, en muchas etapas. Desde mi nacimiento hasta hoy. Mi primera etapa debe haber sido cuando nací, . . . me recuerdo de los tres años cuando murió mi papá.

Yo nací en Sonora en 1929. . . . y tuve una infancia diferente que otras personas. Que yo recuerde cuando tenía seis años mi mamá murió y me regaló con mis padrinos que me bautizaron. Ellos me criaron en (otro lugar) . . ., afuera en el corral amarrada en el trochil del cochi . . ., no entiendo por qué . . . yo no entiendo por qué me tenían amarrada. Yo no recuerdo, si sería traviesa o por qué, o no me querían y yo hasta la fecha no como maizoro, no como galleta de soda, me representan la comida del puerco. La galleta de soda me representa el salvado y la "conflays" o maizoro era el que dejaban en la orilla de las bateas los puercos y era lo que yo comía, pues entonces por eso que recuerdo ese pedazo de mi infancia pero no me recuerdo por qué me tenían amarrada, no recuerdo si me trataban mal o bien mis padrinos, no sé. Pero sí me tenían afuera y sí me acuerdo que me metían en la noche a dormir un lado de la estufa, en el suelo, de eso sí me acuerdo.

Llegó mi hermano me llevó, me dijo, "Te voy a llevar con tu otra hermana, donde la tienen." La tenía mi abuela por parte de mi papá. "Y a estas gentes no me les vuelvas a hablar nunca más, no las recuerdes porque no son buenas personas," es lo único que yo me acuerdo que él me dijo. Y me llevó a una panadería a comer pan, me recuerdo de eso cuando me desató de los puercos y me llevó allá.

Me llevó con mi nana, la mamá de mi papá, y de ahí en adelante pues tuve una vida muy dura con mis . . . , con mis tíos. . . . Y ellos me dieron una vida muy dura.

No me daban de comer también. Me daban de la comida que se les echaba a perder como que si les caía grillos y yo no me los quería comer porque tenía grillos, pero me los tenía que comer y me daban una tortilla de maíz al día, eso es todo. No me compraban ropa, no me compraban zapatos. Nunca tuve un par de zapatos y sí me hacían trabajar bastante. Recuerdo que vivíamos en un cerro y tenía que acarrear yo el agua desde abajo, del principio del cerro subir dos botes de agua en palanca, no sé si sepa qué son. Un palo, un palo aquí, ¿no? para agarrar el agua y levantarla y subir tenía que llenar barricas de agua, y ellos tenían una frutería y tenía que estar la fruta, la verdura limpia. Para eso cargaba yo agua. Y pues la golpeaban a uno en ese tiempo así se usaba, los papás o los que les estaban criando, no recuerdo por qué me pegaban, quizás sería, no quería hacerlo al modo de los niños.

Y mi vida fue muy dura. A los diez y seis años me casé con alguien que no era ni mi novio, no, quería salir de mi casa por lo mal que me trataban. Me casé en Nacosari con un hombre veinte años mayor que yo. Tuve tres hijos con él, y me casé bien. Me sacó de la casa, pero para casarme fíjate, y nos casamos en Nacosari, y entonces ya me vine a vivir a Esqueda. Era un hombre pobre que no tenía nada, nada no tenía para vivir, absolutamente nada. Entonces yo creo que yo viví, yo nací con eso en la mente que yo podía hacer algo. Y . . ., y siempre trataba de hacer algo aunque no tenía con qué hacerlo. Hacía toda mi ropa para los niños en la mano. Todo cocía en la mano. Quizás eso lo traigo yo en mí, pero yo batallé mucho con mi primer esposo, era muy tomador, y él no tenía nada y lo poquito que podía ganar era para tomar, y yo duraba semanas sin comer, pepenando quelites en las orillas de las vías de los trenes, en las acequias para poder sobrevivir. Y así tuve a mis tres hijos. Cuando mi hija mayor se puso muy mala de tos ferina, me vine a Agua Prieta, a curarla. Mandé a pedirle a mi hermana que mandara el pasaje del tren y llegué y ya la niña estaba bastante mala ya no sobrevivió, se me murió en cinco años. Entonces vi que yo podía vivir de otra manera. Empecé a lavar y a planchar ajeno y supe que podía ganar dinero, entonces decidí divorciarme y me divorcié.

My life has had several stages. From my birth until now. My first phase was from the time I was born up until I was three years old when my father died.

I was born in Sonora in 1929. . . . I had a childhood that was different from that of other people. From what I remember, I was six years old when my mother died, and she gave me to my godparents, [who had baptized me]. They raised me in [another place] outside in the corral, tied to a pig trough. I don't understand why. I don't understand why they had me tied up. I don't understand if I was always misbehaving or if they didn't like me. To this day, I don't eat cereal that reminds me of corn flakes. I don't eat soda crackers because they remind me of the feed that was given to the pigs. Soda crackers represent to me the pig slop, and corn flakes, or maizoro, is what the pigs left on the edge of the troughs. And that's what I would eat. That's why I remember that time of my childhood, but I don't remember why they had me tied up. I don't remember if they treated me good or bad, my godparents, I don't know. But they did have me outside, and I remember that they would take me inside at night to sleep by the stove, on the floor, and that I do remember.

My brother came and took me away. He told me he was going to take me to where my other sister was living. My grandmother had her. My grandmother on my father's side had her. "Don't ever speak to these people ever again . . . Don't remember them because they are not good people," my brother said to me. And he took me to a bakery to eat bread. I remember that, when he untied me from the corral and took me there.

He took me to my grandmother [my father's mother]. And from then on I still had a difficult life with my uncles. [My relatives] gave me a difficult life.

They didn't give me much to eat. They would give me the food that spoiled on them or that was ruined by crickets, and I didn't want to eat it because the food had crickets in it. But I had to eat, and they gave me one corn tortilla per day, that's all. They wouldn't buy me clothes; they wouldn't buy me shoes. I never had a pair of shoes, and they made me work very hard. I remember we lived on a mountain, and I would have to haul water up from below, from the edge of the mountain; I had to carry up two cans of water on a stick. . . . I had to fill barrels of water. They had a fruit stand, and the fruit had to be cleaned. That's why I had to carry the water. And they used to beat you in those times, that's the way it was—the parents or those whoever were raising you. I don't know why they would hit me. Maybe it was because I did it in a child-ish way.

And my life was very difficult, very hard. At sixteen years of age, I married someone who was not my boyfriend. No, I just wanted to leave the house because I was treated so badly. I got married in Nacosari with a man twenty years my senior. I had three children with him, and I was married the right way. He took me out of the house, but to marry me. We got married in Nacosari, and then I went to live in Esqueda. He was a poor man who didn't have anything . . . he had nothing on which to live, absolutely nothing. Then I believe that I lived . . . it dawned on me that I could do something else with my life. I always tried to do things, even though I didn't have anything to do it with. I made all the clothes for my children by hand. Everything I sewed was by hand. Maybe I carry that in me. But I really struggled with my first husband. He was a drinker. And he didn't own anything, and the little that he earned, he used it for drinking, and I would go weeks without eating. Just picking wild spinach from the edge of the train rails and on the banks of the creeks and irrigation ditches so that I would survive. And that's the way I had my three children. When my older daughter became very ill with whooping cough, I came to Agua Prieta to seek a cure. I sent a message to my sister who lived there to send me the fare for the train, and when I arrived, my daughter was very ill, and she did not survive. She died at age five. Then I saw that I could live in a different way. I began to wash and to iron for other people, and I found out that I could earn money. So I decided to get a divorce, and I divorced.

As the realization grew in Señora Ortiz that there was another way to live, she, like Señora Hernández, rejected the life that she had suffered and made a move, again to another border town, Agua Prieta, where she was able to survive through her own labor. In the following section of her narrative, she describes the abject poverty of her life with her first husband, the desperate struggle of bearing children, and her scraping together of bits and pieces of leftover materials to make do in the struggle to survive. As she describes the birth of her first daughter, however, another construct emerges that moves her narrative away from the singularity of gender as a primary conceptual or organizational category. In her telling, Señora Ortiz speaks of the owner of the vineyard where her husband worked, a woman of means, who attended to Señora Ortiz's birth experience, supplied blankets for the newborn, but who also allowed the workers and their families to live out in the open, under the trees, without even the most minimal housing, and who further had a store that sold supplies to the workers, which they paid for from their meager wages. The intersection of class and gender is played out in the juxtaposition of these two women, one who enjoyed a life of privilege, perhaps because of gender, and the other who embodied multiple systems of gender, class, and racial oppression—eking out an existence with only a cup, a plate, and a spoon as her only possessions.

Pero así es, mi vida ha sido muy dura. Con mi primer, voy a volver para atrás, cuando viví con mi esposo el trabajaba en . . . una vinatería, no sé si será. Es donde hacen vino, donde hacen mezcal de ese fuerte. Yo vivía abajo del árbol. Mi primer hija la tuve yo colgada en el árbol, yo.

Me llevaron partera, me colgaron en el árbol y me ponían una rodilla en la cintura, me ponían la mano arriba del estómago pa' bajo. Tres días duré colgada para tener a la niña. Duré un mes y yo no me podía mover, porque me dolía todito. Día y noche allí colgada y con los dolores. Y yo chamaca todavía.

Amarrada con una sábana, de aquí así, y luego la cuelgan en un gancho del árbol, allí. Y luego va la partera y le pone la rodilla en la cintura y le pone las manos aquí, cada dolor le bajan aquí, y es para sostenerle la cintura. Y esa niña la tuve colgada en el árbol. Ya los otros dos no, pues ya había tenido la primera, ya sabía como tenerlos los otros dos. . . . Allí me daban, me daban pura manzanilla. . . . Pero yo duré tres días. Y había una señora en ese rancho, ella tenía, la de la vinatería, tenía dinero, tenía muy buena casa. Y ella fue la que llevo sábanas, toallas. Y ella nomás movía la cabeza, pero pues ¿qué iba a hacer? Estaba muy lejos de la civilización, allá en el cerro, muy lejos. Y pues yo no sabía nada, y así duré, tuve a la niña y yo la crié como Dios me dió a entender. . . .

Abajo del árbol y nevando, una nevada tremenda . . . se estaba derritiendo la nieve, y yo, me tenían en una lona, arriba del árbol, y tenían cobijas, para que no me entrara mucho aire y cuando nació la niña igual con puras cobijas colgadas de los árboles, que la señora llevó para niña no tuviera frío. Pues porque no tenía casa. Yo vivía y dormía debajo del árbol. La vinatería, todos los que trabajaban allí vivían abajo de los árboles. Las únicas casas que estaba allí eran la de la señora, la dueña de la vinatería. Y así el que la agua la pasaba a uno debajo de los árboles, la nieve, todo. Así vivía un, y yo no mas tenía tres cajoncitos de esa que vendían la comida, nomás tenía una taza, un plato, una cuchara, un sartén, cuatro piedras, una hoja.

Las cuatro piedras las ponía yo, atizaba yo allí. Y las hojas era para poner el sartén arriba, echar tortilla, una bandejita que amasaba para hacer tortilla, y esta señora, la dueña de la vinatería tenía una tiendita para venderle comida a los trabajadores. Pues le vendía allí de a poquito, según a lo que le pagaban. No ganaban nada, nada no ganaban, apenas pa' mal comer. Yo molía el café en una, en una vasito de cerveza tecate, que esa era la lámina más gruesa, siempre andaba yo buscándola, y con un marrito ahí molía yo el café. Y pa' rayar queso, cuando llegaba a tener queso. En una lámina así, le hacía agujeritos, pues con un cuchillo, con un clavo, y quedan piquitos atrás. Y se raya bien suave el queso. Cuando llegaba uno a tener queso, que llega a ir uno a un rancho donde vendían queso.

That is the way my life has been . . . very difficult. With my first . . . I'm going to regress here, when I lived with my first husband, he worked in a winery, where they make wine and that very strong mescal. I used to live under a tree. When I had my first daughter, I was hung from a tree.

They had a midwife, and they tied me to the tree, and someone would put their knee to my back, or a hand above my stomach to push down. Three days, three days, I stayed hanging from the tree, to have my baby. I couldn't move for a month after that because everything hurt. Day and night, there I was hanging and with labor pains, and I was still very young.

They tied me with a sheet, which they would hang on a hook to a tree. And then the midwife put her knee to my waist, and she would put her hands here [on my stomach]; with each pain she would press down and would also grab my waist. And that child I had hanging from a tree. The next two children, I did not because I had already had the first one, and I knew how to give birth. I had only chamomile tea to drink the whole time I was in labor. . . . It lasted three days. There was a lady on the ranch [the winery], she had some money, and she had a good house. She's the one who took sheets and towels. She would just shake her head. What else could she do? We were far away from civilization, up there in the mountains. And I didn't know anything. I survived, and I had the child and raised her in the way God has let me know I should. . . .

And after that, we continued living under the tree. . . . Sometimes there was a tremendous snow, and the snow would melt, and I had only a tarp and blankets hanging from the tree, so that not too much air would blow on me, and on the newborn baby. I covered her with blankets that the lady had taken, so that the child would not be cold. So, because I didn't have a house, I lived and slept under the tree. At the winery, all who worked there lived under trees. The only house that was there belonged to the owner of the winery. So, one would weather rains and snow, there under the tree, everything. That's the way we lived. All I had was three little boxes of the kind that is used to sell produce, and I had only one cup, one plate, one spoon, one pot, four rocks, and a grill.

I would place the four rocks on the ground, and I would build a fire, and the grill was for me to place a can on top or to make tortillas, as I had a little basin where I could mix the dough. And this lady, the owner of the winery, had a little store to sell food to the workers. She would sell a little at a time, according to how much they could pay her. They didn't earn very much, only enough to eat and not very well. I would grind the coffee in an aluminum can, the thickest aluminum; I was always looking for Tecate beer cans [because they were the best], and with a little mallet I would grind the coffee. Also, when I would grate cheese, whenever I happened to have cheese. In the aluminum, I would make little perforations with a knife or a nail, which left sharp edges in the back, and it served to grate cheese very well.

The remainder of Señora Ortiz's narrative is also not for the weak of heart, yet she pressed on with determination and perseverence, seeking to make her surroundings better in whatever small way she could. After the death of her daughter, she struggled with her two remaining children and eventually remarried. This marriage has endured the test of time, and at the time of the interviews they were celebrating their forty-first anniversary.

After recounting the first years of her second marriage, she tells of her sister's lingering illness and painful death. At that point, despite her own abject poverty, Señora Ortiz took on the five siblings, raising them as brothers and sisters to her own five children.

[Ella] tenía cáncer. Y entonces me la llevé a vivir a la casa, y ella estaba tan enferma que me la llevé pa' Hermosillo porque me pasaron para allá, creo. Pues que no habían, no habían buenos doctores en aquel tiempo en Agua Prieta. Que la llevara al Hospital General de Hermosillo, y nos fuimos con Manuel, me fui yo, me llevé todos los niños de ella, me llevé a los míos y fuimos a vivir a Hermosillo con los primos mientras estaba ella internada cuando ya me dijeron que ya no tenía remedio que ella, ya estaba muy avanzado el cáncer entonces dije pos no, pues mejor me voy a estarme en mi casa en Agua Prieta. Y no teníamos dinero pa' venirnos. Manuel trabajaba allá pero pa' mantener a tantos chamacos pues no se alcanzaba. Entonces lo que hice es que nos vinimos en el camión como pudimos hasta Cananea, hasta allí nos llegó el dinero. . . . Yo hice una carta para Douglas, a las casas donde yo trabajaba y les dije, "Mi hermana va a llegar mañana, por favor si pueden llevarles algo de comida." No pos cuando yo llegué, tenía la casa llena de comida. Todas las que escribí llegaron con cajas de comida. . . . Y sí, respondieron muy bien las trabajadoras, ahí me apuntan y cuando yo vaya voy y trabajo por la comida que les dieron. Nunca me la cobraron, hasta dinero les dieron.

Si, siempre duró como dos años. Muy mala. Después ya tuve que dejar de trabajar, no pude ya. Es que ella necesitaba . . ., no teníamos dinero pa' tenerla en un hospital, entonces ella necesitaba de atención. Tenía que cambiarla, porque ella tenía cáncer, pues cuando tienen cáncer tienen desechos del cáncer que se la está comiendo por dentro. Tiene uno que estarles cambiando, hasta con las madres de allí de Douglas fui a parar a pedirles sábanas, fundas, lo que tuvieran pa' ponerle zapeta, porque no las podía lavar, las tenía que quemar. Todas las mañanas quemábamos toditita la ropa que le quitábamos a ella.

Pues, porque una, que yo no iba a poder yo lavar, tenía muchos chamacos, y tenía mucho trabajo yo para estarla lidiando, lavarla. Mejor la quemaba porque era un deshecho muy apestoso el que tenía ella del cáncer. Y como no estaba atendida por doctores, entonces yo empecé a vender todo lo que . . ., muebles de ella. Empecé a vender para comprarle la inyección pa' que aguantara el dolor. Después que ya no tenía nada que vender, me decía yo, me gritaba y me decía, "Vete a robar. Roba, y tráeme la medicina, no aguanto." Y pues batallando, batallando. Y ya después, pues ya les pedía dinero con las que trabaja yo. Les decía luego les pago. Y sí me daban dinero. Y venía y le compraba la medicina, pero tenía que traerle doctor porque solamente el doctor podía ponerle la inyección profunda para aguantar el dolor. Y así batallé con ella dos años.

[My sister who lived in Agua Prieta] developed cancer. And I took her to live at my house, and she was so ill that I had to take her to Hermosillo because they referred me over there, I believe—because there were, there were not any good doctors at that time in Agua Prieta. We went with Manuel, and I went, and I took all of her children, and all of mine, and we went to live in Hermosillo with our cousins, while she was hospitalized. When they told me that she had no hope for recovery, that the cancer was very advanced, then I said, well, it would be better if I went back to my home in Agua Prieta. And we didn't have enough money to return. Manuel worked over there, but in order to support so many kids, well, it wasn't enough. So what I did was that we came on the bus as far as we could, up to Cananea, is where our money got us. . . . I mailed a letter to Douglas, to the houses where I worked, and I said, "My sister will be arriving tomorrow, please take some food if you are able to." And indeed, the women that I worked with responded very well. . . . "Write it down," [I said], "and when I go, I will go work for the food that you gave them." They never charged me, and they even gave them money.

Still, she was quite ill for two years. I had to quit my job because she needed . . . we didn't have very much money to have her in the hospital, and she needed attention. I had to change her clothes because she had cancer. When one has cancer, there's a lot of tissue and body waste from the cancer that is eating you inside, and one has to be changing bedclothes and clothes often. I even had to go to the nuns in Douglas to ask for sheets and pillowcases, whatever they could spare, so that I could use them as diapers for her because I couldn't wash them; I had to burn them. Every morning we burned all the clothes that we took off her.

For one thing, it was impossible for me to be washing, with the ten kids, and a lot of work to be taking care of her and washing also. It was better for me to burn the garments because it was a body waste that smelled very bad. And she was not being attended to by any doctors. I started selling all that she had . . . furniture, whatever. I started to sell everything to buy her injections so that she could stand the pain. Later when I had nothing more to sell, she would scream and plead with me, "Go and steal if you have to, but bring me the medicine. I can't stand the pain." And I was just struggling and struggling. So then, I would just ask for money from the people that I had worked with. I would tell them I would pay them later, and they would give me money. So I would buy her the medicine, but I would also have to bring a doctor because only a doctor could give her the deep muscular injection to calm the pain. And that's how I struggled with her for two years.

Señora Ortiz continues to struggle now in her life, albeit in different circumstances and with the wisdom garnered from her years behind her. As a much sought after seamstress, she often works eighteen-hour days on her sewing—churning out, at times, five dresses a day. She tells me that she finds sleep a waste of time and that she can get by on three or four hours a night. Her sewing room, a converted carport, houses dignified wedding dresses, glitzy evening gowns, and frilly little girl frocks. As her clients come to the door, she retrieves items from among the piles of cloth, patterns, and half-finished designs. She owes her success in part to the low rates she charges. She tells me that she is often told that she should charge more for her work, but she refuses, saying that if she herself wouldn't pay a particular price, why should she expect others to pay? Her humble yet stalwart nature is embodied in her confidence to face any adversity and overcome any obstacle:

Doy gracias por lo que no tengo, y si tengo, gracias por la comida que tengo. . . . Si tengo pa' ahora bien y si no tengo también. Yo le digo a Manuel que si viene una hambre muy grande, él se muere, y yo no, yo no me muero, de hambre no. . . . porque voy entre la basura, allá hay muchos quelites, muchas ramitas que antes las corto y las pongo a cocer, y me las como. Ya lo hice por mucho tiempo. Y puedo hacerlo ahora también. Y las puedo cortar y las lavo y las coso con agua y sin sal, y al final me las como. Y no me muero de hambre. No pienso en la comida, en lo que tengo que comer y todo eso. No. Pa' mi la comida, para comer yo, yo hago comida pa' todos pero no hago comida para mi. Porque yo, yo la comida para mi, la comida y la cama son segundo y tercer tiempo. . . Que una recámara bonita . . . la cama que sea, allí me acuesto. ¿Por qué yo me voy a estar matando por una recámara bonita? . . . Yo con la camita que tengo con eso me basta y me sobra, para que más, pero yo no me ando matando para dormir a gusto, donde quiera duermo ahí, en el piso. Dormí muchos años en el suelo, en el monte, no puedo vivir diferente.

Por eso a mi no me gusta que los anillos, aretes, collares, relojes, no me, no porque no pueda hacerlo o pueda comprar, pero no estoy impuesta a esas cosas. O un vestido elegante, . . . me siento otra, no soy yo. Porque así viví, y no, no creo que yo pueda cambiar. . . . Pero, mi cuñada la que vive en Agua Prieta me dice, "Tú te fuistes a Estados Unidos, y vienes, vienes lo mismo." Pues yo no le hallo ninguna diferencia a Estados Unidos y México. Nomás que aquí no me muero de hambre, y aquí si viviera en Agua Prieta sí.

If I have food now, fine, and if I don't have it, fine also. . . . And I tell my husband that if one day there is a famine, he will die, and I won't die of hunger because I will go to the garbage, and there's a lot of wild spinach, a lot of herbs, a lot of edible weeds that I can cut and cook, and I will eat them. I did it before, and I can do it again. I can cut them, and I can wash them and cook them in water, without salt, and I will eat them. And I will not starve. I don't think about food or about what I have to eat and all of that . . . because, for me, food and a place to sleep, they are in second and third place. A beautiful bedroom is not for me, and I don't want it. I will sleep on whatever bed there is, and I'm not going to kill myself in order to sleep comfortably. I'll sleep anywhere, there, on the floor. I slept many years on the ground, on the mountain; I can't live too much different from that.

That's why I don't like rings and earrings and necklaces and watches, not because I can't buy them. I'm just not used to those things or an elegant dress . . . I feel like it's not me. That's who I am, and I don't think I can change. . . . But my sister-in-law who lives in Agua Prieta tells me, "You went to the United States, and you come back the same." I don't see any difference between the United States and Mexico. Only that here I don't starve, and in Agua Prieta I might.

The Fracturing of Gender Ideologies

In the last sentence of the previous extract, Señora Ortiz consciously foregrounds her border identity, describing how her life isn't much different on this side of the border, except that the specter of hunger does not hang over her.

Even though we can read abstractly about issues such as accommodation and resistance, domination and subordination, the affirmation of identities, and the realignment of practices that are transformed with deterritorialization, the narratives of these women stun us into reading across domains to discover how institutional fault lines intersect with the lived experiences of women. The dynamic process and struggle of these women's lives resonate with the reconfiguration of emergent identities and practices as we witness such impacts on the poor, the oppressed, and the displaced. As these women told their stories of raising their children and their own life stories, however, it was impossible to gloss over the gendered nature of their experiences. The stories of both of these women touched raw nerves in me, exposing a side of life that researchers often keep obscured and silenced. Because of the very personal nature of the narratives, I struggled and still struggle with how I can respectfully tell their story. To tell their story is to name their silenced lives, as McLaughlin and Tierney (1993) explain, and to make explicit the multiple identities that they, as mothers, as socializers of children, and as key personages in the lives of school-age children, have actively fashioned for themselves in the face of overwhelming adversity and suffering. I came away from interviews with these women emotionally drained by the powerful impact of going beyond superficial interactions. But if I had been so forcefully affected, I knew that others could also be transformed in fundamental ways. I also came away with a profound concern that their stories not reductionistically reaffirm patronizing stereotypes of the role of women in Mexican society. Their stories elude any unidimensional retelling, and the multiple levels of interpenetration of gender, class, and race in them help us redefine strategies of representation where, despite shared histories of deprivation, the exchange of meanings may not be unilineal (cf. Bhabha 1994). In the two narratives, the preimmigration experiences of these women were embedded within a gendered ideology that they hope to have left behind. The relocation across a literal border, in both cases, from Sonora to Arizona, reconfigured their own resistance to and accommodation within particular constellations of their roles as women. However, their discourses go beyond the resistance/accommodation dyad, inscribing their experiences within a complex dynamic of the patriarchal nature of one form of gendered ideology and within their own appropriation and construction of identities that both resisted and accommodated. The apparent naturalness and naturalizing of the gendered power dimensions that these women narrate permeate other cultural domains, articulating with other inequalities and leading us to examine the permeability of "boundaries between gender and other categories of difference" (Yanagisako and Delany 1995:10). As Sylvia Yanagisako and Carol Delany note, the naturalizing of gender inequality, for example, is commonly based on observing "similarities" in the relations between women and men in different societies. These "similarities" are adduced as evidence of a common "human condition" that can lead to patronizing representations of the female "other" (ibid.:16). For this reason, I have tried to read across domains, taking the broad discursive construct *una mujer acomedida* as a discourse emerging from a patriarchal stricture that Señora Hernández and Señora Ortiz retransformed into a resource strategy that allowed them to survive a harsh economic reality.

Both of these women embody the complex centrifugal and centripetal forces that are part of a multiplex reading of structure and agency. On the one hand, by adopting a discourse of being accommodating women, serviceable women, hard-working women, they have been able to transform their economic circumstances in the transnational movement where this "work ethic" is positively evaluated. Both Señora Hernández and Señora Ortiz have enjoyed modest success in their own home-based work, Señora Hernández cleaning houses and Señora Ortiz working as a seamstress. On the other hand, these women incorporated a process of adaptation into their existence—or, in other words, making lemonade when life gave them lemons—which has helped them to survive circumstances that might make others wither. Both are incredibly resourceful in transforming whatever product is at hand, making it do, embellishing it, and stretching it to its ultimate use. However, because women who are poor and uneducated are not often seen as resources within the household, schools do not often validate their life experiences or draw on their multiple funds of knowledge. These women's life histories reveal the rich repositories of knowledge that belie any superficial reading of their "at risk" factors. Poverty, lack of English skills, lack of education have not prevented them from transforming their circumstances. Señora Ortiz's sewing skills offer abundant evidence of a self-constructed knowledge that implicates mathematical processes she has internalized. Adapting her skills to whatever is at hand, she is able to construct elaborate geometric designs into her sewing of folklórico dresses, to create sophisticated tailoring of women's clothes, and to fashion elaborate dresses for quinceañeras and weddings. In her narrative, she talks of sewing with thread that she had unraveled from flour sacks, of caring for her one needle as if it were made of gold because it was her only one, and of taking apart clothes to find out how they were sewn. Señora Hernández is sought after for her meticulousness in cleaning and is very often the sole breadwinner of the family because her husband works at odd jobs. Her children, however, are dedicated students, involved in mariachi and music, and the strength of her knowledge bases have had an impact on their educational success.

What can we learn about language from these stories? First of all, for me, the emotional pull of these stories had to do with the fact that they were told in Spanish. Simply the use of another symbolic system to tell a story affected how I interpreted and visualized the images. A story told in one language conveys a very different picture when it is translated. We cannot simply map one set of words over another. When I read the translations, although the narratives continue to be powerful, I don't experience the women's lives in the same way. Yet when I write about them, it must be in English because that is the language in which my academic discourse resides. In some way, different languages do create different worlds. In these narratives, I experience very personally the notion that Spanish and English are embedded in dimensions that are not an overlay of each other. Like the transcripts of household discourse reveal, I, too, see English as the medium of functional communication, of professional development, and of economic mobility. But with Spanish, the roots of feeling, of emotion, and of identity pull me back and tie me to a social memory, never having lived these women's lives or suffered their adversity. Language is funny that way.

CHAPTER 7

Household Language Use

THE PUSH AND THE PULL

I overheard my twelve-year-old daughter, Briana, talking to one of her friends on the telephone one day, and the concluding part of her conversation went something like this:

Uh huh, yeah.
OK, well.
Yeah, OK, well.
Bye.

I knew from her conversations with her friends, most of whom are second-generation Hispanics and English dominant, that they often used expressions such as "Come on, well," or "Give it to me, well." Briana's use of "OK, well" was not uncommon to her speech, but it did make me think of when I first noticed that it was not quite standard English. When I switched schools in eighth grade from a school that was 95 percent Hispanic to a school that was 95 percent Anglo, I found that even though I spoke English fluently, there were subtle differences, and this was one of them: no one at my new school said, "OK, well." Later, when I became interested in language forms, I thought that this speech habit was an example of what is sometimes referred to as a calque—that is, a literal translation into another language of an idiom or common speech form. In Spanish, it is common to use the adverb *"pues"* as a tag after particular expressions such as *"Bueno, pues"* or commands such as *"Dámelo pues"* (give it to me) or *"Vente pues"* (come on). I had translated these expressions literally with *well* substituting for *pues:* hence, "Bueno, pues" became "OK, well."

The interesting thing is, though, that I had never heard Briana or her friends ever say "Bueno, pues." They obviously were not translating the expression. They were simply using a language form that was common in the school they attended, and that adults in their surroundings also used. The fact that an English speaker from another part of the country might find this particular construction somewhat strange did not occur to them: it was English as they heard and used it. Norma Mendoza-Denton, in reviewing the sociolinguistics of Latinos in the United States, reports on phonological variants in Chicano English that are not the result of phonemic filtering from a Spanish substrate (1999:379). In many ways, the English that children speak in Tucson is marked not by code-switching, but by particular phonological markers of Chicano English (cf. Giles 1979).

Centripetal and Centrifugal Forces in Language Use

How can we think about children's use of language along and across borders? Norma Mendoza-Denton affirms that the voices of Latinos in much current work in sociolinguistics

> variously interrogate racism, crossing/passing, and issues of borders, bringing into focus a sociolinguistics not so much defined by homogenous speech communities, but one constituted through contact across boundaries, borders, and isoglosses. A linguistics of contact (Pratt 1987) allows us to glimpse not only along and across the borders of groups that traditionally have been imagined as "different" from each other (sometimes to their surprise) but also to investigate borders that are not national or linguistic, but material and embodied. It is in the close analysis of contact that we will find the articulation of different levels of semiotic systems, where subtle linguistic cues work in tandem with material culture to index history and ideology. (1999:388)

In this chapter, I explore the "different levels of semiotic systems" within households. In considering the evolution of language systems, Bakhtin emphasizes that language serves as a focal point for the battle between forces that propel cohesion and those that thrust disunity into the system:

Every concrete utterance of a speaking subject serves as a point where centrifugal as well as centripetal forces are brought to bear. The processes of centralization and decentralization, of unification and disunification, intersect in the utterance; the utterance not only answers the requirements of its own language as an individualized embodiment of a speech act, but it answers the requirements of heteroglossia as well. . . . Every utterance participates in the "unitary language" (in its centripetal forces and tendencies) and at the same time partakes of social and historical heteroglossia (the centrifugal and stratifying forces). (1981:272)

So what does that mean? I would like to imagine these swirling oppositional propulsions that Bakhtin terms "centripetal" and "centrifugal" within the metaphorical interactional double helix, the dialogical staircase that I have described. Centripetal pressures for unification and centrifugal processes of diversity are captured by a multidimensional metaphor that incorporates forces for change as well as forces for maintenance. We can think about these swirling processes in several ways. For example, the effort to preserve unifying forces of language and ideology are present on several levels. Proponents of "unitary language" measures underscore the consolidating effects of linguistic homogeneity. English unequivocally links the household to the larger national sphere and marketplace outside of its doors. In a piece for the *Los Angeles Times,* Ron Unz, the Silicon Valley high-technology entrepreneur and chairman of the English for the Children campaign in California, argued, "Although English is not and never has been America's official national language, over the past twenty years it has rapidly become the entire world's unofficial international language, utterly dominating the spheres of science, technology and international business. Fluency in Spanish may be a significant advantage, but lack of literacy in English represents a crippling, almost fatal disadvantage in our global economy" (Unz 1997:M6).

Lack of access to English, as the legitimated medium of communication, effectively precludes assimilation into sanctioned interaction. Interestingly, in the transcription of language use in many of the homes I studied, I found that English does fulfill this referential and instrumental role. English is used as the medium of interaction with the wider social sphere, as well as for much of the ordinary daily interaction at dinner table conversations and homework sessions. Within each house-hold, however, there exists varying degrees of acceptance of this notion of unification. Forces that press toward mainstream patterns and to-ward economic upward mobility coalesce in a propulsion of transforma-tions of Mexican identity that align with these orientations. On the other hand, these assimilative forces are countered with a resistance against the symbolic domination of the superordinate group. These centrifugal forces impulse a consciousness of identity and self-affirmation.

These processes are in evidence upon a careful analysis of transcrip-tions of household discourse. The contradictions of opposing forces set the stage for multiple language and literacy ideologies.

HOUSEHOLD DISCOURSE

I would like to present language data from two households to illustrate this process. The first case involves the Aguilar children. Their involve-ment in dense familial networks, of Spanish kinship terminology for nanas, tatas (grandfathers), tíos, and tías, a predilection for tostadas and chorizo, and ritualized participation in piñatas and baptisms are evident from tapes of dinnertime conversations. The place names that family members mention (Pío Décimo, Menlo Park) are situated in heavily Mexican-origin areas of the city, locating most of the children's inter-actions within this particular context. Yet the bulk of their communica-tion is in English. The transmittal of mores—including the mother admonishing the children to engage in sibling solidarity and family unity, as well as an extended segment on spiritual values—is in English. A similar process appears in the second transcript, documenting the Gómez family interactions. Although Spanish is the mother's first lan-guage, she addresses her children in English the majority of the time. Again, the processes of referring to food and family in Spanish, but making other communications in English are evidenced. We also get a glimpse of one form of language socialization identified in a study by Ann Eisenberg (1986) on Mexican immigrant families: teasing. In both households, the father engages in a marked degree of teasing, verbal play, and humorous remarks. In the Gómez household, the teasing shifts to Spanish, and the child attempts to tease the father back with an ungrammatical Spanish phrase. Eisenberg claims that teasing is a method of interacting without dependence on the functional exchange of information. It essentially reenforces the bonds between interlocutors and includes statements about the density of the relationships involved. These two case studies are illustrative for two reasons. First of all, I think they strip away the veneer of the "ethnic other." An unspoken undercurrent in dominant discourses assumes that within these households somehow things are done and talked about in a radically covert, nonmainstream way. These two tapes, in fact, however, reflect patterns that have been found in research on dinnertime conversations in two-parent, English-speaking, European American, financially comfortable families (Ochs and Taylor 1992). Similar research reports on the collaborative narrative activity as a "linguistic medium for constituting the family as well as different identities within a family" (Ochs and Taylor 1992:447; see also Ochs et al. 1992). The topics, as well as the joint productive narration of events, are highly analogous.

The second issue demonstrated in these tapes is the importance of the symbolic manipulation of emblems of identity. As is apparent, the living heteroglossia of differential linguistic domains is an active force in these naturally occurring conversations. In a methodological note, these lengthy transcriptions are not given in their complete form. (For extended transcriptions, see González 1992.) They are also not marked with linguistic transcription conventions because my intent is not a fine-grained linguistic analysis. Only pauses and unintelligible comments are noted.

BREAKFAST TABLE CONVERSATION. Father (FA), Mother (MO), seven-year-old twins, Lisa (LI) and Louie (L), and nine-year-old Eric (E).

53.   L: I love your breakfast, Mama.

54.   LI: I love the chorizo.

55.   L: I love the chorizo, too.

56.   E: I love the potatoes.

57.   FA: Tortillas?

58.   E: I'll do one just for them, Dad.

59.   MO: Lisa said we haven't had tostadas in a long time.

60.   E: Tostadas.

61.   MO: We haven't had tostadas in a long time.

62. L: I said that before . . . So why don't we have them?

63. FA: Well, tell her to starve! She should know how to cook by now!

64. LI: Nuh-uh. I only know how to cook chocolate chip cookies. Huh, Mama?

65. E: Who?

66. LI: I learned at Tía Yolanda's.

67. FA: You better get with it. You better start learning 'cause you're gonna be getting married pretty soon.

68. LI: Nuh-uh. I won't get married. I'll just cook. I won't get married.

69. L: If you . . . Just start cooking!

70. MO: She doesn't want to get married. She doesn't want to have problems and you guys.

71. *[Edited out]*

[Pause]

72. L: Do old mans have tatas? Do . . . ummm, like if they're old, like if I had . . . if I was old, and if I was old, like an old tata.

73. MO: Like Tata?

74. L: Do I still have to call her Nana?

75. LI: Yeah!

76. FA: If you're old, your Tata and Nana won't be alive.

77. MO: They die after they get a certain age.

78. L: They die?

79. FA: They don't die. They go to heaven.

80. MO: Heaven.

81. E: They might have a heart attack.

82. L: How do they get to go to heaven?

83. MO: Their body gets old.

84. L: And it feels like they might die?

85. MO: . . . takes them up there to heaven.

86. E: 'Cause He wants them to die?

87. L: He gets His hand out.

88. LI: Well, that's mean.

89. MO: Huh?

90. LI: That's mean that He wants them to die.

91. L: He doesn't want them to die.

92. MO: He takes them up to heaven to take care of them.

93. L: Why?

94. MO: He loves them right? It's a high experience.

95. LI: And Godses houses are nice.

96. E: Oh! Fireworks!

97. LI: I wanna go up there again.

98. MO: Tata Memo died of a heart attack, and God didn't want him to stay in this world suffering from his heart, getting sick all the time and having heart attacks, so God took him up to heaven with Him. And he can rest up in heaven with Him. Up in heaven there is a better world than here.

[All three children talk at once.]

99. FA: We're gonna get old, and then you guys are gonna have to push us around in a wheelchair.

[Children laugh]

100. FA: And you're going to have to make breakfast for us and . . .

101. LI: Nuh-uh. Doctors are.

102. MO: Louie, Lisa, and Eric are going to be . . .

103. E: But you guys are going to be living in that other house. Or are you gonna be living here?

104. MO: This is our home. You guys move out.

105. LI: No. We're going to stay in this house! I love this house!

106. FA: No way. You've only got two more years, Lisa.

107. LI: You guys move out while we stay here. How about this guys?

108. L: No! I wanna stay with Mama and Daddy. They give me my heart so happy.

109. E: Are you chicken? Chicken! Chicken! Cluck, cluck.

110.   FA: Yep, you'd become a little angel.

111.   L: You guyses have become a little angel.

112.   FA: You become a little angel when you go up to heaven.

113.   L: I know!

114.   FA: I can't picture Eric being a little angel.

115.   E: What? What?

116.   MO: There's two ways you can go. Up in heaven with God or down to h-e-l-l with the devil.

117.   E: I know. I'm going up. I'm going up.

118.   LI: I'm going up. I'm going up!

119.   MO: You've got to be nice . . . help Mom and Dad.

120.   E: I'm going down. . . . I'm kidding!

121.   MO: That's right. That's right. The way that you have been behaving lately, you're going down.

122.   E: I'm going up.

123.   MO: You'll get all burned up.

124.   LI: I'm going down.

125.   L: Nuh-uh.

126.   MO: It's all fire.

127.   FA: It's all fire down there.

128.   L: Does he die?

129.   E: All people stay there.

130.   MO: The good people go up to heaven, and God's place is beautiful, all the animals and all the fruit.

131.   LI: When we go up, and there is water?

132.   MO: All the dads, our brothers and sisters, and everybody loves one another. It's a beautiful world. They don't have cars, they don't have nothing. It's just beautiful.

133.   E: You just fly.

134.   LI: Do they have anything like, uhh . . .

135A.   FA: My brother died.

135B.   L: Tata Memo died of a heart attack.

136.   E: Whose brother, Dad?

137.   LI: *La Bamba* was a true story, huh, Mama?

138. E: Lisa, Lisa.

139. FA: You know how you have a Tío Beto, a Tío Chuy?

140. LI: Uh-huh.

141. FA: Well, you used to have a Tío Louie, and Tío Louie got sick and he died, and he's up in heaven, but when I die, I'm going to see my brother again.

142. LI: And when I die, I'm gonna see my Daddy and my Mama.

143. FA: Oh, come on, Lisa.

144. LI: I'm going to see my Tata Memo.

145. FA: Give me a break, Lisa.

146. LI: I'm going to see you when you're in heaven and I'm in heaven, *[unintelligible]* and Nana Durán, Nana Durán...

147. MO: Nana Durán is still alive.

148. LI: I know, but how come . . .

149. FA: You're going to see *all* your tatas.

150. MO: Yeah, you're going to see your tatas.

151. FA: Tata Memo, Tata Luis, and Tata Frank, all together.

152. MO: *[Laughs. This is an "inside" joke, referring to the fact that the grandmother has married several times.]*

153. E: Daddy, I want to still be a family.

154. MO: Nana is training for her tatas. *[Laughs]*

155. LI: I want to still be a family.

156. MO: Yeah.

157. FA: Do you think they'll fight up there?

158. MO: *[Laughs]*

159. E: We're not going to fight.

160. MO: For another, you never dreamed you guys would have so many tatas, huh?

161. E: God is nice to give her a lot of tatas, huh?

If we think of each strand of the double helix, each interactional node—offering endless options for both caregivers and children, donors and recipients—interacts in a dynamic process. One example is evident in lines 149–61, in which the father and mother are making ironic remarks (actually to each other) concerning the number of tatas the children have because of their grandmother's multiple marriages. The children pick up on this irony and make the seemingly innocent observation, following the spiritual turn of the conversation, that it was God who had given her all of her husbands. In another example of the dialogical emergence of household ideologies, the parents, in response to a topic shift by children, take the opportunity to transmit their views on death, God, the afterlife, the children's responsibilities to them in old age, and the eternal consequences of misbehavior (lines 72–149). Also of significance is the interjection (line 137) of the association of the movie *La Bamba* with discourse concerning death. This movie, which at the time was one of few films with a positive image of a Latino hero, was a favorite among the children that I interviewed, being supplanted in more recent years by the movie about Selena, and seemed to satisfy a need for video and media images of the familiar and accustomed.

In the following segment, we can observe the give and take between parents and children, each participant interweaving and modifying interpretations and stances.

162. LI: At school, I'm nice, Mama, but the kids are being mean to me.

163. MO: That's OK. That's OK. God's watching them, and God will take care of them.

164. LI: And God will put them . . .

165. L: There's this girl, and she pinches me, and she pinches me.

166. MO: Well, you know what? You turn around, and you pinch them back.

167. E: No, you can't, Mom.

168. MO: You pinch her back. You tell her, "Leave me alone."

169. FA: No, you tell the teacher.

170. E: You have to tell the teacher.

In this segment, the mother initially takes the stance that the child who is bullying her daughter will meet with immanent justice and that "God will take care of [her]." Her children's repeated recounting of the bullying prompts her to modify her position, and she then encourages them to make a stand and "pinch them back." The father then interjects a more formalistic and institutionalized response: tell the teacher. Thus, within one speech segment, strategies of nonintervention, self-determination, and institutionalized response are displayed as behavioral options, a co-narration of a household ideology concerning justice and retribution. The following segment illustrates an example of storytelling as a "theory-building activity" as the Aguilars jointly "construct, deconstruct, and reconstruct theories of everyday events" (Ochs et al. 1992:37).

THE BENT GLASSES STORY.

172.	MO:	Perfect.
173.	LI:	It's all scratched.
174.	MO:	What did you do with it, Lisa? You don't sleep with your glasses.
175.	LI:	I don't sleep with them!
176.	MO:	I'm gonna have to take them in then. You know what? You're gonna have to do without your glasses tomorrow in school.
177.	LI:	I'll go without.
178.	MO:	There's gum and everything. Scoot this back.
179.	E:	If I would have glasses, I wouldn't take care of them, I wouldn't take care of them like that.
180.	FA:	We're not gonna buy her another pair if she's not gonna take care of them.
181.	MO:	*Mira,* Eddie. I can't do it here, I'm gonna have to take it in.
182.	FA:	How are they gonna straighten those out?
183.	LI:	I've got . . .
184.	MO:	They put them in heat and then . . .
185.	LI:	All right. If I gotta tell you, I gotta tell.
186.	MO:	You've got gum on that. Did you sleep with gum in your mouth? You don't sleep with glasses. When you're laying down, when you're like this, . . . this is how she did it. She was watching the TV.
187.	FA:	You could step on them.

188. MO: You know, she was watching the TV, and she was laying down. She moved them over to one side. I can't see . . . see how it touches more on this side? I'm gonna have to take them in.

189. LI: I think I know.

190. MO: You're gonna have to do without your glasses today.

191. LI: *[Sigh]* Just gotta tell.

192. MO: Tomorrow morning I'm gonna take them in.

193. L: That girl hit me with the ball.

194. LI: I just gotta tell, Mom.

195. MO: That's it. It must have hit it right there. The ball there that's it.

196. E: No, it didn't hit her like that, Mom. It, he threw it; he was trying to hit me, he was trying to get me out, and Lisa got in the way, and he hit her, and he hit this thing, this thing, and she was all crying.

197. LI: And it never touched here.

198. MO: Yeah, it hit you. It could have gone in her eye, and she could have been messed up for life. It's dangerous.

199. E: That's why I said not to play with her again.

200. MO: And you too, Eric, the minute she comes here you say, yeah, and you go out and play. Mark is too big for you guys. Mark will get you guys in a lot of trouble. He can go play with kids his own age. You too.

201. L: I remember when Eric used to play with . . .

202. MO: Sandy is fine for you to play with, but Mark is too big. Mark should find his own friends.

203. L: Yeah, but when he comes to the house, he just wants us to play with him.

204. E: And when he wants his other friends to play . . . Mom, Mom.

205. MO: Which one?

206. LI: And this one Manny, he comes to play with him. Why don't you play with him? Why doesn't he play with Manny?

[Pause]

207. MO: Pass the bread.

208. FA: It looks like it's starting to get mold on it.

209. E: Let me see.

210. FA: I can't really taste.

211. E: Mold, when there's mold, it's old.

212. FA: Is it mold, or is it just . . . huh?

213. E: Uh-huh. Yeah. Mold.

214. MO: I ate a few.

215. FA: I ate a couple, I shhhhh . . . gawwww.

216. L: How many did you eat?

217. MO: I'm gonna take this back.

218. L: Get some other ones.

219. E: I thought you couldn't even have strange food.

220. MO: I'm taking these back and get another box.

221. FA: Where were they?

222. MO: *[Name of grocery store]*

223. L: Get them at [name of a grocery store].

224. LI: [Name of second grocery store]? Or you can change ketchup if it doesn't come out.

225. E: Shut up. Maybe you've got the wrong one.

226. FA: I still don't have my sense of taste, and I can't tell.

227. E: You don't have your sense of breath!

228. MO: *[Laughs]*

229. E: What's so funny? All I said is that.

230. FA: You don't have no sense at all.

This extended segment on the bent glasses (lines 173–99) is another illustrative example of theory building. The mother is upset by the apparent lack of care that Lisa has demonstrated for her glasses and engages in a series of exploratory suspicions as to how the damage was done. All three children engage in a mutually constructed explanation absolving Lisa of blame (lines 193–99). The mother extends this rationalization, however, as a justification for not playing with older children and conveys her desire that only age mates are appropriate as playmates.

As stated previously, each household is permeated with its own household ideology that it in some form communicates to children. In this tape, several factors pertaining to survival strategies are transmitted to the children. In the mundane occurrence of finding mold on the bread (lines 208–22), the parents communicate to the children the underlying assumption that there remains a certain amount of control in dealing with the vagaries of life. Rather than merely tossing the bread in the trash, the mother comments that she is going to return the bread to the supermarket. Chalking it up as a loss and disregarding the issue would have been the easier course, but the notion of making the effort to rectify the situation subtly influences the children. Lisa immediately decides that if the ketchup does not flow out, it can also be returned. Louie pipes in that a different vendor might have a better product. A nascent sense of autonomy and control over the environment seems to be taking root, which is further reinforced by the parents' constant references to doing homework and doing well in school before being interested in girls, and the parents' marked awareness of all of the children's friends and everyday happenings. The Aguilars stress that one can impact and control one's immediate environment by adherence to certain principles and tenets that will bring desired results. The children are enjoined to strive to be Thunderbird of the Month (a school honor similar to "student of the month"), and all of the transcripts from this household evidence constant interaction concerning schoolwork, the quality of homework, and detailed questioning on daily occurrences. The parents direct language toward the children (line 114) and carefully evaluate complaints about harassment by other children, revealing a comprehensive involvement in their offspring's routines.

The next segment illustrates the multiple social spaces within which children move, as the Aguilars easily shift from talk about piñatas at Pío Décimo (a bilingual preschool program) to heartfelt hopes for a University of Arizona basketball team victory.

258. E: Over at Pío Décimo, Daddy.

259. L: I wanna go.

260. LI: ——'s gonna graduate at Pío Décimo. She called his name.

261. MO: You go and you shake hands.

262. L: And then they clap. Yay! *[Claps]*

263.   E: Remember when I was graduating ... Did you see me up there in the stage?

264.   L: I saw you.

265.   MO: Did you go to the graduation?

266.   L: Uh-huh.

267.   LI: Nuh-uh.

268.   L: Uh-huh!

269.   LI: I didn't see you! Did you see me?

270.   E: But I know I went to the Halloween party.

271.   L: Halloween party?

272.   E: Yes. I hit the piñata.

273.   LI: Ooh, I hit the piñata.

274.   L: Did you break it?

275.   E: Did I break it?

276.   LI: Yes.

277.   FA: It popped back to Javier.

278.   E: Oh, yeah. You're right! I did break it.

279.   LI: You broke her nose real hard, I remember.

280.   L: I didn't even have a chance to break it. That was my piñata!

281.   LI: Oh, what a lie!

282.   MO: Louie, you're gonna need those shoes.

283.   E: I'm done.

284.   LI: I'm full. I can't eat more.

285.   MO: You didn't touch your potatoes.

286.   L: I love the potatoes.

287.   E: I'm done.

288.   FA: The Wildcats are gonna be on TV today.

289.   L: Whooo!

[Edited out]

297.   FA: They're playing in Oklahoma.

298.   E: Ooh! Who they playing against? Who are they playing against? Oklahoma?

299.   FA: Yep.

300. E: Ooh, oh! This is gonna be a tough one!

301. FA: It sure is.

302. L: I hope the Wildcats win.

303. MO: Yeah.

THE GÓMEZ FAMILY. Father (FA), mother (MO), two sons, Ricky (R) and David (D), nine and seven years old respectively at the time of taping are looking over a school project that David has brought home, a picture of a turkey filled in with different types of beans and grains.

1. MO: Ricky, David, come set the table. Come get the . . . David, show Dad your turkey.

2. D: OK. Dad, look at my turkey.

3. FA: *[Aside]* That's David's.

4. D: Dad, my turkey.

5. FA: *Awwright!* Let's see it.

6. D: It's made out of food and . . .

7. FA: *Heeeeyyy.* Looks good enough to eat, buddy.

8. D: Yeah.

9. FA: What do we have there . . . we've got . . . we've got beans . . . and macaroni . . . and we've got lentils.

10. D: What are lentils?

11. FA: These things right here. *Son lentejas.* Do you know what lentejas are?

12. D: No.

13. FA: They're called lentils. Those little . . . like little flying saucers that your Nana makes?

14. MO: It's a type of bean.

15. FA: It's a bean, but it's small. It's like this, too; these are lentils, too. Right here.

16. D: They're different ones.

17. FA: Uh-huh.

18. MO: Some of those could be peas. Aren't they peas?

19. FA: Yeah, these are peas cut in half?

20. D: What? These?

21. FA: Yeah, those are peas. This, oh, that's red rice, it looks like.

22. D: Colored.

23. FA: Yeah that's what it is. That turned out real nice, bud.

24. D: Yeah. Thank you.

25. R: Daddy, I got a hundred on my spelling test.

26. FA: You did what?

27. R: Got a hundred on my spelling test.

28. FA: Oh, yeah? What words did you have to spell?

29. R: I had a whole bunch. Twenty-five words.

30. FA: Twenty-five words? Wow!

31. R: But they were review words.

32. FA: Did you get a hundred the first time?

33. R: *Mmmhhhmmmm.*

34. FA: So what do you do now . . . just kick back and relax?

35. R: *[Laughs]* Yeah, tomorrow.

36. FA: Hey, have you ever seen a fifty-five pound turkey? *[Laughter]*

37. R: —— already told me that.

38. FA: What did he say?

39. R: He said, "Have you ever seen a fifty-five pound turkey?" And I said, "Yes," and he says, "Look in a mirror?" *[Father laughs.]*

40. MO: But that's more like a seventy-pound turkey.

41. R: Five.

42. MO: Seventy-five pound turkey? Wow, that's a big one. *[Some silence]* Do you have practice tomorrow, Ricky?

43. FA: No practice.

44. R: No practice.

45. MO: *[To FA]* How do you know?

46. FA: He told me.

47. R: 'Cause Rodney called and said that there was no practice tomorrow and no practice Friday.

48. MO: And you don't have a game Saturday, right?

49. R: Right.

50. MO: When's your next game?

51. R: December seventh.

[Unintelligible conversation between Mother and Father]

52. FA: Put it on the side, buddy.

53. D: Naaaah.

54. FA: You don't want to eat napkin and fork. You put the fork
and the napkin on the side. Like that it looks like you're
going to eat . . . a fork and a napkin for dinner.

[Laughter by children]

55. D: I want a fork for my rice.

56. MO: You have a fork.

57. FA: Well, what is that fork you have in your hand? *[Pause]*
You guys need to have your nails cut. Hey, have you ever
seen a thirty-pound turkey?

58. R: Yeah . . . Dad, he's only twenty . . .

59. FA: Oh, twenty, or whatever . . . Este turkey flaco, acá. [This
thin turkey here.]

60. D: Tú, yo no. [You, not me.]

61. FA: Eres un turkey flaco. [You're a skinny turkey.]

62. D: Tú turkey flaco *[unintelligible material]* chiquito. [You
skinny turkey, a small one.]

63. FA: Eh?

64. FA: ¿Sabes qué es *flaco?* [Do you know what *flaco* means?]

65. R: Weak?

66. FA: No. Not weak.

67. R: Uh . . . skinny?

68. FA: Skinny. Thin.

69. MO: Thin.

70. FA: Not skinny but thin.

71. MO: Thin is . . . skinny doesn't sound too good. *Delgado* is
skinny.

72. FA: Delgado, *[pause]* I guess. Did you guys wash your hands?

[Pause]

73. R: No.

74. D: I'm clean.

75. FA: Huh? *[Loudly]*

76. D: I'm clean.

77. FA: Since when?

78. D: Since today.

79. FA: Go wash them. You haven't washed them all day. Probably since last week sometime. When was the last time you had a bath?

80. D: Yesterday.

81. FA: That's the last time you washed your hands.

[Mother and Father laugh]

82. MO: You're so mean.

[Silence]

83. R: Daddy, you have to serve us some punch.

84. FA: Punch? Who made this Kool-Aid?

85. D: Me.

86. R: David.

87. FA: How much sugar did you put in it?

88. D: A little.

89. FA: How much is that? *[Pause]* Did you measure with something, or did you just put it in?

90. R: He usually just sticks it in.

91. FA: Huh?

92. R: He usually just sticks it in.

93. FA: I'm talking to David.

94. D: I just sticked it in.

95. FA: You stuck it in? With what? A spoon? *[Pause]* It's too sweet, buddy.

96. D: I like it.

97. FA: Well, I know *you* like it, but it's still too sweet. *[Pause]*

98. R: Mom, could you make me a burro?

99. MO: ¿De eso?

100. R: Yeah.

101. MO: ¿De carne?

102. R: Yeah, carnita.

103. MO: Ricky! ¡Tiene mucho caldo y se te va a tirar! Así cóme-
            telo. [You have a lot of soup, and it's going to spill! Get
            busy and eat.]

In both of these households, we can see how the father's teasing of
the children lends a jocular air to mealtime conversations. This light-
hearted treatment of instructive conversations is evidenced in the father's explanation of what lentejas are, drawing on the experiential store
of the child. He refers to Nana's cooking of little flying saucers, a
colorful metaphor that piques the child's interest. Mr. Gómez did not
speak Spanish when he and Mrs. Gómez first married (according to
Mrs. Gómez), but he has taken an active interest in his children's bilingual abilities, quizzing them on the meanings of certain words. He
does, however, defer to his wife's judgment, as in the case of the seman-
tics of the word *flaco*. He adds an unconvinced "I guess" when his wife
differentiates *thin* from *skinny*.

Cleanliness and hygiene is a frequent topic of discourse. Both families
stress washing and mildly ridicule the malcreants who fail to perform
their hygienic duties adequately. Significantly, it is not only parents, but
siblings as well who dispense these norms. Research on the influence of
siblings in teaching one another points to the fact that children spend as
much time with siblings as with parents and that they learn new ways to
approach situations by watching one another. The Aguilar and Gómez
children are alert sentinels for maintaining their siblings' appropriate
behavior.

Both households are also keenly interested in sports, both for boys
and girls. All of the children in both households play on soccer or Little
League teams, and both families, as evidenced in the Aguilar tapes, are
loyal University of Arizona Wildcat fans.

I believe these transcripts illustrate the push-pull effect of centripetal
and centrifugal forces for and against unity and assimilation. Mores and
values, as noted, speak of middle America. One reader of the transcripts
noted that the pseudonyms *Ricky* and *David* are appropriately representative of the "Ozzie and Harriet" portraiture represented. Yet, under
this veneer, the children are guided toward an identification of their
Mexican-ness, not through overt proclamations, but by symbolic trans-

actions of the association between feelings and Spanish in family, food, and identity. Dinner table conversations, expunged of the diacritical emblems, differ very little from those reported in European American families. Quantitatively, the differences in topic and language patterns are quite small. Qualitatively, however, they take on a transcendent symbolic importance to valorize the social identities constitutive of self-hood. The exploitation of affective tools in the symbolic resistance to being engulfed by a dominant culture carves out personhood in incongruous circumstances. The interplay between emotion, language, ideology, and child developmental processes in these households demonstrates intricate dynamics that cannot be reduced to unilineal causative models.

THE TIES THAT BIND

Even though I was quite aware that Mexican-origin parents are intensely preoccupied with their children's success, the degree of earnest, sustained, and concentrated effort on raising children in these households is so marked that it is evident at every turn. The parents' involvement with their children is so acute that it requires an amplification of the term *child rearing*. Parents do not simply "rear" or "raise" their children. Children are an extension of life. There is no point at which your children cease to be your responsibility. One mother once remarked to me (in Spanish, translation is given): "I don't understand how the Americanos can turn out their children as soon as they reach eighteen. My son has a friend whose parents told him he was on his own now, and so he's living with us. My children will be my children always. Whenever they need something, they know that I'm here." Another mother, Mrs. Cisneros, echoed those sentiments when detailing her dealings with her over-eighteen sons:

El problema de los [hijos] grandes es que a veces se van y . . . como en un viernes . . . y yo me preocupo si no vienen o no me hablan. Pero, como ellos son mayor de edad, según ellos, si ellos quieren venir, vienen, y si no, no. Ya según ellos, como ellos dicen, uno no tiene que mandarlos ya. . . . . Y pues lo que yo hago a veces es dejarlos afuera . . . a dormir afuera. Porque, yo les digo, como yo trabajo, como yo trabajo el sábado, ellos salen el viernes, les digo que si no llegan a venir, allí se van a quedar afuera. O aprenden de

que tienen que venir . . . o se van a quedar afuera. . . . Ya no quieren
entender . . . Es que yo quiero saber como llegan. Si llegan cayén-
dose o si llegan derecho. . . . Yo me doy cuenta si han llegado
tomados. . . . Dan el olor a lo que toman . . . al licor. . . . A veces . . .
les digo que se vayan y ellos pueden poner sus propias reglas. Pero
es muy difícil, porque echarlos uno así nomás, y decir, bueno no me
hiciste caso . . . toma tus garritas y vete . . . es difícil para mi. Nomás
estarles diciendo, y estarles diciendo, y a ver hasta cuando re-
capaciten. . . . Es difícil agarrarlos y apucharlos a la calle. Porque es
lo que uno trata de evitar, de que no . . . pues si están hechos a
perder, que no se echen mas a perder. Y yo pienso que si uno los
echa a la calle, mucho mejor para ellos.

The problem with the older children is that sometimes they go out,
and, like on a Friday . . . and I worry if they don't come, or they
don't call. But, since they are of legal age, according to them, like
they say, one can't order them around. . . . And so now what I do
sometimes is to leave them outside . . . to sleep outside. Because I
tell them, since I work, since I work on Saturday, and they go out
on Friday, I tell them that if they don't come home [in time], that
they're going to stay outside. They either learn that they have to
come, . . . or they're going to stay outside. They don't want to
understand. . . . It's that I want to know how they come home . . . if
they come home falling down or straight. I am aware of how they
arrive: whether they've been drinking or not. They give off the
odor of what they have drunk . . . of liquor. Sometimes, I tell them
that they should go, and they can have their own rules. But it is
very difficult because just to throw them out just like that, and say,
"Well, you didn't listen to me . . . take your clothes and go," that
would be very difficult for me. [I can] just keep on telling them and
keep on telling them, and see when they will reflect on it. It's
difficult to take them and push them into the street because that is
what one tries to avoid . . . that they not . . . well, if they're taking
the wrong road, one doesn't want them to get even *worse*. And I
think that if one throws them out into the street, well, they would
like it even better.

This cementing of the parent-child bond throughout the life cycle is
one underlying proposition for socialization activities. Mexican-origin

parents usually do not make the assumption that there are only a few years provided in which to transmit all of the caregiver's repertoire of knowledge into the young learner's receptive field. Mrs. Cisneros made it quite clear that although she was having serious problems with her son, throwing him out on the street would not solve his problem. In the Aguilar tape number one (lines 104–6), the father jokes with Lisa that she has "only two more years" to live in the household, and the mother insists that "you guys move out," both ironic commentaries underscoring the implicit supposition that they will be "close," either geographically or affectively. It is this bond that gives rise to the clustering of households that has been documented in the literature (Vélez-Ibáñez 1996:148). Many of the families in my small sample had at least two other closely related households living on the same street or in the same neighborhood. Children ease into adulthood knowing that a full array of familial resources will always be available to them. In kinship terminology, the family becomes a corporation, in the anthropological sense, in that it never dies. It is a mechanism whereby information and support can be received and given throughout the life cycle. This lifetime guarantee of close family ties is implicit in exchange, ritual, and language behavior.

TELEVISION AND TELENOVELAS

One significant source of Spanish-language input in these households is television. Telenovelas are a pivotal element in the receptive language to which children in U.S.–Mexican households are exposed, and expressive language sometimes involves discussions of the storyline. Both immigrant and native-born families reported watching telenovelas, and homework activities were sometimes relegated to hours that did not interfere with the novelas. The telenovelas have had a resounding effect on children. Prior to the introduction of the Spanish International Network to Tucson in the early 1980s, programs in Spanish were few and far between. I remember the *Teatro Mexicano* on Sunday morning with Henry and Tony Villegas, a token nod by the local media, as the one time we would hear Spanish on television. The first telenovelas that aired in Tucson in the late 1960s, *Simplemente María* and *Natacha,* were broadcast at 11:00 P.M. on Friday and Saturday nights, and very early on Sunday morning. In spite of the inconvenient hour, they enjoyed immense popularity, prompting a local priest to comment on how attendance at early morning mass on Sunday morning had declined since the airing of the shows. The presence of an entire network (currently there are two, Univisión and Telemundo) whose programming was entirely in Spanish marked a qualitative shift in the quantity and quality of Spanish spoken in the area. Children are exposed to conversational patterns that reflect the standardized Spanish that networks air. This exposure is one of the most significant differences in the language socialization of both children and their parents. Additionally, a lifestyle unfamiliar to many native-born households in the borderlands is open to inspection. One native-born woman in her fifties, born and raised in Tucson, commented to me that her exposure to telenovelas unveiled a new perspective of Mexico and Mexicans to her. Her youthful experience of life across the border had consisted of trips to Nogales and northern Sonora, and one particularly harrowing and unfortunate trip to Guadalajara. Her memories were not positive. Seeing the novelas revealed a whole category of lifestyles that she confessed she had not seen represented in her borderlands experience. In *Hispanic Nation* (1996), Geoffrey Fox claims that for Hispanic audiences in the United States, "telenovelas offer not only catharsis and companionship but also, especially for recent immigrants, continuity with their home cultures. Not only are they in a familiar language; they refer to familiar dilemmas and types of relationships. The novelas also offer a readily comprehended narrative structure in which the wicked are ultimately punished, the virtuous rewarded, and the viewer can easily tell who is which; such a morally orderly universe can offer comfort to people in a confusing new land" (49).

Spanish-language talk shows, CNN news broadcasts, and information shows on these channels provide a range of spoken Spanish for children that often interrogates the dominant themes of English-language news. By accessing a realm of discourse not in English-language media, children are given multiple perspectives of current events. Fox sees that the noticieros (news)

> do not directly challenge these assumptions, but they do treat events from an angle so different that it tends to undermine them. In particular, the noticieros focus much more closely and sympathetically on the sufferings of the poor in Latin America. . . . Even more prominent attention is given to Hispanics in the United

States. Person-in-the-barrio interviews, stories on neighborhood programs and cultural events, and interviews with Hispanic politicians and community workers, professionals, and artists appear on almost every broadcast . . . Of course news is not the only way that television shapes the Hispanic-American collective consciousness. The variety programs, talk shows, and novelas all serve to reinforce certain values such as family loyalty, and to create the illusion of a common televised territory of all Spanish speakers. (1996:44–47)

For children and young people, Spanish-language programming is often the only source of news about topics that interest them. For instance, the spate of public interest on the chupacabras phenomenon was reported mainly on Spanish-language media, as was Howard Stern's "dissing" of Selena. Many who had never heard of Howard Stern were indignant over his remarks about the then recently deceased Selena, and the incident was publicized widely on Spanish talk shows. News shows are ever vigilant in the search for human rights abuses against any Latino group in the United States, and children are exposed to a significant amount of discourse concerning such topics as Proposition 187 in California or immigrant reform enactments.

HOMEWORK AND LANGUAGE

In addition to mealtime conversations, I was also able to collect recordings of homework sessions. In another clash of competing processes, the transcripts of homework sessions embody a contest between agency and structure in maternal-child discourse, as well as a contradictory stance between language and literacy ideologies. Interactions surface on the one hand as fostering an open and transformative approach to learning experiences and on the other as regimenting and restricting behavior and appropriate responses, pointing to the need for conceptualizing a space between structure and agency. This vacillation between authoritarian educational strictures and a more open constitutive process is one key to explain the variants in homework language use in the households. The constraints that parents use to delimit acceptable and appropriate knowledge and ways of learning were forged within an institutional setting within which they themselves were constrained. The symbolic domination of the institution reproduces, in this sense, not the defeat of subordinate classes, but the validation and legitimization of certain forms of knowledge, certain ways of reproducing knowledge. Language socialization in homework sessions—when the stakes imply success in the adult world and when adults reproduce what they view as dominant cultural capital—takes on a qualitatively different form. Mothers, fiercely attempting to ensure success for their children, often resort to the discursive practices sanctioned by the voice of the school and reproduce the forms, modes of thinking, style, and meaning legitimated through their own institutional experience. In order to illustrate the contrast between these two approaches, I present two excerpts. In one tape of the Escobedo family (lines 146–71), Marina (MO) personalizes the story that Anthony (A) has just read by relating the characters to his classmates. The children are drawn into the story by the likening of their own friends' characteristics to the storybook, and they are given wide latitude in responding to questions and preferences:

146. MO: OK, now, tell me about the story. What do you think the moral of this story is? Make pretend you're that hippopotamus and you're going to everybody. And how many people at school do you like the way they look? Huh?

147.　A: I don't know.

148. MO: Is there anybody at school that you like the way they look. Who?

149.　A: I don't know.

150. MO: No, tell me. This is a part of the story. Who do you like the way they look at school? One of your friends. Who?

151.　A: Fernando.

152. MO: You like the way Fernando looks?

153.　A: No.

154. MO: What do you like about Fernando?

155.　A: My friend.

In contrast, in lines 55–102, the boys' responses (with the addition of brother Sergio [S]) and actions are evaluated only in terms appropriate to the school. For example, even though Richard doesn't like a brown mouse, it must be colored brown because the directions insist on it. The

jack-o-lantern must be standardized as only such pumpkins are accepted as suitable:

55. MO: OK, wait a second Anthony, let me go on. OK, what does
it say? The first one says, "Oh my, it's getting late." And
it's getting late, so what do you do?

56. S: Draw a turkey, and it's getting late. Draw it?

57. MO: OK, well, I guess. Wouldn't that be it?

58. S: Yeah.

59. MO: Well, draw me a turkey and draw me it getting late.
Richard, that's the silliest jack-o-lantern I've ever seen.

60. R: I always draw something silly.

61. MO: You always draw something silly?

62. R: Yeah.

63. MO: How about, *ssshhhhh.* How about putting your name up
on the top, and I'll give you another one.

64. R: You mean like mine.

65. A: *[Anthony begins to read story again.]*

66. MO: What is this word here? I saw you skip over it. Glorious.

67. A: *[Anthony continues reading.]*

68. MO: Draw me a mouse on there, too.

69. S: I see a muscle man up there.

70. MO: I know, but you're gotta make a brown mouse down there
eating the cheese.

71. S: Copy that muscle man. *Lookit,* Mom!

72. MO: Wait, Anthony.

73. S: That's how you do it. That's the one he said, you gotta
draw a . . . a . . .

74. MO: OK, it says draw a picture, make a brown mouse. You
have to make a brown mouse down at the bottom. Use
your pencil first. Where's your pencil? Didn't Mama give
it to you?

75. S: You left it in the . . .

76. MO: Anthony has it.

77. A: *C'mon, Richard!*

78. MO: It's not yours, either. Yours doesn't have an eraser.

79. R: *Well,* I had this one in my . . . bag.

80. MO: No. Yeah, but where did you put the other one? Where's your other pencil?

81. R: I don't need the pencil.

82A. MO: Here it is.

82B. A: I don't need the pencil no more.

83. MO: OK, fine. Then go on and read.

84. S: The turkey says, "Oh my, it's getting late."

85. A: *[Anthony continues reading.]*

86. S: Ma, I said "Oh my, it's getting late." What's next?

87. MO: Draw a picture of it getting late.

88. S: Oh!

89. A: *[Anthony continues reading.]*

90. MO: Use crayons, Sergio.

91. S: I'm going to draw up there, and then I'll color it.

92. MO: OK.

93. S: I'm gonna, I'm gonna play it. OK, Ma, I'm done.

94. A: *[Anthony continues reading.]*

95. R: "The second one says . . . 'Thanksgiving is near.'"

96. MO: *Very good!* You read that. "The second one said, 'Thanksgiving is near.'" Where's the mouse, Richard? Oh, that's cute, but you didn't color it brown.

97. R: I didn't like it . . . color it brown.

98. MO: Well, I like a brown mouse. It says to draw a brown mouse.

99. R: I don't wanna.

100. MO: Where's the color brown? Yes, you do. There's a big old brown crayon there. Now tell me another story, huh?

101. A: *[Anthony reads.]*

102. MO: You better listen to this story while he's reading it cause I want you to tell me all about it when he's done.

In a second family, the Gamboas, the institutional template is almost painfully evident as the mother (MO) and seven-year-old Vanessa (VA) and nine-year-old Gabriel (GA) engage in dialogue. In lines 35–110, the mother's well-intentioned pedagogy to "think it out" turns a simple request for information into a drawn out litany that reproduces the "recitation script" often found in classrooms:

14. GA: Journals. . . . Mom.

15. MO: Huh?

16. GA: How do you spell "journals"?

17. MO: Huh?

18. GA: How do you spell "journals"?

19. MO: J-o-u-r-n-a-l-s.

20. GA: After "r," what?

21. MO: n-a-l-s.

22. GA: What's cooking?

23. MO: Nothing yet.

24. GA: *Uhhhhhhh. [Complaining]*

25. MO: *Well! I'm helping you here! You said to help you!*

[Pause]

26. VA: Pet . . . I . . . have . . . a . . . new . . .pet.

27. GA: Journals.

28. VA: Make?

29. MO: Met. *Do it later, Gabriel! That's very sloppy!*

30. GA: Well, I don't got any pencils.

31. MO: Well, you can do neat with pen, too, just as well as you can with a pencil.

[Pause]

[Mother goes back to preparing dinner.]

32. MO: Where did you put the hamburger meat, Gabriel?

33. GA: In the refrigerator.

34. *[Both children continue to articulate sporadic words from homework. No interaction for several minutes]*

35. GA: Mom! How do you spell "every"?

36. MO: Think it out.

37. GA: Huh?

38. MO: Think it out.

39. GA: *Uhhhh.* I don't know how to spell it. *[Pause]* Uhh. V-e-r-y?

40. MO: Right. *[Pause]* I told you you knew how.

41. VA: My shoe came off.

42. GA: ... was ... good ... yesterday ... yesterday ... mmmm ... we ... lost ... a ... scrimmage ... game.

43. VA: Mom, I'm on my second word, number two.

44. MO: OK.

45. VA: h ... -a ... h ... -a. Mom. Mom.

46. MO: What?

47. VA: Come over here. ... Mom, come over here.

48. MO: *Just a minute, Vanessa!*

49. GA: Mom, how do you spell "practice"?

50. MO: P-r-a ... think it out.

51. GA: I don't know ... I can't think ... *[Complaining tone]*

52. MO: Gabriel! You've always wanted me to give you big words to spell out. Now think it out.

53. GA: Uhhhh ... p-r-a-

54. MO: Yeah.

55. GA: t-i-s?

56. MO: No.

57. GA: P-r-a-c-t-i-s.

58. MO: No.

59. GA: Well, that's how you spell practice.

60. MO: Yeah, but there's another letter that sounds like a "s" besides "s."

61. GA: C?

62. MO: Yeah.

63. GA: t-i-s?

64. MO: No. You just *said* what the letter was, Gabriel.

65. GA: P-r-a-s-c ...

66. MO: No. You said it right the first time, except for the "s." Now spell it out again.

67. GA: P-r-a-c-e?

68. MO: You're not thinking; you're just guessing.

69. GA: *No!* I'm thinking.

70. MO: Well, say it again.

71. GA: P-r-a-c- . . . k?

72. MO: You said it right the first time . . . Now think how you said it the first time.

73. GA: I said: p-r- . . . a- . . . s.

74. MO: No. That's not what you said the first time.

75. GA: C? P-a-r . . . p-r-a-c. . . .

[Pause]

76. MO: "-tis."

77. GA: . . . t-i-s.

78. MO: I just finished telling you another letter . . .

79. GA: H?

80. MO: I just finished telling you another letter that sounds like "s." *[Pause]* You said it, Gabriel. *[Pause]* What other letter can make the sound of "s"? Besides "s"? *[Pause]* You said it earlier.

81. GA: C?

[Pause]

82. MO: C what? There's a silent letter at the end.

83. GA: E?

84. MO: Now spell it again.

85. GA: P-r-a-c . . .

86. MO: Not "z".

87. GA: C, I said.

88. MO: Oh, OK, p-r-a-c . . . what?

89. GA: E? But that's what I said. -t-i-s.

90. MO: There you go again, using the "s."

91. GA: But first you said . . .

92. MO: Spell it again.

93. GA: P-r-a-c-c . . .

94. MO: You're just guessing. You're not thinking.

95. GA: But first I said . . . "p-r-a-c-e."

96. MO: No, it's not c-e.

97. GA: Uh-huh.

98. MO: Now think of the word. *Prac*-tice. Now spell it out. . . . *[Pause]* You're not thinking, you're just jabbering off words . . . letters. Try spelling it on the paper. If you see it on the paper, then you'll know it. Spell it on the scratch sheet of paper, there. Right there on one of those papers there.

99. GA: One of these?

100. MO: Yeah. You said you want me . . . you want to learn how to spell words. Well, you have to think them out.

101. GA: Write the alphabet?

102. MO: *No!*

103. GA: Write what?

104. MO: *Practice!* See if you can put it on there and see if you spell it right. Think it out. *[Pause]* Sound out the word in your head.

105. *[Mother turns attention to Vanessa. Unintelligible phrases]*

106. MO: You still haven't figured it out? *Practice.* P-r-a-c-t-i-c-e.

107. GA: Oh.

108. MO: *Oh!* Now you know how you said it before, except you kept on saying "s."

109. GA: P-r-a-c-t . . .

110. MO: Yes.

In these homework examples, mothers have internalized certain forms of what has been identified as a central feature of classroom discourse. Mehan (1979, 1982) describes a three-part structure of classroom events within which students mark the boundaries of interactional sequences: Initiation, Reply, and Evaluation. Similarly, Tharp and Gallimore (1988) identify what they term the "recitation script" in which a tripartite division of communicative resources occurs. As the script is enacted, the teacher assigns a text, in either oral or written form. The student is then to absorb the text and recite it. After the student's recitation, the teacher evaluates the student's performance. Thus, a teacher's initiatory elicitation cues a student's reply, which in turn invokes a teacher's evaluation. This three-part structure seems to result from the kinds of questions teachers ask. Although an entire corpus of literature has grown around the supposed discontinuity between the discourse features of the language spoken in the home and the discourse features of the language used in school, these homework transcripts indicate that the households of these students are often attempting to incorporate and validate school discursive practices. The following exchange in the Escobedo family parallels the classroom recitation "known information question" (Heath 1983) script:

67. MO: OK, Anthony, gimme your book. *[Unintelligible phrase]* What did Jack do with the cow he was supposed to sell?

68. A: He got stuff instead of money.

69. MO: OK. Why do you think Jack's mother was angry when she saw her beans?

70. A: Because, because he didn't get money instead of, umm, he didn't get . . . he didn't, he didn't get money, but he got a beanstalk, beans, magic.

71. MO: Yeah, but she didn't believe they were magic, did she? So she got angry, right? What kind of plant grew from the bean?

72. R: A beanstalk.

73. MO: How do you think Jack felt when he saw the giant?

74. A: Scared.

75. R: Scared.

76. MO: What did the heart do when Jack tried to take it?

77. A: It said, "Master, Master."

78. MO: It said "Master." What, what did, what did the . . .

In many ways, it would appear that this type of interactional display is what educational institutions promote as adequate and conducive home-learning techniques. For example, one publication from the Office of Education called *Parental Involvement in Education* (Coleman 1991) links the presence of "social capital" to school success, in which the concept of social capital is extended to include the attention and involvement of adults in children's learning. The underlying premise of this extension is the assertion that schools must assume a new role: rebuilding social capital (ibid.:13). The publication contends that through the involvement of parents in a school's functioning, a more robust community will emerge, one in which a high level of community consensus exists concerning the rules, norms, and standards that are part of this social capital. It is, in essence, a call for strong communities imbued with the authority to act in a way that is consistent with school norms. The assumption here is that social capital in the form of a particular type of parental involvement in children's schooling is infused *from the school to the community*. The school is seen as providing the catalyst for the type of involvement that the school defines as parental interest. It ignores the fact that parental involvement in their children's education may be quite high, but that it may take forms other than those validated by the school.

The data from the households in my sample reflect this contention. As is obvious from the length of the time provided for homework sessions (often hours at a time), parents take their children's education very seriously. Witness Marina's unabashed glee when Richard performs a task competently:

110. MO: Wait a minute, Anthony. Very good, Richard! You wrote in these letters, numbers, you knew the numbers all by yourself? Wow!

111.   R: I counted all those things.

112. MO: You counted them! Oh, guy, Richard, that's really good! I didn't know you could do that. He's good, yeah, he knew the numbers, the numbers, himself; he didn't ask me for help, he didn't ask me for help. He did it himself. OK. You can color the pictures now, OK.

Every household I interviewed, immigrant and native born, placed an inordinately high value on the child's succeeding in school, and other studies on the value of education in Latino communities cite a similar ethos (Goldenberg and Gallimore 1995; Reese et al. 1995). The manifestation of this concern, however, took forms other than the traditional barometer of parental interest: classroom visits. One mother declared that her way of helping her son scholastically was by not requiring him to carry out heavy household chores. She felt that she could not contribute to his advancement because of her own limited education, but she could offer him what she had: her time. In order to free him for homework, she took over the chores that would have been expected of him. Other parents went to great lengths to ensure that their children were properly outfitted for school, at the sacrifice of other items that the household needed. All faithfully either met their child personally or had an immediate family member meet the child after school and chatted every day with their children about the day's events. Because PACE mothers were required to spend a certain amount of time volunteering in their child's class, classroom visits were frequent. Several mothers additionally accompanied the class on field trips or taught them special skills.

All of these examples point to the fact that a great deal of social capital is invested in these children in terms of encouragement, attention, and interest in school matters. There is no need to inject into the community an interest in their children's education because *it is already there*. Interest and motivation can be manifested in countless other ways besides bringing parents into the institutional setting. This is an example of how a theoretically good idea such as social capital can come to a halt in the quest for silver bullets. For example, in a section detailing how social capital in the family can be built, the Office of Education monograph states:

> Yet one area in which schools can act concerns homework. Schools demand homework, and assume that parents will reinforce the school's demands and provide a setting in which children can meet the demands. But to expect that parents know how to reinforce the school's demands, and know how to provide a setting conducive to the child's completing homework is a serious error. There are specific, concrete points that parents do not know. How long does the school expect an average child in a given grade to spend on homework? What time is best for doing homework? What kind of setting should the parents attempt to provide? What are the pros and cons of rewards contingent upon finishing homework? Should a specific period of time be set aside for homework, or should the child be free as soon as the homework is finished? What rules are best about telephone calls during the homework period?
>
> What is true of homework is true of other contexts of parental

involvement with the child's schooling. The principal point is that parents are unskilled in helping their children to succeed in school. Even well-educated parents often lack the knowledge of what practices in the home will most help their children to succeed in school. The school, on its own or with the aid of specialized professionals, can help parents help their children. (Coleman 1991:18)

The transcripts included in my study cogently demonstrate that parents have learned *too well* what the schools demands of homework. In an attempt to reproduce the routinized interactional sequences of the school setting, these mothers reproduce the dogma of how "learning" is to take place. In the transformational irony of parental homework sessions, mothers themselves come to embody the voice and authority of the school. The "habitus" of the household, in addition to the school, becomes a site for the validation of institutional dominant ideologies as well as a site for cultural reproduction. The authority of the household and the authority of the school merge into one.

The statement that "parents are unskilled in helping their children to succeed in school" is the most telling indictment of this authoritative approach. Social capital can validate household pedagogies in which the array of household investment in learning is the baseline, not an artificial rendering of the demands of educational institutions. The schooled definition of "parental involvement" is often based on preconceived notions of what constitutes "good parenting." The parents in this sample appear to have internalized this model and based their interactions on what the school expects. The disjunction between the open-ended language practices and formulations evident in other socialization situations collides with the mechanistic roles imparted in homework situations. Parents, in their quest to ensure their child's ability to succeed in school, adopt a tactic opposed to the active construction of selfhood for the child that appears in other contexts. That is, rather than allowing for the differential development of areas that define the child's selfhood, parents impose structures that tend to curtail self-creation.

One other important point that emerges from looking at the transcripts in combination with the interview data is the clash between language ideologies and literacy ideologies. Although both of these mothers emphasized that they would like their children to be fluent in Spanish, their emphasis on English literacy completely overshadows any other concern. They display a literacy ideology that places a premium on English skills as a conduit to future economic success. Thus, although both support bilingual education, they nevertheless enact within their own households the ideological stance that the English for the Children campaign espouses: a lack of literacy in English is an almost fatal disadvantage in our global economy. In true Gramscian fashion, the consent of the subaltern is instrumental in validating the dominant ideology. Antonio Gramsci, the social theorist, argued that power is maintained through both consent and force. In this case, the hegemony of the school is reproduced in and by the consent of well-meaning parents. I would contend that this vacillation between institutionally legitimated patterns of interaction and the personalized and constitutive configurations of other types of discourse is part of the larger, overarching process previously identified as disambiguation. Mothers can be seen fluctuating between a resilient construction of personal identity and a desire to fit into the structures that can facilitate survival and success for their children, as centripetal and centrifugal forces clash again within households. Academic success is predicated as the one narrow avenue to "making it." For this reason, mothers appear to conform to whatever methods the school has legitimized as conduits to the world of upward mobility. Like Willis's "lads," these women are social agents who "are not passive bearers of ideology, but active appropriators who reproduce existing structures only through struggle, contestation and a partial penetration of those structures" (1981 [1977]:175).

If we are to accept a definition of social capital measured in terms of shared norms and standards that direct academic behavior, these transcripts demonstrate that these mothers are acutely aware of the norms and behaviors of the schools. There is no deficit in the evaluative scheme that they have internalized through their own schooling experience. They become, in essence, the guardians of their perceived notions of cultural capital, enacting conservative language routines.

From a study of the transcripts, it is readily apparent that defining social capital in terms of institutional goals and behavioral scripts directly suppresses the transmission of the parent's inventory of knowledge. Rather than affirming relationships and social and affective networks, such a definition can effectively derail the inventory of resources available within the household. If, however, social capital is redefined as the value attributable to relationships that facilitate the transmission of knowledge, then an investigation of the children's networks and relationships takes on paramount importance. In the Escobedo tape, the child's affective networks emerge spontaneously as they discuss the pictures that they want to draw for their ninos (godfathers):

287. A: I'm gonna draw pictures for my Nino Rudy.

288. R: No, for your Nino Giro.

289. A: I gonna draw one for my . . .

290. MO: Rudy.

291. R: Nino Rudy.

292. A: Nino Rudy.

293. R: Nino Rudy?

294. A: Yeah, I'm gonna draw one for him.

295. R: Your, your, your, your Nina, ah, Vera gave you the money.

296. A: I know, but I'm gonna, I'm drawing both of 'em. *[Pause. In a sing-song way]* Storybook story, storybook story, storybook story, storybook story.

As has been noted, many Mexican-origin children are tied to a number of functional networks that contribute to the child's emergent competency. Shifting the value of social capital from standardized norms to living networks engenders a reappraisal of the resources that children have within their own households. In elaborating a framework for social capital, Stanton-Salazar defines social capital as the value attributable to either a social tie or a network that facilitates "access to tangible institutional resources and opportunities" (1997:10). Drawing on the concept of "funds of knowledge" (González et al. 1995; Moll 1992; Vélez-Ibáñez and Greenberg 1992), Stanton-Salazar outlines institutionally based funds of knowledge crucial to school success. He suggests that students should be nurtured in an empowering network orientation that recognizes the strategies embedded in households and communities. These strategies enable students to "successfully negotiate different sociocultural worlds and the often conflictive relations between such worlds, and to acquire a heightened measure of resiliency" (Stanton-Salazar 1997:27). Rather than underestimating the array of knowledge domains upon which the child can draw, a "funds of knowledge" approach redirects the focus to a solid pedagogical technique: starting from what is available and building on that foundation.

CHAPTER 8

Where's the Culture?

As a reader of this text, you may have noticed that I have not used the term *culture,* except to describe others' conceptualizations of it. There is a reason for this: *culture* has lost much of its utility as a way to describe the diversity within societies. A useful concept at one time, it has become more of a burden than a tool in recent years. In her essay "Writing against Culture," Lila Abu-Lughod explains that individuals often improvise daily decisions and do not always adhere to "cultural" norms and prescriptives: "the particulars suggest that others live as we perceive ourselves living, not as robots programmed with 'cultural' rules, but as people going through life agonizing over decisions, making mistakes, trying to make themselves look good, enduring tragedies and personal losses, enjoying others, and finding moments of happiness" (1991:58).

Anthropology's contribution of the concept of culture to the social sciences was a welcome antidote to existing notions of inherited and therefore immutable racial differences. The idea that something external to the human organism, something called "culture," could contribute to perceived human diversity was a startling and pivotal affirmation. Even after several decades of tinkering with the concept of culture, it is astounding to realize that it is a fairly recent construct, so embedded is it in our thinking. The concept has evolved through several transformations, often to the detriment of Latino populations.

Latinos and Culture

It is unfortunate that early anthropological studies of Latinos, which sought to objectify the culture of Mexicans and other Latino groups, contributed to the pernicious notion that the etiology of Latino student failure in schools and on standardized tests was related to a culture apparently not conducive to academic achievement. Shrouded in the mantle of social science inquiry, Latinos and Latino households were appointed as "objects of research" and dispassionately dissected for public consumption (e.g., Heller 1968; Madsen 1964; see Romano 1968 for a critique of the anthropology and sociology of Chicanos). The fact that the objects of research themselves had no voice in either co-constructing the authoritative text or on commenting in its aftermath was of little concern. Reacting to this crisis of misrepresentation, Latino scholars and communities countered that these cultural interpretations were stereotypical, patronizing, and misunderstood. By explaining educational achievement disparities and differential social mobility through recourse to forces within the culture, in the domestic realm and hence outside of the public purview, the dominant writing of social theory legitimized the marginalization of Latino students. Although we might hope that these deficit conceptualizations regarding the households of Latino students would belong to the dustbin of history, we can still find evidence in current teacher-training programs that Latino students' culture within their households continues to be viewed as deficient in cognitive and social resources for learning (González 1995).

Culture and "Multicultural Awareness"

As Latino and other scholars directed academic attention to educational disparities of minority children, there emerged a discourse that centered on educators' coming to "know" their students' culture. Predicated on the assumption that classroom cultural and linguistic patterns should be in congruence with cultural and linguistic community patterns, researchers and practitioners sought to bridge the discontinuity gap. However, reports on cultural awareness programs indicate that these approaches may simply succeed in forming new sets of stereotypes, albeit more positive or benign, to replace previous sets of stereotypes. Within workplace settings, for instance, sensitivity sessions are often couched in the rubric of essentialized differences between groups. One example, reported in a periodical for federal employees, cites a participant's comments on how the audience was told that whites "know through counting and measuring," Asians "know through striving toward transcendence," and blacks, Hispanics, and Arabs "know through symbolic imagery and rhythm" (Harris 1995, 12–13). As an outgrowth of the "cultural difference" approach, which was useful in its debunking of "cultural deficit" models of student achievement, this paradigm nonetheless focused primarily on micro-interactional processes rather than on issues of power and hegemony. Levinson and Holland note that by

> Neglecting to emphasize how communication styles, cognitive codes, and so on were the cultural practices of *variably* empowered groups, historically produced within relations of power, the cultural difference approach tended to essentialize the cultural repertoires of minority groups. As Ogbu (1981) has pointed out, the absence of such a critical analysis permitted confident reformists to attempt amelioration of school-based conflicts in cultural styles through remedial programs and "culturally responsive" pedagogies. The deeper structural context of cultural production and school failure remained obscure and largely unaddressed. (1996:8, emphasis in original)

These "cultural mosaic" approaches are often superficial and decontextualized, and do not address underlying power imbalances. Because the theoretical basis for "cultural mismatch" studies has not been adequately interrogated, they often continue to be the basis for preservice and in-service teacher training on cultural diversity. In the case of teacher in-services, practitioners rely on a "transmission" model for learning about their students—a method disengaged from firsthand experience and often boxed into preexisting molds.

The whole notion of culture as it has been translated into educational arenas proves problematic. Although "multicultural education" has been implemented in school districts across the country for more than two decades, this approach generally has relegated notions of culture to observable surface markers of folklore, assuming that all members of a particular group share a normative, bounded, and integrated view of their own culture. The concept of culture emphasized in schools focuses on how shared norms shape individual behavior. Yet prevailing trends in anthropological literature have moved away from univocal and harmonious visions of culture and focus on the processes of lived experiences rather than on standardized rules for behavior. Rather than uniform categorizations of a shared group culture, issues of contestation, ambiguity, and contradiction are now often the focus of ethnographic analysis. Because ethnographic theory has not often been transferred into elementary school arenas, a multicultural curriculum has continued to define culture as dances, food, ethnic heritage festivals, and international potlucks. Although these affirmations are undoubtedly positive in fostering tolerance and identity, there is an unspoken assumption of a normative and clearly defined culture "out there" that may not take into account the everyday lived experiences of students' lives (see Moll and González 1997).

Processual Approaches to Culture

In contrast to static and frozen ideas about human groups, processual approaches to culture that take into account multiple perspectives can reorient educators to consider the everyday lived experiences of their students. Processual approaches, as Renato Rosaldo notes, are marked by stressing the case history method and show how ideas, events, and institutions interact and change through time. Such studies "more nearly resemble the medical diagnosis of a particular patient rather than lawlike generalizations about a certain disease . . . and resist frameworks that claim a monopoly on truth" (1989:92).

As I have tried to demonstrate, the households from which students emerge are intersected by multiply mediated constructs that can belie a harmonious and homogenous set of shared cultural practices, and we cannot assume cultural uniformity as a canon of knowledge that simply has to be transmitted transgenerationally. By adopting a dynamic view of social processes, educators can validate the experiences of Latino students, regardless of generation, class, or language preference. Processual approaches to culture question the shared, bounded, timeless nature of culture. Processual approaches focus on the *processes* of everyday life in the form of daily activities as a frame of reference. These daily activities are a manifestation of particular historically accumulated "funds of knowledge" that households possess. Instead of individual representations of an essentialized group, household (and hence cultural) practices are viewed as dynamic, emergent, and interactional (see González 1995). Sally Falk Moore, an early proponent of the term *processual,* explains that process conveys an analytic emphasis on continuous production and construction without differentiating in that respect between repetition and innovation. A process approach does not proceed from the idea of a received order that is then changed. Process is simply a time-oriented perspective on both continuity and change. . . . An event is not necessarily best understood as the exemplification of an extant symbolic or social order. Events may equally be evidence of the ongoing dismantling of structures or of attempts to create new ones. Events may show a multiplicity of social contestations and the voicing of competing cultural claims. (1987:729)

As anthropological social theory has moved away from previously accepted ways of thinking about culture, curricular practices in schools often have not. In his book *Assessing Cultural Anthropology*, Robert Borofsky summarizes the repackaging of culture: "It is now clearer than ever, for example, that cultures are not homogeneous, stable units—tending to be in equilibrium, tending to endure in the same form through time and/or tending to involve people with mostly shared understandings" (1994:9). Colson nicely summarizes this antiessentialist view, commenting: "Values once thought to be fundamental for guiding the way particular people dealt with each other and their environment have turned out to be situation and time linked, rather than eternal verities that can be used to predict behavior over time, under all circumstances" (1984:7, cited in Vayda 1994:322).

Culture in the Borderlands

Even though the fluidity of cultural practices has been the grist of the anthropological mill for the past several years, what has changed is not the mobility but the theoretical lens through which they have been observed. Within the context of a borderlands area, the concept of culture becomes even more contested and multiplex. Because of the permeability of the border and because borderlands are riddled with emergent practices and mixed conventions that do not conform to normativity, they can be fertile soil for observing flux and fluidity, literally and metaphorically. Gupta and Ferguson, for instance, interrogate the "assumed isomorphism of space, place and culture," noting that "The fiction of cultures as discrete object-like phenomena occupying discrete spaces becomes implausible for those who inhabit the borderlands. Related to border inhabitants are those who live a life of border crossings—migrant workers, nomads, and members of the transnational business and professional elite. What is 'the culture' of farm workers who spend half a year in Mexico and half a year in the United States?" (1992:7).

In his provocative and dazzling work *The Location of Culture* (1994), Homi Bhabha argues for examining "border lives" as exemplars of moments "of transit where space and time cross to produce complex figures of difference and identity, past and present, inside and outside, inclusion and exclusion" (1). It is these "in-between" spaces, he argues, that

> provide the terrain for elaborating strategies of selfhood—singular or communal—that initiate new signs of identity, and innovative sites of collaboration, and contestation, in the act of defining the idea of society itself.
>
> It is in the emergence of the interstices—the overlap and displacement of domains of difference—that the intersubjective and collective experiences of *nationness,* community interest, or cultural value are negotiated. How are subjects formed "in-between," or in excess of, the sum of the "parts" of difference (usually intoned as race/class/gender, etc.)? How do strategies of representation or empowerment come to be formulated in the competing claims of communities where, despite shared histories of deprivation and discrimination, the exchange of values, meanings and priorities may not always be collaborative and dialogical, but may be profoundly antagonistic, conflictual, and even incommensurable? (ibid., emphasis in original)

If Not Culture, Then What?

Even though the reductionistic use of *culture* may have led to the abuse and misuse of the term, how can we discard a construct that has been so useful in conceptualizing difference? By dismantling culture as we know it, do we not risk a "one size fits all" approach? Although we may agree that cultural spaces are contested, fluid, and permeable, must we obliterate the space completely? In some ways, it appears that the idea of *identity* has replaced the use of *culture,* at least in studies of students and schooling.

Language and Culture

Because language has been seen for many years as being tightly bound up with culture, "language and culture" have been regarded as an impenetrable fusion of two domains. Yet language is not coextensive with culture (Sapir-Whorf revisited), nor, as Wittgenstein suggested, do the limits of one's language coincide with the limits of one's mind.

As I have tried to argue, it is through and by language (and discursive practices) that selfhoods are constructed, identities forged, and social processes enacted. As a constitutive force, language shapes the shifting ethnoscapes and multiple identities that morph from the interculturality of multiple knowledge bases. Elinor Ochs explains the persistence of viewing our social worlds through the prism of language:

> The Sapir-Whorf hypothesis promotes the notion that language does not merely mirror "reality," it also shapes it. While deterministic interpretations of this generalization have been refuted, there lingers among anthropologists and sociologists of language the notion that nonetheless language does structure the phenomenological world. . . .
>
> . . . In this perspective, members of societies are agents of culture rather than merely bearers of a culture that has been handed down to them and encoded in grammatical form. The constitutive perspective on indexicality incorporates the post-structural view that the relation between person and society is dynamic and mediated by language. In an intellectual era that brought paradigms such as practice theory and cultural psychology into academic parlance, we have come to entertain the notion that, while person and society are indistinguishable, they are integral. Person and society enter into a dialectical relation in that they act on each other, draw upon each other, and transform each other. In such paradigms, while society helps define a person, a person also helps to (re)define society. (1996:417)

The idea that language can *create* social worlds, although one of the tenets of postmodernism, is not particularly new. In fact, the creative force of language has resonated throughout the history of textual production. "In the beginning was the Word," begins the gospel of John, "and Word was with God, and the Word was God. . . . All things were made by him: and without him was not any thing made that was made." The imagery of the Word as containing the power to create a world, a creative act indexed through reference to a symbolic system, has impacted emotions and minds for centuries. Language, however, must be estimated in its larger semiotic sense, taking into account written and spoken language in all of its permutations in this age of hypermedia and electronic symbolic systems. To encode this larger semiotic system, the notion of "text" has been adopted, as Allan Luke explains: "Texts are moments when language connected to other semiotic systems is used for symbolic exchange. All texts are located in key social institutions: families, schools, churches, workplaces, mass media, government and so on. Human subjects use texts to make sense of their world and to construct social actions and relations required in the labor of everyday life. At the same time, texts position and construct individuals, making available various meanings, ideas and versions of the world" (1995:13).

In some sense, as Susan Philips intimates (1993), macrosociological processes are the accumulation and sum total of microinteractional processes. Within our every interaction, every face-to-face encounter, every dialogical act, every discursive practice embodied in music, art, or drama, we create and re-create selves and others. Students in Ann Locke Davidson's (1996) study *Making and Molding Identity in Schools* actively resisted or accommodated the constitution of Mexican-ness that has been constructed and mediated for them by social scientists, media images, school policy, and day-to-day linguistic practice. In this vein, Luke argues that all language has a *refractive* rather than transparent effect, "mediating, interpreting and reconstructing versions of the natural and social world, identity and social relations. If this is the case, then the possibility of an ideologically disinterested and nondistorting text is at best debatable. By this account, all texts are normative, shaping and constructing rather than simply reflecting and describing" (1995:18–19).

Thus, through discursive practices, people given semantic labels such as *immigrants* can be constructed as undesirable, criminal, dirty, and shiftless, their accented language as uneducated or ignorant. Language, then—or, as Foucault calls it, Discourse—is also implicated in perpetuating relations of power. As the premiere symbolic system, language in the form of text conveys a powerful emotional resonance, shaping and molding our "take" on the everyday stimuli that surround us. The power of the word echoes into the chambers of our innermost subjectivities. Gabriel García Márquez, the Colombian Nobelist, in a speech to the First International Congress of the Spanish Language in Zacatecas, Mexico, in April 1997, related a foreshadowing of his own experience with the "power of the word":

> When I was twelve I was almost run down by a bicycle. A passing priest saved me by shouting, "Watch out!"
>
> Without stopping, the priest called to me, "Did you see the power of the word?"
>
> I learned it that day. And we know now that ever since the time of Christ, the Mayans had known it, too, and with so much clarity they even had a special god of words. That power has never been as great as it is today. Humankind will enter the third millennium under the sway of words. (1997:E2)

From "Language and Culture" to Language Ideologies

As I mentioned in the introduction, I have adopted throughout this text the framework of "language ideologies" (Woolard, Schieffelin, and Kroskrity 1998)—that is, a connection of language with social process, with a special attention to the power dimensions that inhere in both.

One of problems with the term *culture* is that it has often been reduced to simplistic and formulaic expressions. For good or ill, the idea of language ideologies does not reduce well, and complexity is inscribed within the concept. We cannot give up completely on trying to understand the double-sited nature of intersubjectivities, acting and being acted upon, to shape and legitimate practices, and the conceptualization of language ideologies is one avenue that may prove fruitful to pursue.

CONTESTED LANGUAGE IDEOLOGIES WITHIN THE BORDERLANDS

As I have argued, processes of refiguring our social worlds mitigate against a view of cultures as bounded entities containing equally distributed and shared knowledge. Instead, as the narratives and transcripts have indicated, internal diversity helps us to reconceptualize cultures as emerging from contested and contesting language ideologies, within historically situated contexts. Within the borderlands, ideas about language and child rearing are neither uniform nor fixed. Several themes relating to language emerged not as a coherent and integrated whole, but as sometimes contradictory sites for the push and the pull of language in context. One compelling example deals with the concepts of linguistic insecurity and linguistic purity. Many second- and third-generation borderlands mothers may feel "linguistic insecurity" in Spanish because of the erasure of native language skills in the schools until the late sixties. This insecurity is evidenced by a reluctance to engage foreign-born Spanish speakers in a conversation where there is no recourse to English and by the circumscription of Spanish into particular domains. It is born of a sociohistorical legacy of language purism, treating anything but a standard language form as a socially stigmatized, uneducated form of expression, as well as of the absence of Spanish-language instruction in schools. Olga Vásquez, in a particularly open and revealing anecdote, recounts the sting of linguistic disdain when she once checked into a hotel in Spain:

> Vásquez inadvertently asked the hotel clerk to examine her physically when she used, *"Me quiero registrar"* to mean "I would like to check in." The clerk, seizing an opportunity to establish a status differential, curtly informed her that *registrar* meant "inspect" or "search" in *Castellano* (Castilian Spanish) and that she should have said, *"Me quiero inscribir."* This brief interaction communicates much about the social and cultural assumptions underlying the use of language. One could speculate on the influence that Vásquez's physical appearance, her Chicano cadence, and/or her gender may have had on the clerk's response, but there is little doubt that, at least in his own estimation, the clerk's command of standard Spanish afforded him a higher status and the right to correct a guest's use of language. (Vásquez, Pease-Alvarez, and Shannon 1994:3)

Many women in the borderlands report similar humiliation, often emanating from Spanish-language prescriptivists informing them that the Spanish they speak is substandard. Gloria Anzaldúa, the poet laureate of language use in the borderlands, takes up the theme she describes as "linguistic terrorism" in her chapter "How to Tame a Wild Tongue" in *Borderlands:* "Chicanas who grew up speaking Chicano Spanish have internalized the belief that we speak poor Spanish. It is illegitimate, a bastard language. And because we internalize how our language has been used against us by the dominant culture, we use our language differences against each other" (1987:58).

The impact of these language ideologies on native-born children is what one would expect and what is evidenced in the household transcripts: English is privileged for the bulk of communication, yet the safety of hearth and home is inscribed in Spanish. What is the impact on children in the long run? In an article entitled "U.S.–born Latinos Feel Tug to Learn Spanish," appearing in the *Arizona Daily Star,* it is reported that many local Hispanic community college students are filling Spanish classes (Mendoza 1996:B1). One of these students, Patrick Ríos, was profiled:

> "My parents could speak Spanish fluently," said Ríos, twenty, who grew up in Tucson. "But they didn't teach us. Later we actually got into arguments about it. They felt it was better to learn English to fit the Mexican-American nationality."
>
> As a college sophomore, Ríos is confident learning to speak Spanish will advance him in a business career. But it also just feels good, he said.
>
> "I have Mexican friends who totally speak in Spanish to me and I could only reply in English," said Ríos, who now is in a second-year Spanish class.

Aristeo Brito, author and Spanish instructor at Pima Community College, commented in the same article: "It's a renaissance. . . . There is a resurgence of those wanting to reconnect with their heritage." He goes on to reiterate: "It is a generation of Latinos excited about learning to speak a language their parents were criticized for speaking" (ibid.).

For immigrant children, the sociohistorical context differs, but in many ways the result is the same. Ana Celia Zentella and colleagues, for example, note that "Contrary to popular belief, Spanish is being abandoned faster than early twentieth century immigrant languages were lost. The loss of Spanish is accelerated by an anti-immigrant climate in the U.S. and by the global power of English. Most immigrants, in their struggle to survive in an English-dominant society, stress English at the expense of Spanish" (1999:2).

The confluence of these language ideologies—the market value of English, the influence of English-only campaigns, linguistic purism, and linguistic insecurity—influence children in the privileging of English over Spanish, often "at the expense of Spanish." Added to this mix is the impact of the media on children. Children might notice that in the *Star Wars* galaxy, although non-Earth beings may speak other languages, they still understand and speak English. In Spanish-language television programming, advertising for Inglés sin Barreras (English without Barriers), a pricey English-language instruction program, promises success and riches as a consequence of learning English. English is "a jewel that no one can take away from you" and "the passport that no one can rescind," claim the ads. Children are sometimes portrayed overhearing their parents' struggles with lack of employment opportunities and advancement because they don't understand English, and the commercials claim that "every day that goes by without speaking English is money that is lost."

Using the analytical lens of language ideologies rather than culture in the borderlands helps us to connect with the multilayered contested and contesting meanings that connect ideologies to language use. It also moves us away from ideas of culture that have reified cultural traits as evenly distributed within any population. By focusing on language ideologies, we can fracture the "one language, one culture" isomorphism of Spanish-speaking populations, as we become aware of, for instance, the derogation of Chicano Spanish by native Spanish speakers. Intrapopulation issues of class, prestige, and citizenship mark Spanish speakers as segmented by internal divisions and demarcations, obscured by assumptions of homogeneity. Within schooling practices, the study of language ideologies can interrogate language and literacy policies of schools, moving beyond static and fossilized notions of the "culturally relevant." Within educational research, our focus can be on how particular textual productions are legitimated and reproduced in schools and on the ideologies that underlie these productions, as I explain in the next chapter.

CHAPTER 9

Beyond the "Disuniting" of America

IMPLICATIONS FOR SCHOOLING AND
PUBLIC POLICY

> There has always been a tension between the fixed, durable, and inflexible requirements of national boundaries and the unstable, transient, and flexible requirements of people. If the principal fiction of the nation-state is ethnic, racial, linguistic, and cultural homogeneity, then borders always give the lie to this construct.
> —Mathew Horsman and Andrew Marshall,
>   *After the Nation-State*

In a *Newsweek* special issue, renowned biological psychologist Saul Schanberg was interviewed about his research linking physical contact with babies' weight gain and general infant development. He recalled his elderly grandmother's reaction to his discovery of a link between touch and growth. "She said, 'You went to Yale to get a Ph.D. and to get an M.D., and that's what you've learned? To touch a baby is good?'" (Van Boven 1997:45).

In some ways, what I have tried to present may on the surface appear equally commonsensical:

Language is important.
Language can both shape and reflect our social worlds.
People lead complex lives, and talk is one way to get at that complexity.
Language is emblematic of our identity.

Language and emotion are complexly intertwined.

It is important for teachers to learn from parents and for parents to talk to teachers.

What we say and how we say it are decisively and momentously critical to the formative developmental processes of children's growth and maturity.

Implications for Educational Public Policy and Schooling

Other points that I will try to make as I move from the interpretive to the practical may not be quite so commonsensical. Children live in complex worlds, and part of that complexity is inscribed in schooling. Issues of language, identity formation, and child development are at the forefront not only in the household but in classrooms as well. The contradictions that inhere in these issues belie the reductionist approach to controversies at institutional, policy, and governmental levels regarding the multicultural "disuniting of America" (cf. Schlesinger 1992). Many critics view this disunification as taking place within schools and within multicultural curricula. In an incisive overview of the political and moral postures that inhere in pluralism, multiculturalism, and assimilation, Walter Feinberg encapsulates the argument against multicultural education:

> Critics who are concerned about the social effects of structuring public education around specific identities are uneasy about using schools to heighten children's awareness of the importance of certain attributes—skin color, sex, ethnic background, parental income—that they happen to share with some but not all other citizens. They object to schools' contributing to a heightened sense of differences, differences that are constructed within the context of public political formations, and they are concerned that active recognition of the "child's group," instead of broadening the child's awareness of different forms of the good, narrows it. (1998:165)

Yet, as Feinberg rightly notes, "the schools cannot keep all options open, and it is not as if children do not come to school with certain directions, patterns, and identifications already marked" (ibid.:167).

The trope of disunification is also a clarion call for proponents of

English-only movements who view a single language as an axiomatic foundation for the formation of nationhood. In a letter to the editor of the *Arizona Daily Star* (March 24, 2000) responding to a column entitled "Bilingual Ed Is in the U.S.' Best Interest—Si?" a reader reiterated this assumption: "Tom Teepen showed he is apparently unaware that the purpose of a common language and culture is to unite a nation made up of peoples from many parts of the world. . . . In the process, will we find the unity of our country destroyed and 'Balkanized' as is so much of the world?" (Buran 2000:A18).

The idea of "Balkanization" and fragmentation into diverse factions based on language is a common thread of the rhetoric of single nation/single language proponents. Yet the idea of nationhood and a single language as being bound up with each other is a language ideology that begs interrogation. Tove Skutnabb-Kangas, citing Pattanayak (1986), offers us an alternative view of "linguicism" and explains: "D. P. Pattanayak, the Director of the Central Institute of Indian Languages, says in a powerful article (1986) that the Western way of looking at multilingualism is something like this: a country should ideally be monolingual. If it is officially bilingual, that is a pity, but one can live with it. If it has three or more languages, it is underdeveloped and barbaric. In order to become civilized, it should strive towards becoming monolingual" (1988:13).

This polarity of viewing the disunification of multiple languages as chaos and a single language as integral is reminiscent of the evolutionary schemata that assumed that all societies must pass lockstep through stages leading to the highest (Westernized) ideal. Yet the ideas of nation and state and of national identity are as contested and continuously negotiated as are ideas of culture. These concepts have been viewed "to share the same properties of integrity, unity, linearity of time and space, and discreteness" (Wilson and Donnan 1998:7). However, as I explained in the previous chapter, the idea of bounded, unitary, and discrete cultures is a fiction of homogeneity. Similarly, the meaning of nationhood is constructed through Discourses about meaning and value:

> From Lincoln honoring those who have sacrificed for national unity in his Gettysburg Address, to Malcolm X and Noam Chomsky reminding us of national failings, to Martin Luther King Jr. and Jesse Jackson holding out national promise and hope, children

need to see the different meanings nationhood holds for different groups of people. They also need to understand how, despite differences, the idea of the nation provides a framework for a continuing discourse about meaning and value. Ultimately the signifiers of this identity are less important than are the principles of fairness and justice by which we evaluate the past and anticipate the future. (Feinberg 1998:235)

In the borderlands, however, there is a space where the ideas of nationhood and state are most explicitly addressed:

Nations and their individuated members may be in a perpetual condition of becoming, but this is only partially true of the state. The state exists. Its institutions and representatives make and enforce the laws which regiment most daily activities of its citizens and residents, in direct relations of cause and effect. Border peoples, because of their histories, and objectified and subjectified cultures, not only have to deal with the institutions of their own state, but with those institutions of the state or states across the border, entities of equal and sovereign power which overshadow all other relations. (Wilson and Donnan 1998:8)

Thus, the presence of a border and the often unequal power relations of the entities across borders mitigate against a single unified trope of "nationhood." In discussing languages and borders, Bonnie Urciuoli remarks: "In many instances language and group identity are not isomorphic and people do not always see language shift vitiating their cultural identity. Any sense of language mapping onto culture, and culture onto national identity, and thus onto border, must be mediated through macro-micro interstices in relationships" (1995:533).

As children form identities as citizens, they need to understand that there is not a one-to-one mapping between language, culture, and national identity, and that citizen identities are created and re-created through webs of meanings:

Children also need to understand that identity is confined neither to national boundaries nor to groups within them. What (was said above) about the way a nation holds out promise for unifying meaning could also be said of culture or of humankind, with the

exception that nation-states also entail formal and enforceable instruments for collective action. Nevertheless, many features of our
identity are shared across national boundaries and across distinct
cultural groups.

Although webs of meaning become thinner as we move across
distinct and nameable cultural boundaries, and although webs of
mutual aid also thin out as we move across established and recognized national borders, they do not disappear. Every citizen of a
multicultural state carries an identity that is larger than that of this
single nation. When people become members of a public they need
to attend to the extended identities of their fellow citizens. (Feinberg 1998:236)

Feinberg goes on to explain that the formation of a national identity in
the public schools requires certain orientations:

The identity of multicultural nations such as the United States is
defined in part through their role in maintaining existing avenues
of association and developing those through which new individual
and cultural alignments can emerge. Maintaining this identity requires citizens who are willing to deliberate about the way webs of
meaning and mutual aid are constructed and who are able to
evaluate present conditions against future possibilities. (ibid.)

Because I have contended that language socialization be viewed as a
resource for the construction of selfhood, then the deeper structural
functions of ontological discourse do not fragment or disunite. Rather
than exacerbation of differences, we can find that the "language of becoming Latinos" provides the instruments that can bind together and
span the ambiguities and discontinuities of a borderlands existence.
These language practices offer a formative and ongoing definition of
selfhood that is actively constructed and continuously transformed.
Other practices (e.g., music, family, and kinship networks) do not
threaten the fabric of society and need not be obliterated in the name of
Americanization. A construction of ethnic selfhood does not perforce
drive wedges between groups. In the neighborhoods where I worked,
house after house displayed yellow ribbons during the Gulf War, dozens

more than in any other neighborhood in Tucson that I visited during this time, a silent testimony to the thousands of Hispanic servicemen and women enlisted to combat. The ribbons waving in the air, sometimes alongside outdoor nichos or shrines of the Virgin of Guadalupe, bore witness to the harmonious and parallel coalescence of "self" and "other." Strong and effective ontological constructs of identity invigorate rather than diminish, fortify rather than curtail the connections between peoples. It is the opposite tendency, the need to obliterate what is foreign or nonconventional, that erects barriers between groups. The construction of selfhood for children is an integral part of the developmental trajectory of maturation, and this semiotic process must grapple with the inconsistencies of an equivocal and contested world. When identity formation is viewed as a necessary component of sound and healthy child development, the specter of fragmentation into corporate ethnic identities is defused. As children acquire "roots," the branches that can span ontological discourse will burgeon in a continuous self-creation of existence. Articulating theories of identity, language, and contestation as contingent can help to defuse the seductive pull of gangs. As youths define themselves in multiple and complex ways, an adherence to a standardized behavior demanded of unidimensional personas can be problematized. As I have argued, children's identities are fluid, not fixed, and children are exposed to multiple identities within their own households and communities. They are soccer players, folklórico dancers, mariachis, Nintendo addicts, Wildcat basketball fans, Pokémon and Barbie collectors. They forge identities as altar servers in Catholic churches or as members of Christian Bible study groups. They have an ambiguous relationship with Mexico, yet are evocatively bound by the phonetic melodies of language and music. Their grandmothers have struggled and overcome, and their mothers merge and transform multiple ways of being.

By opening up the panorama of possibilities, by enlarging the repertoires of possible identities, the polarization of "either/or" can be eliminated. The seductive pull of gang identities and affiliations are processes of identity formation gone awry. In the age of global capitalism, identity formation is often for Madison Avenue to define, and, as Peter McLaren and Tomaz Tadeu da Silva contend, "[The current historical juncture] is further a site where identity has become annexed by advertising and marketing industries and where the nihilistic extrapolation of the mass-produced image provides the fundamental referents for structuring and 'promoting' human agency" (1993:47).

A Freirian position is useful in understanding that adding multiple possibilities for identity formation is

> not accretive in the sense that it simply promotes other voices to be added to the menu of mainstream cultural perspectives in the form of a depotentiated multiculturalism. In the sense that Freire "thinks from the margins," [he views] the oppressed not as ethno-centric special interest groups to be fulsomely added on to the already harmonious pre-existing pluralism but rather as offering in themselves valid and legitimate articulations of everyday experience ("dialogical angles"). . . . Freire argues that we need to understand the historical contexts, social practices, cultural forms and ideologies that give these discourses shape and meaning. Freire teaches us that contradictions in the larger social order have parallels in individual experience and that educators for liberation must restore the political relation between pedagogy and the language of everyday life. (ibid.:51, 53)

In other words, schools must be sites for the interrogation of knowledge production and not merely sites for its reproduction. What does this mean for teachers in classrooms? It means that although we should continue to acknowledge the diversity of children's experiences, it is also important to *learn from* these experiences. The individual expressions of diversity reflect a larger social order. How can we theorize the everyday and the mundane of children's lives? The answer is both simple and complex: by connecting with the lived practices of students. In work that my colleagues and I have carried out on tapping the "funds of knowledge" in communities, we outline a methodology for expanding our perspectives of communities and households (González 2000; González and Amanti 1997; Moll et al. 1992). It is through recognizing that the internal diversity *within* populations is as great as diversity *between* populations that we can come to acknowledge that the distinctions we make between peoples are arbitrary and, at times, capricious.

Another implication for classrooms is a recognition of the constitutive nature of language. It is important to recognize that every inter-action within a classroom both reflects and constructs a social order. Teachers can *create* through language the worlds that children inhabit in the classroom. The individual and the sociohistorical come together in every language interaction, bringing together the dialogism of Bakhtin and the developmentalism of Vygotsky, as described in chapter 4. Through the power of classroom interaction, teachers have a genera-tive power at their disposal, a power that can be wielded at every moment of contact. Allan Luke helps us to understand how this kind of "critical discourse" can have a powerful impact on classrooms:

> The strength of critical discourse analysis lies in its capacity to show the power relations of apparently mundane texts at work, to represent and interpret instances of everyday talk, reading and writing, whether in a beginning reading lesson, a science discus-sion, a research seminar, a memo or policy statement, or child/ parent conversation in a shopping mall. Language, text and dis-course are not mere educational subfields or areas of interest. They are the very media by and through which teaching and learning and the writing and discussion of research occur. Not only is there no space outside of discourse. There are no means of educational description, classification, and practice outside of discourse. It is extremely difficult, if not altogether impossible, to talk or write about mind and behavior, belief and value, and policy and practice without a social analysis of language, however theorized or under-theorized, however explicit or implicit. It is extremely risky to engage in the construction of texts of curriculum, educational pol-icy and research, without some explicit reflexivity on how and whom we construct and position in our own talks and writing. For these reasons, a critical sociological approach is not a designer option for researchers, but an absolute necessitation for the study of education in postmodern conditions. (1995/1996:40−41)

Teachers can also incorporate the link between language and identity (Messing 1995) into classroom practices. Joshua Fishman, the eminent linguist and scholar, has long written about languages and identities. In some of his recent work, he reiterates the importance of language in identity:

In a century (and even in a decade) marked by ethnic excesses in various parts of the globe, the more evenhanded treatment of ethnicity and the greater awareness of its link to language, to identity, to cultural and intellectual creativity, and even to globalization represents a change that is welcome indeed. The evils of ethnolinguistic violence will probably never totally disappear . . . but the ethnolinguistic link will also always be related to much of what is best and most treasured about humankind. The link between ethnicities and the specific languages that have been traditionally associated with them will always be associated with some of the most positive attributes and achievements of human life. (1999)

Similarly, it is also important not to relegate emotion and feelings to the sidelines in classrooms. Renato Rosaldo remarks that

New classrooms and new readings often arouse stronger feelings than the old ones. One can be tempted into following the dominant culture's conditioning by separating thought from feeling. On the other hand, one can ask: What in the book or discussion has produced these feelings? Rather than wishing them away, teachers can use such feelings as starting points for analysis and intellectual discussion. Consider that matters that are deeply felt can also be deeply thought, and vice versa. In my experience, matters that arouse strong feelings often concern students deeply and can lead to more searching analyses than other issues. (1994:406)

Finally, I believe that we must never underestimate the power of stories in our educational processes: stories of self and stories of others. The stories in this book have a history behind them, are embedded in contradictions and struggle, and interrogate our assumptions about the shared quality and boundedness of human groups. Susan Florio-Ruane urges educators and researchers that to tell a new story is to reinvent narratives of culture, identity, and education. She continues, "If our stories of self are to help us reform institutions or build new communities, we need to be willing to reinvent them, repeatedly and in the company of others, embracing rather than defending ourselves from contact. We must replace outworn renditions of 'who we are' that, in Toni Morrison's words, are 'unreceptive to interrogation, cannot form or tolerate new ideas, shape other thoughts, tell another story, fill baffling silences' (1994:14). Instead, in our scholarship and our teaching, we must risk telling new stories in and by many voices. This is an act of hope" (1997:160).

The Dialectics of the Centripetal and the Centrifugal

Within the social construction of borderlands, some would argue that one of the contradictions of borderland status is that many Latino families have attempted to adapt *too much* to what they perceive is the "American" lifestyle and perhaps have adopted English at the expense of Spanish. We sometimes forget (like Iris Gallardo) that essentialized notions of what it means to be "American" also exist. In Mexico, where stereotypes of norteamericanos abound, the country to the north is often seen as decadent and immoral, its family structure disintegrated. Yet there is grudging admiration for its manufactured goods and services and for its affluent lifestyle. Immigrant children, at times chafing under strict parental authority, sometimes adopt what they view as the more "permissive" ideology of the United States, equating it with First World dominance. Elementary school teachers in the borderlands invariably comment that their recently immigrated students are their "ideal" students, respectful, well-behaved, viewing the teacher as the ultimate authority (cf. Matute Bianchi 1991). However, it doesn't take long, teachers note, before these students realize that their peers don't value their proper behavior, and they begin to act like everybody else. The shock of being uprooted from a safe and familiar territory to an unfamiliar and seemingly hostile new homeland is a psychological trauma that has never been fully explored. For those children who aspire to fit in, conformity in dress, talk, and behavior is all-important.

There are further contradictions. The growing schism between the native-born and immigrant Mexican-origin population is evident at both the school level and the neighborhood level. Longtime Tucson residents blame increased crime rates on the "apartment dwellers," usually immigrant families, who have been moving into long-established neighborhoods. As crime rates soar, families who have lived in the Tucson southside for years find themselves yearning for the way "things used to be." An *Arizona Daily Star* article summed up the problem:

"Often speaking English better than Spanish, the old-timers are proud of their working-class barrios and the fact that their families have lived in this country for two or three generations. . . . The newcomers chastise Chicanos, a term they use to describe Mexican-Americans, for speaking broken Spanish. The immigrants also consider Mexican-Americans to be traitors to their heritage and mock them for having coddled childhoods compared with the upbringing in Latin countries" (Associated Press 1997:B7). Within Tucson high schools and middle schools, the groups that form around identities are often demarcated as either immigrant or native born. The immigrant students continue to speak Spanish among themselves and form their own networks. Although not always polarized, the two groups find they have little in common in terms of interests or ways of talking. In a detailed study of immigrant and U.S.–born youth in a high school in the east end of Houston, Angela Valenzuela examines the social divisions that exist between these two groups. She questioned both groups of students as to why they did not associate with each other. The immigrant youth most commonly answered that U.S–born youth *"son americanizados"* ("are Americanized") (1999:182). Valenzuela explains that the term *Americanized* is a pejorative, and

> as a rather generic label, it is often used to convey a variety of negative perceptions. For example, the statement "Chicanos are Americanized" unpacks into many separate observations: "We never saw drugs until we came to the United States." "We do not have a gang problem in Mexico." "In Mexico, we mostly drink at home. Here, they [Chicanos] go to happy hour." "We take school more seriously than them [Chicanos]." "Smoking, doing drugs, getting involved in gangs, and not taking school seriously is an American phenomenon." "We're more respectful toward our elders." (ibid.)

On the other side of the coin, U.S.–born Mexican-origin students in Valenzuela's study also felt a similar disconnection with immigrant youth. One young female commented: "They talk to each other in Spanish and all. They think they're better than us Chicanos. Can you believe? And she's from Mexico! Mexico sucks! I'd rather be American than Mexican any day" (ibid.:116).

With these multiple centripetal and centrifugal forces swirling around the language wars that are part of our daily lives, is it any surprise that there is no one unified way of thinking about language, identity, and child rearing?

Weaving the Threads Together

And so I have come full circle. I began by trying to find out the *One Truth* about how understanding language use can impact children's school achievement. I found out that there are many partial truths and that there is no *one* correct way to foster educational development. But these partial truths are important and must be rooted in the acknowledgment that language use is not merely cognitive, but is deeply social, ideological, and political, and resonates in children's emotional development. Add to these truths the incredible resilience of Latino families, the funds of knowledge found within households, and the multiple dimensions of what it means to be a woman and mother in the borderlands. I began this study by pointing to the impact that the extended family, most often in the form of the maternal grandmother, could have on language use. I went on to explore the impact of emotion and discovered a deep spirituality inscribed in lives. Indeed, spirituality was a recurrent theme through the study. Some women reported making a pilgrimage to Magdalena, Sonora, on foot or to the Mission San Xavier to fulfill a promise made in return for a blessing. The presence of altars, santos, and nichos is always evident in the women's lives. In response to the growing turn away from traditional Catholicism, some scholars have suggested implications for the schooling and language practices of children, drawing on early work by W. Lloyd Warner (1961), which distinguished between "oral Protestantism and visual Catholicism." Warner argues that the "Protestant final symbol of authority is the *written* word" (1961:62, emphasis in original), especially the written word of the Bible, and that Catholicism is oriented to visually connected symbols. Although I have no doubt that the literacy practices in religious domains can impact children's language use, I would be reluctant to categorize religious symbolism in such bounded terms. What I have suggested, though, is that the mothers and children who have entered into new spiritual realms do so in a dialectic between structure and agency, configuring new identities and emergent practices.

But these themes of emotion, spirituality, motherhood, grandmotherhood, childhood are not the stuff from which social analyses are made. They are not among the "Key Words" that Raymond Williams (1976) identifies as significant in social theory. They were not imposed from above, but erupted from below.

Because our research base of how children engage in language learning in diverse contexts must be expanded, we should be asking more and better questions, rather than assuming simplistic answers. We may find that in researching children, we add to our storehouse of "key words" and begin to think of the elements and emotions of child-life as meaningful theoretically. Are theories of identity that relate to adults just as applicable to children? Are children interpellated in the same way as adults? We need to move children from the "margins to the center of anthropological inquiry," as Marjorie Harness Goodwin has emphasized:

> We need to move children from the margins to the center of anthropological inquiry. Over 40 percent of the world's urban population will be children fifteen and younger by the year 2000, many of whom are especially vulnerable. . . . It is time we take children seriously and use the distinctive practices of anthropology to give voice to their social worlds and concerns. . . . Through language, children of diverse ethnicities, social classes, ages, abilities and genders orchestrate their social organization and socialize one another across a range of activities. Without longitudinal ethnographic studies of children from different ethnic backgrounds in diverse structural settings we will not know how children's lives are shaped by their encounters with family, peers, adults and others expressing various language ideologies, in neighborhoods, schools and after school, or how children change developmentally over time. (1997:5)

Critical theorist Terry Eagleton also argues that children "make the best theorists":

> Children make the best theorists since they have not yet been educated into accepting our routine social practices as "natural," and so insist on posing to those practices the most embarrassingly general and fundamental questions, regarding them with wonderful estrangement which we adults have long forgotten. . . . It is

those children who remain discontent with this shabby parental response who tend to grow up to be emancipatory theorists, unable to conquer their amazement at what everyone else seems to take for granted. (1990:34)

We can look at children and language socialization for insights into social theory (Schieffelin 1990). In more recent work on language socialization, Elinor Ochs addresses the issue of using linguistic resources for socializing humanity. One of the dilemmas that she identifies deals with looking at "human culture" as a universal of human behavior and at "pan-species commonalities in the human accommodation to, and structuring of, social life" (1996:409). Ochs suggests that language socialization is a potent and pervasive process. It is potent because "once novices understand that language has a constitutive potential, they have a semiotic tool not only for constructing a world that abides by historically achieved conventions, but also for transcending that world to create alternative worlds for other interlocutors to ratify or challenge" (ibid.:431).

Dialogism within the Sociohistoric

As part of growing up in families, embedded in communities and enmeshed in popular culture, children develop complex discursive resources for using language to make sense of the social and natural worlds (Luke 1995/1996), which has direct implications for educational policy. Allan Luke points out that "Learning to engage with texts and discourses, then, entails far more than language development or skill acquisition per se. It involves the development and articulation of common sense, of hegemonic 'truths' about social life, political values and cultural practices" (1995/1996:37).

What I have attempted to do is to use transcripts, narratives, and other discursive practices as sites for showcasing how local, regional, and global issues come to be embedded in talk. Concomitantly, the talk that I have highlighted is a window into a sociohistorical context and political economy of a particular borderlands zone. Although I have presented a perspective that views women and children as active agents in constructing their identities, I do not advocate the position that *all* reality is socially and linguistically constituted, that there is no reality outside of our human interactions. To say that language and discourses can create and fashion particular ways of construing our social world does not necessarily imply that there is no reality that is *not* socially constructed. We can construct one version of multiple versions, all imbued with partial "truths." Actually, the discarding and fine-tuning of "partial truths" is part of the process of coming to "know" our world. Similar to children testing language, exploring its dimensions, we as adults, in our life-long learning process, equally explore, discard, refine, and adopt "realities" or portions of realities into our everyday ideologies. Although we may incorporate aspects of others' "partial truths," in the end we are left with our own personalized contour and interpretation of the multiple experiences and discourses to which we have been exposed. Abu-Lughod and Lutz remind us that "To take language as more than a transparent medium for the communication of inner thoughts or experience, and to view speech as something essentially bound up with local power relations that is capable of socially constructing and contesting realities, even subjectivity, is not to deny non-linguistic 'realities.' It is simply to assert that things that are social, political, historically contingent, emergent, or constructed are both real and can have force in the world" (1990:13).

Because I have assumed that language and emotion are tightly interwoven, it is important to acknowledge how language can index both affirmation of self and resistance to minority status. In the language wars that rage on in schools, policy cannot be reduced to language methodology, and we have not even begun to understand the complex ways that children respond to language in its various forms. We must also be aware, as I have illustrated, of how ideologies of language are themselves contested within communities. In many ways, Spanish is indexical of identity, heritage, tradition, and a construction of selfhood. English is given an instrumental load, a commodity to be traded for access to the larger communicative sphere. In her study of New York Puerto Rican language use, Bonnie Urciuoli (1996) similarly reports on an "inner sphere" of talk among intimates within the household and barrio, and on an "outer sphere" of language use with institutions and gatekeepers. The idea of Spanish as tied to intimacy is not intrinsic to that language alone, however. Hill (1985) reports on the use of Spanish and Mexicano (Nahuatl) by indigenous populations in the Malinche

Volcano region of Mexico. In this case, power and distance are marked by Spanish, and Mexicano is the language of intimacy and identity as a campesino.

Language ideologies in the borderlands include not only conceptions of social power, vis-à-vis the privileging of communication in English, but also a subaltern counterdiscourse that insists that symbolic activity within the realm of personhood is constituted through Spanish. Thus, language ideologies not as metapragmatic discourse or ideas about language but as construed practice are consequential for both social and linguistic processes. The almost impenetrable identification of language with self, of language with a notion of peoplehood, interrogates the idea of how languages not as discrete, distinctive entities but as emblematic of self and community are used to resist the symbolic domination of a prestige language. Children are acutely aware that their participation in activities in which they produce and respond to Spanish are emotionally laden to their parents, ninas, tíos, and grandparents, and that the ties that bind are laced with Spanish inflections. Proponents of initiatives similar to Proposition 227 in California do not take into account this kind of organic language ideology—that is, an ideology that touches the practical and the everyday. For children who are English learners, there is no pedagogical reason for a their first language to be erased so that they can learn a second language, and it is sound practice to build on their existing "funds of linguistic knowledge" (Smith 2000). Indeed, as Secretary of Education Richard W. Riley recently (March 15, 2000) affirmed:

> It is high time we begin to treat language skills as the asset they are, particularly in this global economy. Anything that encourages a person to know more than one language is positive—and should be treated as such . . .
>
> But whatever the approach to teaching English, it cannot be simply a defensive or reactive one. If we see to it that immigrants and their children can speak only English and nothing more—then we will have missed one of the greatest opportunities of this new century, namely, to take advantage of the invaluable asset that helps define a culture.
>
> Our nation can only grow stronger if all our children grow up learning two languages. The early school years are the best and

easiest time for children to learn language . . . I can assure you that when they enter the workforce in several years we will regret the inability of our children to speak two languages. Our global economy demands it; our children deserve it. (Riley 2000)

This positive affirmation of the necessity for bilingualism and biliteracy, or for multilingualism and multiliteracy, acknowledges language issues as a necessary component for preparing the citizens of the future. Yet there are other reasons to foreground language other than the global economy. Language as symbolic of selfhood and of an "imagined" community can be read as a marker of identity, the diacritica that both marks membership and resists the marking of the language. For children in the borderlands, the process of becoming Latino is necessarily diverse and nonlinear. We must be wary of theoretical postures that reduce the complexity of Latino experiences or that assume that market value is the only worth of a language. But we must also be aware that ideologies of languages and social practices are mutually constitutive and that children both enact and resist social relations in their language use within a discursive field that is neither unified nor fixed.

In some ways, it might be said that some of the mothers and children described in this study are on their way to complete assimilation: that the mothers may stand, in the traditional metaphor, with one foot on each side of the border, but that the children are firmly planted on the U.S. side. By adopting the metaphor of the borderlands, I have tried to show that both culture and the border are more mythologized than real and that the borderlands trope goes beyond a spatiotemporal referent. Hybridity, in one sense or another, is ubiquitous in our postmodern condition, as we draw and distill from multiple knowledge bases. These mothers and children, then, are no different than other social actors who mediate between "structure" and "agency." Regarding the tension between "structure" and "agency," I have tried to illustrate that they are not fixed polarities, but rather that a mutually constructed interplay of links exists between the two. In the swirls and scaffolding of the dialogical staircase, the interactional double helix, we can apprehend the deconstruction of oppositions and the dialectical relations between received past and emergent present.

Yet in the shifting landscapes of "repertoires of identity," not all possibilities are open to us. As much as we may "choose" to construct ourselves as white and middle class, dominant discourses preclude, for instance, a young man of color entering certain shops without being regarded with suspicion. As much as Mexican-origin children may adapt to the admitted essentialization of middle-American family values, their very "looks" define the attention/disattention given to them. Disattention may be even more pernicious than negative attention. Within malls and supermarkets, the averted eye contact and other subtle paralinguistic cues that index a lack of affinity are not overt and easily dismissed. Their cumulative effect, however, is the erasure of personhood. The oohing and aahing over babies in the street is not often lavished on children of color. It is the blond, blue-eyed baby who catches the eye, elicits the comments, receives the approving nods. For impressionable children, the disattention is part of the construction of minority status. Our mutual interaction, at times couched only in paralinguistic nuances, is a constant source of sensory and extrasensory stimuli, creating and re-creating, affirming and disaffirming our identities.

Unfortunately, the wrong kind of attention can be just as pernicious. As I write these words, there plays out in the local scene an incident that encapsulates how certain identities are *created for* minority youth. In April 2000, a middle school teacher claimed to have been shot by a "young Hispanic male with a shaved head." Because of the fear of school violence, parents and students were stunned and shocked. The next day, it was revealed that the teacher had shot herself and had invented the description of the shooter. One Hispanic mother told the *Arizona Daily Star* that she has a daughter who attends the school and also a son who fits the given description. "If my son would have gone to pick up my daughter at school yesterday, he would have been in jail" (Duarte 2000:A15). We shape and are shaped by these discourses, for good or ill.

Yet these discourses do not spring from nowhere. In the same time frame, the *Tucson Citizen* reported on the "Corridor of Fear" along Sixth Avenue, the main street of the south side of Tucson. "At least eighteen people have been shot to death and dozens wounded along South Sixth since 1995, records show" (Teibel and Cieslak 2000:A1). The article reported that shots are fired routinely, every night, and that residents are afraid to venture out after dark. An editorial cartoon that appeared the next day depicts the gathering of a working-class Mexican family, with children ready to hit a piñata; the family disgustedly looks on as one youngster tries to shoot the piñata with a gun, while the mother laments, "This is *not* the southside I grew up in" (Fitzsimmons 2000:B6). Bonnie Henry, a local newspaper columnist who grew up on the southside, describes the avenue that I myself remember:

> For years we chugged up and down South Sixth Avenue packed inside those hot, dusty buses on the Old Pueblo line.
>
> Past the Veterans Hospital where my aunt used to work.
>
> Past the Safeway, where my mom and grandma shopped every Friday night. . . .
>
> Past Santa Cruz Catholic Church, where half the passengers in the bus—old ladies dressed all in black—would make the sign of the cross. . . .
>
> Count 'em and weep. Seventeen people have been shot to death along South Sixth Avenue in the last five years. . . .
>
> What have you done to my street? (Henry 2000:B1)

Early on in this book, I bemoaned the pain of gangs and drugs and violence, begging the question "Why?" Why are our kids killing each other, and why do parents shake their heads in stunned disbelief? No, I do not have the *one* answer. But I do believe that we do not need to know or understand the causes before we can actively engage a problem. Although I began this study with a faith in the healing power of theory, I found that grand theories are inadequate to explain the contradictions of our daily lives. Although theory can inform practice, I believe that it is just as important that practice inform theory. How can we find what works and then theorize about why it has worked? As Saul Schanberg's grandmother suggests at the beginning of this chapter, why must we spend years of study to discover something that is so basic, so human? What is important is connection with children, with young people, with their lives, and what matters to them. We must understand they are multidimensional beings, formed and being formed within contexts of discourses and histories. What we should be about is big people helping little people to become big people, theorizing the practices that nurture and support.

However, although language and discursive practices are imbued with a powerful creative force, they do not imprison us within their confines, simply because we have the same potent arms at our disposal: words. Counterdiscourses, counterstories, contestations as well as resistance and accommodations are ever in process and ever shifting, and children must hear these stories. They must know that their repertoire of identities includes identities as mathematicians, as scientists, as engineers, as professionals, and as laborers, mothers, and fathers engaged in productive citizenry. We can create these discourses.

I end by reiterating the power of the word that Gabriel García Márquez affirms: "humankind will enter the third millennium under the sway of words."

Notes

Chapter 1

1. Fregoso (1993:65) cites a paper by James Clifford, "Borders/Diaspora" presented at the "Borders/Diaspora" conference, University of California, Santa Cruz, April 1992, as the source for the phrase "paradigm of transcultural experience."

2. The chupacabras, the goat bloodsucker that is said to leave a trail of carcasses in its wake, received a good deal of media coverage on Spanish-language television stations and was a popular image among children for a time.

Chapter 3

Author's note: Portions of chapter 3 and chapter 4 appear in Norma González, "Blurred Voices: Who Speaks for the Subaltern?" in *On Becoming a Language Educator,* edited by Chris Casanave and Sandra Schecter, 75–83 (Mahwah, N.J.: Lawrence Erlbaum, 1997).

Chapter 4

1. I admit to a bias in highlighting this particular group because my two youngest daughters played in the Mariachi Aguilitas.

Chapter 5

Author's note: Portions of this chapter were previously published in Norma González, "Contestation and Accommodation in Parental Narratives," *Education and Urban Society* 29 (1) (1996): 54–70.

1. "Legal Alien" by Pat Mora is reprinted with permission from the publisher of *Chants* (Houston: Arte Público, University of Houston, 1984).

Chapter 6

1. La Paloma is an exclusive resort hotel.

Chapter 8

Author's note: Portions of this chapter were previously published in Norma González, "What Will We Do When Culture Does Not Exist Anymore?" Special anniversary issue, "Reflections on the Future Work of Anthropology and Education," *Anthropology and Education Quarterly* 30 (4) (1999): 431–35.

References

Abu-Lughod, Lila. 1990. "The Romance of Resistance: Tracing Transformations of Power through Bedouin Women." *American Ethnologist* 17 (1): 41–55.

——. 1991. "Writing against Culture." In *Recapturing Anthropology: Working in the Present,* edited by R. G. Fox, 137–62. Santa Fe: School of American Research Press.

Abu-Lughod, Lila, and Catherine Lutz. 1990. "Introduction: Emotion, Discourse, and the Politics of Everyday Life." In *Language and the Politics of Emotion,* edited by L. Abu-Lughod and C. Lutz, 1–23. Cambridge: Cambridge University Press.

Allende, Isabel. 1985. *The House of the Spirits.* New York: A. A. Knopf.

Alvarez, Robert R., Jr. 1995. "The Mexican–U.S. Border: The Making of an Anthropology of Borderlands." *Annual Review of Anthropology* 24: 447–70.

Anderson, Benedict. 1983. *Imagined Communities: Reflections on the Origin and Spread of Nationalism.* London and New York: Verso.

Andrade, Rosi A. C., and Luis C. Moll. 1993. "The Social Worlds of Children: An Emic View." *Journal of the Society for Accelerative Learning and Teaching* 18 (1–2): 81–125.

Annerino, John. 1999. *Dead in Their Tracks: Crossing America's Desert Borderlands.* New York: Four Walls Eight Windows.

Anzaldúa, Gloria. 1987. *Borderlands/La frontera: The New Mestiza.* San Francisco: Spinsters, Aunt Lute.

Associated Press. 1997. "Mexican-Americans Often at Odds with the New Immigrants." *Arizona Daily Star,* April 20, B7.

Baca Zinn, Maxine, and Bonnie Thornton Dill. 1994. *Women of Color in U.S. Society.* Philadelphia: Temple University Press.

Bakhtin, Mikhail. 1981. *The Dialogic Imagination.* Translated by C. Emerson and M. Holquist. Austin: University of Texas Press.

——. 1984. *Problems of Dostoevsky's Poetics.* Vol. 8. Translated by Caryl Emerson. Minneapolis: University of Minnesota Press.

Bannon, John Francis. 1976. *The Spanish Borderlands Frontier 1513–1821.* 1963. Reprint. Albuquerque: University of New Mexico Press.

Barth, Frederik, ed. 1969. *Ethnic Groups and Boundaries.* Boston: Little and Brown.

Behar, Ruth. 1993. "Women Writing Culture: Another Telling of the Story of American Anthropology." *Critique of Anthropology* 13 (4): 307–25.

Berger, Joseph. 1988. "Baby Talk Proves to Be Instructive." *Arizona Daily Star,* June 10, D1, D11.

Besnier, Niko. 1990. "Language and Affect." *Annual Review of Anthropology* 19: 419–51.

Bhabha, Homi K. 1994. *The Location of Culture.* London and New York: Routledge.

Bloom, Lois. 1973. *One Word at a Time.* The Hague: Mouton.

Bodine, Ann. 1975. "Androcentrism in Prescriptive Grammar." *Language in Society* 4: 129–46.

Borofsky, Robert, ed. 1994. *Assessing Cultural Anthropology.* New York: McGraw-Hill.

Bourdieu, Pierre. 1977a. "The Economics of Linguistic Exchange." *Social Science Information* 16 (6): 645–68.

——. 1977b. *Outline of a Theory of Practice.* Cambridge: Cambridge University Press.

Brown, Penelope, and Stephen Levinson. 1978. "Universals in Language Usage: Politeness Phenomena." In *Questions and Politeness: Strategies in Social Interaction,* edited by E. N. Goody, 56–289. Cambridge: Cambridge University Press.

Bruner, Jerome S. 1985. *Child's Talk.* New York: W. W. Norton.

Buran, Dorothy. 2000. "Bilingualism a Bad Idea." *Arizona Daily Star,* March 24, A18.

Buriel, Raymond. 1975. "Cognitive Styles among Three Generations of Mexican-American Children." *Journal of Cross-Cultural Psychiatry* 6: 417–29.

——. 1987. *Academic Performance of Foreign- and Native-Born Mexican Americans: A Comparison of First-, Second-, and Third-Generation Students and Parents.* Report to the Inter-University Program (IUP) for Latino Research, Social Science Research Council. New York: Social Science Research Council.

Calderón, Héctor, and José D. Saldivar, eds. 1991. *Criticism in the Borderlands: Studies in Chicano Literature, Culture, and Ideology.* Durham, N.C.: Duke University Press.

Cameron, Deborah. 1990. *The Feminist Critique of Language: A Reader.* London: Routledge.

Cheek, Lawrence. 1989. "Tucson's Dirty Little Secret: Our Love/Hate Relationship with Mexican Culture." *City Magazine* (February): 34–43.

Clancy, Patricia. 1986. "The Acquisition of Communicative Style in Japanese." In *Language Socialization across Cultures,* edited by B. Schieffelin and E. Ochs, 212–50. Cambridge: Cambridge University Press.

Coleman, James. 1991. *Parental Involvement in Education.* Washington, D.C.: U.S. Department of Education. U.S. Government Printing Office.

Collier, Jane, and Sylvia Yanagisako. 1989. "Theory in Anthropology Since Feminist Practice." *Critique of Anthropology* 9 (2): 27–37.

Colson, Elizabeth. 1984. "The Reordering of Experience: Anthropological Involvement with Time." *Journal of Anthropological Research* 40: 1–13.

Davidson, Ann Locke. 1996. *Making and Molding Identity in Schools.* Albany: State University of New York Press.

Dobson, James. 1970. *Dare to Discipline.* Wheaton, Ill.: Tyndale House.

Donnan, Hastings, and Thomas M. Wilson. 1999. *Borders: Frontiers of Identity, Nation, and State.* Oxford: Berg.

Duarte, Carmen. 2000. "Teacher's Blaming of 'Hispanic' Stirs Anger." *Arizona Daily Star,* April 12, A15.

Eagleton, Terry. 1990. *The Significance of Theory.* Oxford: Basil Blackwell.

Eisenberg, Ann. 1986. "Teasing: Verbal Play in Two Mexicano Homes." In *Language Socialization across Cultures,* edited by B. Schieffelin and E. Ochs, 182–98. Cambridge: Cambridge University Press.

Ekman, Paul, Wallace Friesen, and Phoebe Ellsworth. 1982. "What Are the Similarities and Differences in Facial Behavior across Cultures?" In *Emotion in the Human Face,* 2d ed., edited by P. Ekman, 128–43. Cambridge: Cambridge University Press.

Erickson, Jim. 1997. "City's Ethnic Barriers Carved into the Landscape, Experts Say." *Arizona Daily Star,* January 30, A1.

Feinberg, Walter. 1998. *Common Schools/Uncommon Identities: National Unity and Cultural Difference.* New Haven: Yale University Press.

Fischer, Kurt W., Phillips R. Shaver, and Peter Carnochan. 1990. "How Emotions Develop and How They Organize Development." *Cognition and Emotion* 4 (2): 81–127.

Fishman, Joshua, ed. 1999. *Handbook of Language and Ethnic Identity.* Oxford: Oxford University Press.

Fishman, Pamela M. 1978. "The Work Women Do." *Social Problems* 25: 397–406.

Fitzsimmons, David. 1996. "Wheel of Misfortune" (cartoon). *Arizona Daily Star,* March 14, A12.

———. 2000. Untitled cartoon. *Arizona Daily Star,* April 26, B6.

Florio-Ruane, Susan. 1997. "To Tell a New Story: Reinventing Narratives of

Culture, Identity, and Education." *Anthropology and Education Quarterly* 28 (2): 152–62.

Floyd-Tenery, Martha. 1993. "Looking Inside la Casa: Transformation of the Teaching and Learning Context." Ph.D. diss., University of Arizona.

Foley, Douglas. 1991. "Reconsidering Anthropological Explanations of Ethnic School Failure." *Anthropology and Education Quarterly* 22 (1): 60–86.

Foucault, Michel. 1970. *The Order of Things: An Archaeology of the Human Sciences.* New York: Pantheon.

———. 1972. *The Archaeology of Knowledge and the Discourse on Language.* New York: Pantheon.

———. 1978. *The History of Sexuality.* Vol. 1. New York: Random House.

———. 1980. *Power/Knowledge: Selected Interviews and Other Writings 1972–1977.* Brighton, Sussex: Harvester.

Fox, Geoffrey. 1996. *Hispanic Nation: Culture, Politics, and the Constructing of Identity.* Secaucus, N.J.: Carol.

Fox, Richard. 1995. "Editorial: The Breakdown of Culture." *Current Anthropology* 36 (1): 1–11.

Fregoso, Rosa Linda. 1993. *The Bronze Screen: Chicana and Chicano Film Culture.* Minneapolis: University of Minnesota Press.

Frijda, Nico H. 1986. *The Emotions.* Cambridge: Cambridge University Press.

Gal, Susan. 1987. "Codeswitching and Consciousness on the European Periphery." *American Ethnologist* 14 (4): 637–53.

García Márquez, Gabriel. 1997. "Power of the Word." *Arizona Daily Star,* August 10, E2. Originally published in the *New York Times.*

Gecas, Víctor. 1979. "The Influence of Social Class on Socialization." In *Contemporary Theories about the Family: Research-Based Theories,* vol. 1, edited by W. R. Burr, R. Hill, F. I. Nye, and I. L. Reiss, 365–404. New York: Free Press.

Giles, Howard. 1979. "Ethnicity Markers in Speech." In *Social Markers in Speech,* edited by K. Scherer and H. Giles, 251–89. Cambridge: Cambridge University Press.

Gleason, Jean Berko. 1987. "Sex Differences in Parent-Child Interaction." In *Language, Gender, and Sex in Comparative Perspective,* edited by S. Philips, S. Steele, and C. Tanz, 189–99. Studies in the Social and Cultural Foundations of Language, no. 4. Cambridge: Cambridge University Press.

Goldenberg, Claude, and Ronald Gallimore. 1995. "Immigrant Latino Parents' Values and Beliefs about Their Children's Education: Continuities and Discontinuities across Cultures and Generations." *Advances in Motivation and Achievement* 9: 183–228.

Gómez-Peña, Guillermo. 1986. *Border Culture: A Process of Negotiation toward*

Utopia, La Línea Quebrada = The Broken Line. Tijuana and San Diego: Centro Cultural de La Raza.

González, Norma. 1992. "Child Language Socialization." Ph.D. diss., University of Arizona.

———. 1995. "Processual Approaches to Multicultural Education." *Journal of Applied Behavioral Science* 31 (2): 234–44.

———. 1996. "Contestation and Accommodation in Parental Narratives." *Education and Urban Society* 29 (1): 54–70.

———. 1997. "Blurred Voices: Who Speaks for the Subaltern?" In *On Becoming a Language Educator,* edited by C. Casanave and S. Schecter, 75–83. Mahwah, N.J.: Lawrence Erlbaum.

———. 1999. "What Will We Do When Culture Does Not Exist Anymore?" Special anniversary issue, "Reflections on the Future Work of Anthropology and Education." *Anthropology and Education Quarterly* 30 (4): 431–35.

———. 2000. "The Funds of Knowledge for Teaching Project." In *Classics of Practicing Anthropology 1978–1998,* edited by P. J. Higgins and J. A. Paredes, 247–54. Oklahoma City: Society for Applied Anthropology.

González, Norma, and Cathy Amanti. 1997. "Teaching Anthropological Methods to Teachers: The Transformation of Knowledge." In *The Teaching of Anthropology: Problems, Issues, and Decisions,* edited by C. Kottak, J. White, R. Furlow, and P. Rice, 353–59. Mountain View, Calif.: Mayfield.

González, Norma, Luis C. Moll, Martha Floyd-Tenery, Anna Rivera, Patricia Rendón, Raquel Gonzales, and Cathy Amanti. 1995. "Funds of Knowledge for Teaching in Latino Households." *Urban Education* 29 (4): 443–70.

Goodenough, Ward. 1971. *Culture, Language, and Society.* Reading, Mass:: Addison-Wesley.

Goodwin, Marjorie Harness. 1990. *He-Said-She-Said: Talk as Social Organization among Black Children.* Bloomington: Indiana University Press.

———. 1997. "Children's Linguistic and Social Worlds." *Anthropology Newsletter* 38, no. 4 (April): 1, 4–5.

Gupta, Akhil, and James Ferguson. 1992. "Beyond 'Culture': Space, Identity, and the Politics of Difference." *Cultural Anthropology* 7 (1): 6–23.

Harris, Christine. 1995. "Culture Shock: Is Diversity Training Really Curbing Bias?" *Federal Times,* January 23, 1, 12–13.

Heath, Shirley Brice. 1983. *Ways with Words.* New York: Cambridge University Press.

Heller, Celia Stopnicka. 1968. *Mexican-American Youth: Forgotten Youth at the Crossroads.* New York: Random House.

Henry, Bonnie. 2000. "'50s South Sixth Safe and Sane." *Arizona Daily Star,* April 30, B1.

Heyman, Josiah M. 1994. "The Mexico–United States Border in Anthropology: A Critique and Reformulation." *Journal of Political Ecology* 1: 43–65.

Hill, Jane H. 1985. "The Grammar of Consciousness and the Consciousness of Grammar." *American Ethnologist* 12 (4): 725–37.

———. 1993a. "Hasta la Vista, Baby: Anglo Spanish in the American Southwest." *Critique of Anthropology* 13 (2): 145–76.

———. 1993b. "Is It Really 'No Problemo'?" *Texas Linguistic Forum* 33: 1–12.

———. 1995. "Mock Spanish: A Site for the Indexical Reproduction of Racism in American English." University of Chicago Lang-cult-Site, http://www.cs.uchicago.edu/discussions/l-c.

———. 1998. "Language, Race, and White Public Space." *American Anthropologist* 100 (3): 680–89.

Hoffman, Eva. 1989. *Lost in Translation: A Life in a New Language.* New York: E. P. Dutton.

Holland, Dorothy, William Lachicotte Jr., Debra Skinner, and Carole Cain. 1998. *Identity and Agency in Cultural Worlds.* Cambridge, Mass.: Harvard University Press.

hooks, bell. 1994. *Teaching to Transgress: Education as the Practice of Freedom.* New York: Routledge.

Horsman, Mathew, and Andrew Marshall. 1995. *After the Nation-State: Citizens, Tribalism, and the New World Disorder.* London: HarperCollins.

Irvine, Judith. 1996. "Language and Community: Introduction." *Journal of Linguistic Anthropology* 6 (2): 123–25.

Izard, Carroll E. 1977. *Human Emotions.* New York: Plenum.

Keesing, Roger M. 1994. "Theories of Culture Revisited." In *Assessing Cultural Anthropology,* edited by R. Borofsky, 301–10. New York: McGraw-Hill.

KGUN News at 10:00. 1999. Interview with Steven Holmes. Tucson, Arizona, March 19.

Krashen, Steven. 1981. *Second Language Acquisition and Second Language Learning.* New York: Pergamon.

Kroskrity, Paul V. 1993. *Language, History, and Identity: Ethnolinguistic Studies of the Arizona Tewa.* Tucson: University of Arizona Press.

Lakoff, Robin. 1975. *Language and Woman's Place.* New York: Harper and Row.

Leavitt, John. 1996. "Meaning and Feeling in the Anthropology of Emotions." *American Ethnologist* 23 (3): 514–39.

LeDoux, Joseph E. 1996. *The Emotional Brain: The Mysterious Underpinnings of Emotional Life.* New York: Simon and Schuster.

Levinson, Bradley A., and Dorothy Holland. 1996. "The Cultural Production of the Educated Person: An Introduction." In *The Cultural Production of the Educated Person,* edited by B. A. Levinson, D. E. Foley, and D. Holland, 1–54. Albany: State University of New York Press.

Limón, José E. 1991. "Representation, Ethnicity, and the Precursory Ethnography: Notes of a Native Anthropologist." In *Recapturing Anthropology: Working in the Present,* edited by R. G. Fox, 115–35. Santa Fe: School of American Research Press.

López, Enrique Hank. 1971. "Back to Bachimba." In *The Chicanos,* edited by E. Ludwig and J. Santibañez, 261–79. Baltimore: Penguin.

Luke, Allan. 1995/1996. "Text and Discourse in Education: An Introduction to Critical Discourse Analysis." In *Review of Research in Education,* vol. 21, edited by M. W. Apple, 3–48. Washington, D.C.: American Educational Research Association.

Lutz, Catherine, and Geoffrey White. 1986. "The Anthropology of Emotions." *Annual Review of Anthropology* 15: 405–36.

Madsen, William. 1964. *The Mexican-Americans of South Texas.* New York: Holt, Rinehart, and Winston.

Marcus, George E., and Michael Fischer. 1986. *Anthropology as Cultural Critique: An Experimental Moment in the Human Sciences.* Chicago: University of Chicago Press.

Markus, Hazel Rose, and Shinobu Kitamaya. 1994. "The Cultural Construction of Self and Emotion: Implications for Social Behavior." In *Emotion and Culture: Empirical Studies of Mutual Influence,* edited by S. Kitamaya and H. R. Markus, 89–130. Washington, D.C.: American Psychological Association.

Martínez, Oscar J. 1991. *Troublesome Border.* Tucson: University of Arizona Press.

Martyna, Wendy. 1983. "Beyond the He/Man Approach: The Case for Nonsexist Language." In *Language, Gender, and Society,* edited by B. Thorne, C. Kramarae, and N. Henley, 25–37. Rowley, Mass.: Newbury House.

Matute-Bianchi, María Eugenia. 1991. "Situational Ethnicity and Patterns of School Performance among Immigrant and Nonimmigrant Mexican-Descent Students." In *Minority Status and Schooling: A Comparative Study of Immigrant and Involuntary Minorities,* edited by M. A. Gibson and J. U. Ogbu, 205–47. New York: Garland.

McLaren, Peter, and Tomaz Tadeu da Silva. 1993. "Decentering Pedagogy: Critical Literacy, Resistance, and the Politics of Memory." In *Paulo Freire: A Critical Encounter,* edited by P. McLaren and P. Leonard, 47–89. London: Routledge.

McLaughlin, Daniel, and William G. Tierney. 1993. *Naming Silenced Lives: Personal Narratives and the Processes of Educational Change.* New York: Routledge.

Mehan, Hugh. 1979. *Learning Lessons: Social Organization in the Classroom.* Cambridge, Mass.: Harvard University Press.

———. 1982. "The Structure of Classroom Events and Their Consequences for

Student Performance." In *Ethnography and Education,* edited by P. Gilmore and A. A. Glatthorn, 59–87. Washington, D.C.: Center for Applied Linguistics.

Mendoza, Mónica. 1996. "U.S.–Born Latinos Feel Tug to Learn Spanish." *Arizona Daily Star,* September 8, B1.

Mendoza-Denton, Norma. 1999. "Sociolinguistics and Linguistic Anthropology of U.S. Latinos." *Annual Review of Anthropology* 28: 375–95.

Messing, Jacqueline. 1995. "The Simultaneity of Experience: Multiple Identities and Symbolic Uses of Language among Mexican-Americans." M.A. thesis, University of Arizona.

Miguélez, Armando. 1983. "El Teatro Carmen (1915–1923): Centro del Arte Escénico Hispano en Tucson." *Revista Chicano Riqueña* 11 (1): 53–67.

Miller, Peggy. 1986. "Teasing as Language Socialization and Verbal Play in a White Working-Class Community." In *Language Socialization across Cultures,* edited by B. Schieffelin and E. Ochs, 199–212. Cambridge: Cambridge University Press.

Moll, Luis C. 1992. "Bilingual Classrooms and Community Analysis: Some Recent Trends." *Educational Researcher* 21 (2): 20–24.

Moll, Luis C., Cathy Amanti, Deborah Neff, and Norma González. 1992. "Funds of Knowledge for Teaching: A Qualitative Approach to Developing Strategic Connections between Homes and Classrooms." *Theory into Practice* 31 (2): 132–41.

Moll, Luis C., and Norma González. 1994. "Lessons from Research with Language Minority Children." *Journal of Reading Behavior* 26 (4): 439–56.

———. 1997. "Teachers as Social Scientists: Learning about Culture from Household Research." In *Race, Ethnicity, and Multiculturalism,* edited by P. M. Hall, 89–114. New York: Garland.

Moore, Sally Falk. 1987. "Explaining the Present: Theoretical Dilemmas in Processual Ethnography." *American Ethnologist* 14 (4): 727–36.

Mora, Pat. 1984. *Chants.* Houston: Arte Público, University of Houston.

Morrison, Toni. 1994. *Lecture and Speech of Acceptance, upon the Award of the Nobel Prize for Literature in Stockholm 1993.* New York: Knopf.

Myerhoff, Barbara. 1978. *Number Our Days.* New York: Touchstone.

Ochs, Elinor. 1986a. "From Feelings to Grammar: A Samoan Case Study." In *Language Socialization across Cultures,* edited by B. Schieffelin and E. Ochs, 251–72. Cambridge: Cambridge University Press.

———. 1986b. "Introduction." In *Language Socialization across Cultures,* edited by B. Schieffelin and E. Ochs, 1–13. Cambridge: Cambridge University Press.

———. 1996. "Linguistic Resources for Socializing Humanity." In *Rethinking Linguistic Relativity,* edited by J. J. Gumperz and S. C. Levinson, 407–37. Cambridge: Cambridge University Press.

Ochs, Elinor, and Bambi Schieffelin. 1984. "Language Acquisition and Social-ization: Three Developmental Stories and Their Implications." In *Culture Theory: Essays on Mind, Self, and Emotion,* edited by R. A. Shweder and R. LeVine, 276–322. Cambridge: Cambridge University Press.

———. 1989. "Language Has a Heart." *Text* 9 (1): 7–25.

Ochs, Elinor, and Carolyn Taylor. 1992. "Mother's Role in the Everyday Recon-struction of 'Father Knows Best.'" In *Locating Power: Proceedings of the Second Berkeley Women and Language Conference,* edited by Kira Hall, Mary Buchholz, and Birch Moonwoman, 447–62. Berkeley: Berkeley Women and Language Group, University of California.

Ochs, Elinor, Carolyn Taylor, Dina Rudolf, and Ruth Smith. 1992. "Story-Telling as a Theory-Building Activity." *Discourse Processes* 15 (1): 37–72.

Ogbu, John. 1978. *Minority Education and Caste: The American System in Cross-Cultural Perspective.* New York: Academic.

———. 1981. "School Ethnography: A Multi-Level Approach." *Anthropology and Education Quarterly* 12 (1): 3–20.

———. 1987. "Variability in Minority School Performance: A Problem in Search of an Explanation." *Anthropology and Education Quarterly* 18 (4): 312–34.

Ogbu, John, and M. E. Matute-Bianchi. 1986. "Understanding Sociocultural Factors: Knowledge, Identity, and School Adjustment." In *Beyond Lan-guage: Social and Cultural Factors in Schooling Language Minority Students,* 73–142. Los Angeles: Evaluation, Dissemination, and Assessment Center, California State Department of Education.

Pattanayak, Debi P. 1986. "Educational Use of the Mother Tongue." In *Lan-guage and Education in Multilingual Settings,* vol. 25, edited by B. Spolsky, 5–15. Clevedon, England: Multilingual Matters.

Paz, Octavio. 1961. *The Labyrinth of Solitude: Life and Thought in Mexico.* New York: Grove.

Pence, Angélica. 1996. "Friend: Oscar 'Shouldn't Have Died.'" *Arizona Daily Star,* July 31, B1.

Philips, Susan U. 1987. "Part I: Introduction." In *Language, Gender, and Sex in Comparative Perspectives,* edited by S. U. Philips, S. Steele, and C. Tanz, 15–25. Cambridge: Cambridge University Press.

———. 1993. *The Invisible Culture: Communication in Classroom and Community on the Warm Springs Indian Reservation.* 1983. Reprint. New York: Longman.

Philips, Susan U., Susan Steele, and Christine Tanz, eds. 1987. *Language, Gen-der, and Sex in Comparative Perspective.* Cambridge: Cambridge University Press.

Pinker, Steven. 1995. *The Language Instinct.* New York: Harper Perennial.

Poyer, Lin. 1988. "Maintaining 'Otherness': Sapwuahfik Cultural Identity." *American Ethnologist* 15 (3): 472–85.

Pratt, Mary Louise. 1987. "Linguistic Utopias." In *The Linguistics of Writing: Arguments between Language and Literature,* edited by N. Fabb, D. Attridge, A. Duranti, and C. McCabe, 48–66. Manchester: Manchester University Press.

Preciado Martín, Patricia. 1983. *Images and Conversations: Mexican Americans Recall a Southwestern Past.* Tucson: University of Arizona Press.

Reese, Leslie, Silvia Balzano, Ronald Gallimore, and Claude Goldenberg. 1995. "The Concept of 'Educación': Latino Family Values and American Schooling." *International Journal of International Research* 23 (1): 57–81.

Riley, Richard. 2000. "Excelencia para todos—Excellence for All: The Progress of Hispanic Education and the Challenges of a New Century." On-line at http://www.ed.gov/Speeches/03-2000/000315.html.

Romano, Octavio. 1968. "The Anthropology and Sociology of the Mexican-Americans: The Distortion of the Mexican-American History." *El Grito* 2: 13–26.

Roosens, Eugeen. 1989. *Creating Ethnicity: The Process of Ethnogenesis.* Vol. 5. Newbury Park, Calif.: Sage.

Rosaldo, Renato. 1989. *Culture and Truth: The Remaking of Social Analysis.* Boston: Beacon.

———. 1994. "Cultural Citizenship and Educational Democracy." *Cultural Anthropology* 9 (3): 402–11.

Sachs, Jacqueline. 1987. "Preschool Boys' and Girls' Language Use in Pretend Play." In *Language, Gender, and Sex in Comparative Perspective,* edited by S. U. Philips, S. Steele, and C. Tanz, 178–88. New York: Cambridge University Press.

Sapir, Edward. 1915. *A Sketch of the Social Organization of the Nass River Indians.* Ottawa: Government Printing Office.

Schieffelin, Bambi B. 1990. *The Give and Take of Everyday Life: Language Socialization of Kaluli Children.* Cambridge: Cambridge University Press.

Schieffelin, Bambi, and Elinor Ochs. 1986a. "Language Socialization." *Annual Review of Anthropology* 15: 163–91.

———, eds. 1986b. *Language Socialization across Cultures.* Cambridge: Cambridge University Press.

Schlesinger, Arthur Meier. 1992. *The Disuniting of America.* New York: W. W. Norton.

Schulz, Muriel. 1975. "The Semantic Derogation of Women." In *Language and Sex: Difference and Dominance,* edited by B. Thorne and N. Henley, 64–75. Rowley, Mass.: Newbury House.

Sheridan, Thomas. 1986. *Los Tucsonenses: The Mexican Community in Tucson, 1854–1941.* Tucson: University of Arizona Press.

Skutnabb-Kangas, Tove. 1988. "Multilingualism and the Education of Minority Children." In *Minority Education: From Shame to Struggle,* edited by T. Skutnabb-Kangas and J. Cummins, 9–44. Clevedon, England: Multilingual Matters.

Smith, Patrick H. 2000. "Community as Resource for Minority Language Learning: A Case Study of Spanish-English Dual Language Schooling." Ph.D. diss., University of Arizona.

Stanton-Salazar, Ricardo D. 1997. "A Social Capital Framework for Understanding the Socialization of Racial Minority Children and Youths." *Harvard Educational Review* 67 (1): 1–40.

Stellar, Tim. 2000. "Changing Face of Tucson: It's More Hispanic." *Arizona Daily Star,* January 2, A1 and A12.

Suárez-Orozco, Marcelo. 1991. "Hispanic Immigrant Adaptation to Schooling." In *Minority Status and Schooling: A Comparative Study of Immigrant and Involuntary Minorities,* edited by M. A. Gibson and J. U. Ogbu, 37–61. New York: Garland.

Tannen, Deborah. 1990. *You Just Don't Understand: Women and Men in Conversation.* New York: Ballantine.

Tapia, Javier. 1991. "Cultural Reproduction: Funds of Knowledge as Survival Strategies in the Mexican American Communities." Ph.D. diss., University of Arizona.

———. 2000. "Schooling and Learning in U.S.–Mexican Families: A Case Study of Households." *Urban Review* 32 (1): 25–44.

Teibel, David L., and David J. Cieslak. 2000. "Corridor of Fear: Gunfire along South 6th Ave. Common." *Tucson Citizen,* April 25, A1.

Tharp, Roland, and Roland Gallimore. 1988. *Rousing Minds to Life: Teaching, Learning, and Schooling in Social Context.* Cambridge: Cambridge University Press.

Thorne, Barrie, Cheris Kramarae, and Nancy Henley, eds. 1983. *Language, Gender, and Society.* Rowley, Mass.: Newbury House.

Unz, Ron. 1997. "Bilingualism vs. Bilingual Education." *Los Angeles Times,* October 19, M6.

Urciuoli, Bonnie. 1995. "Language and Borders." *Annual Review of Anthropology* 24: 525–46.

———. 1996. *Exposing Prejudice: Puerto Rican Experiences of Language, Race, and Class.* Boulder, Colo.: Westview.

Valdés, Guadalupe. 1996. *Con respeto: Bridging the Distances between Culturally Diverse Families and Schools.* New York: Teacher College Press.

Valenzuela, Angela. 1999. *Subtractive Schooling: U.S.–Mexican Youth and the Politics of Caring.* Albany: State University of New York Press.

Van Boven, Sarah. 1997. "Giving Infants a Helping Hand." *Newsweek,* special issue (spring–summer): 45.

Vásquez, Olga, Lucinda Pease-Alvarez, and Sheila Shannon. 1994. *Pushing Boundaries: Language and Culture in a Mexicano Community.* Cambridge: Cambridge University Press.

Vayda, Andrew P. 1994. "Actions, Variations, and Change: The Emerging Anti-Essentialist View in Anthropology." In *Assessing Cultural Anthropology,* edited by R. Borofsky, 320–30. New York: McGraw-Hill.

Vélez-Ibáñez, Carlos G. 1988. "Networks of Exchange among Mexicans in the U.S. and Mexico: Local Level Mediating Responses to National and International Transformations." *Urban Anthropology and the Study of Cultural Systems in World Economic Development* 17 (1): 27–51.

———. 1996. *Border Visions: Mexican Cultures of the Southwest United States.* Tucson: University of Arizona Press.

Vélez-Ibáñez, Carlos G., and James B. Greenberg. 1992. "Formation and Transformation of Funds of Knowledge among U.S. Mexican Households." *Anthropology and Education Quarterly* 23 (4): 313–35.

Vigil, James Diego, and John M. Long. 1981. "Unidirectional or Nativist Acculturation—Chicano Paths to School Achievement." *Human Organization* 40 (3): 273–77.

Vygotsky, Lev S. 1978. *Mind in Society: The Development of Higher Psychological Process.* Cambridge, Mass.: Harvard University Press.

Wald-Hopkins, Christine. 1990. "Our Need to Belong Is Frustrated by Who We Are." *Arizona Daily Star,* September 4, A11.

Warner, W. Lloyd. 1961. *The Family of God: A Symbolic Study of Christian Life in America.* New Haven: Yale University Press.

Weedon, Chris. 1987. *Feminist Practice and Poststructuralist Theory.* Oxford: Basil Blackwell.

West, Candace, and Don H. Zimmerman. 1983. "Small Insults: A Study of Interruptions in Cross-Sex Conversations between Unacquainted Persons." In *Language, Gender, and Society,* edited by B. Thorne, C. Kramarae, and N. Henley, 103–17. Rowley, Mass.: Newbury House.

Wierzbicka, Anna. 1994. "Emotion, Language, and Cultural Scripts." In *Emotion and Culture: Empirical Studies of Mutual Influence,* edited by S. Kitamaya and H. R. Markus, 133–95. Washington, D.C.: American Psychological Association.

———. 1999. *Emotions across Languages and Cultures: Diversity and Universals.* Cambridge: Cambridge University Press.

Williams, Raymond. 1976. *Keywords: A Vocabulary of Culture and Society.* London: Fontana.

———. 1977. *Marxism and Literature.* Oxford: Oxford University Press.

Willis, Paul. 1981. *Learning to Labour: How Working Class Kids Get Working Class Jobs.* 1977. Reprint. Westmead: Saxon House.

Wilson, Thomas M., and Hastings Donnan. 1998. "Nation, State, and Identity at International Borders." In *Border Identities and State at International Frontiers,* edited by Thomas M. Wilson and Hastings Donnan, 1–30. Cambridge: Cambridge University Press.

Woolard, Kathryn A. 1998. "Introduction: Language Ideology as a Field of Inquiry." In *Language Ideologies: Practice and Theory,* edited by K. A. Woolard, B. Schieffelin, and P. Kroskrity, 3–47. Oxford: Oxford University Press.

Woolard, Kathryn A., Bambi Schieffelin, and Paul Kroskrity. 1998. *Language Ideologies: Practice and Theory.* Oxford: Oxford University Press.

Yanagisako, Sylvia Junko, and Carol Lowery Delaney. 1995. "Naturalizing Power." In *Naturalizing Power: Essays in Feminist Cultural Analysis,* edited by Carol Lowery Delaney, 1–22. New York: Routledge.

Yengoyan, Aram. 1986. "Theory in Anthropology: On the Demise of the Concept of Culture." *Comparative Studies in Society and History* 24 (2): 368–74.

Zentella, Ana Celia. 1987. "Language and Female Identity in the Puerto Rican Community." In *Women and Language in Transition,* edited by J. Penfield, 167–79. Albany: State University of New York Press.

———. 1997. *Growing Up Bilingual.* Malden, Mass.: Blackwell.

Zentella, Ana Celia, Auris Bourdón, Ida Campanella, Arlene González, Michele Marrero, Elyes Pérez, and Daisy Rosenblum. 1999. "Would You Like Your Children to Speak English and Spanish? ¿Quieren que sus hijos hablen el inglés y el español?" On-line at http://www.hunter.cuny.edu/blpr/bilingualism.html.

Index

Aguilar family, 28, 64–67; Becky (mother), 28; daughter, 28; Pete (father), 28; sons, 28; transcript of household conversation, 133–44

alcohol, teenagers and, 35–36

ambiguity of language socialization, 59–60

Americanized, fear of becoming, 89–90, 180

anthropological study, why children make best theorists, 191–92

Arizona-Mexico border. *See* borderlands

barrio, 17–18; families chosen for study, 20, 39

Barrio Anita (Tucson neighborhood), 28

Barth, Frederick, work on ethnicity, 64

Benavides family: children, 86–87; Maricela, 86–88, 91–92

bilingual, advantages of children being, 194–95

birthdays: becoming too Americanized, 89–90; celebration of, 87–88

borderlands: ambiguity surrounding being Mexican, 57 59, 60; as analytical tool, 12–14; as artificial line, 7–8; contested language ideologies within, 175–78, 194; culture in the, 171–72; defined, 6–7; hegemony and resistance, 8–9, 19; meaning of nationhood, 182–83; as metaphor, 10–14, 195; mystique of Mexicanness, 57–58; nursery rhymes and, 12; schism between immigrant and native-born population, 188–89; Spanish language enjoying a renaissance, 177–78; women of the, 11

bullying, conversation on, 138–39

Catholic Church, role in childhood memories, 82–83, 190

Cheek, Lawrence (author), 9–10

child rearing: bonding with child for life, 149–51; conflicts between mother and grandmother on, 42–43; education, importance of, 85; family get-togethers, importance of, 87–88, 90; religious beliefs playing a part, 36–39, 40; spending time with children, 79; wanting better life for children, 86; views on, 35–36

children: researching for language use, 191; why they make best theorists, 191–92

chupacabra (goat bloodsucker), 199n

Cisneros family, 26–28, 101–105, 149–51; Abelardo (father), 26–27; daughters, 27–28; María del Carmen (mother), 26–27, 149–51; sons, 27

classrooms: immigrant Mexican-origin population and, 188; multicultural awareness programs in, 168–70; power of stories in, 187–88

culture: concept of, 167; identity replacing concept of, 172–73; in the borderlands, 171–72; language and, 173–75; Latinos and, 167–68; multicultural awareness and, 168–70; problems in multicultural awareness programs, 168–70; problem with the term, 175; processual approaches to, 170–71

dances. *See* folклóricos

diminutive, use of between parent and child, 103–105

discipline, views on, 35–36, 42

double helix, metaphor of, 60–63

drugs, worries of parents about children doing, 33–34, 35–36

Durazo, Leticia (*folklórico* teacher), and dance studio, 92–96

economic hardships, impact on parenting, 84

education: importance of, 85; Mexican immigrants in Tucson and, 97–99; multicultural, arguments against, 180; public policy implications of multiculturalism, 180–88

emotional elements, and language socialization, 43–44

emotions and language socialization: ambiguity of, 59; biological nature of, 60–61; brain's role in, 48; can be socially constructed, 46–47; of "Christmas Cheer," 47; cognitive processes and, 46; functionalist Darwinian paradigm and, 46; Mexican-origin children and, 54–56; of minority status, 47–48; part it plays, 45–48, 193; schools of thought on, 46–47; sociohistorically constructed, 47–49

English language: as dominant language in borderlands, 177–78; parent's emphasis on children having skills in, 164–65; as unifying force, 181; as unofficial international language, 131

Escobedo family, 23, 33–37, 154–56; homework conversation, 154–56; 166; Marina (mother), 23; Raul (father), 23; sons, 23

Espinel, Luisa, 9, 67

ethnicity, diacritical features of, 64

evangelical Christians, in study, 36–39, 40

families in language socialization study: Aguilar family, 28, 33–42; Cisneros family, 26–28; Escobedo family, 23, 33–37; Gallardo family, 24–25, 77–82; Gamboa family, 31; Gómez family, 30–31; Linares family, 24; Martínez family, 25–26; methodology used, 19–22, 39; Robles family, 29–30; Salazar family, 28–29, 37–39, 82–86

family get-togethers, importance of, 87–88, 90

family reunions, function of, 88

fathers, role in lives of children, 15

folklóricos (dances), 92–96; dance classes, 92–96, why important cultural function in lives of girls, 92–96

Frederic II (emperor of Rome), 51–52

Fregoso, Rosa Linda, on borderlands, 10

frugality, children adopting practice from mothers, 92

Gallardo family: daughter, 24–25, 78–79; Iris (mother), 24–25, 39, 77–82; Luis (father), 24–25, 78; son, 25, 78–79

Gallego, Soledad, 92

Gamboa family, 31–32; homework conversation, 156–60; Irene (mother), 31–32; Mark (father), 32

gangs, role they play in identity formation, 184

God: conversation regarding, 135–38; imagery of words to describe, 174

Gómez family, 30–31, 132; Herlinda (mother), 31; household conversation, 144–48; Ralph (father), 31; sons, 31

Gómez-Pena, Guillermo, on borderlands, 10–11

González, Norma (author), personal narrative, 3

grandparents, and influence on language use in grandchildren, 42–43, 190

hegemony, 8–9, 19

Hernández, Señora, personal narrative of poverty-stricken life: in English, 107, 108–109, 111–13; in Spanish, 106, 107–108, 110–11, 113–14

homework, 153–64; family conversations on, 154–56, 156–60, 166; helping children find success in school and, 163–64; parent's involvement with, 160–61; structure of conversation and language use, 160–61

hooks, bell (author), quote on social theory, 4

household activities, transmission of knowledge through, 82

household chores, children and, 23, 24, 25, 26, 27; parent's helping with, 163

household language use: breakfast table conversation, 133–44; bullying, conversation on, 138–39; dinner conversation, 144–48; God, conversation on, 135–38; homework and, 153–64; language forms and, 129–30

household living conditions, shifts in, and changes in study subjects, 41–44

identity formation: children exposed to multiple possibilities in, 184–85; importance of language and, 186–87

immigrants of Mexican-origin: children in the classroom, 99–100, 188; cross-border experiences of, 99–103; and Mexican-origin population, 97; views on native Mexican Americans, 189

immigrant women, testimony of harsh life: Señora Hernández, 106–14; Señora Ortiz, 114–25, 137–28

interviewing subjects, problem of
being native anthropologist and,
32

language ideologies: and the borderlands, 176–78; replacing concept of
culture with, 75
language socialization: children learn
differently, 52; and construction of
selfhood, 183–84; discarding of
paradigm, 18–19; emotional elements of, 43–44, 45–48; homework conversations, 153–64; new
paradigm for studying, 17, 191–92;
sociohistoric dialogue, 192–98
language use: and centripetal and
centrifugal forces, 130–31, 148,
188–90; creating social worlds,
174; and culture, 173–75; impact
on school success, 190–92
Latinos: and culture, 167–68; as defined by author, xv-xvi
Legal Alien (Mora), 76
Linares family: Ana María (mother),
24; daughters, 24; Ramón (father),
24
Location of Culture, The (Bhabha),
172
Los Tucsonenses (Sheridan), 4–5

Mariachi Cobre (local Tucson group),
68, 69–70
mariachi music, importance in Tucson Hispanic culture, 69, 70
Martin, Patricia Preciado (author), 8
Martínez family, 25–26; Clara
(mother), 26; daughters, 25–26;
Eddic (father), 26; grandfather, 26;
Oralia Acosta (grandmother), 25;
son, 26

methodology used to study families,
19–22, 39, 41
Mexican Heritage Project, 4
Mexican-origin children: ability to
understand Spanish even if not
fluent, 65–66; classroom behavior
of, 188; and cross-border experiences, 102–103; exposed to multiple possibilities for identity
formation, 184–85; leisure activities and, 23, 24, 26; viewed differently from white counterparts,
196
Mexican-origin households: and the
barrio, 17–18; living under bud-
getary constraints, 79–81; schism
between immigrant population
and, 188–89; school success, emphasis on, 162–63; strong bond between parent and child, 149–51
Mexican-origin parents, and involvement with children once grown,
149–51
Mexicans: mystique of, 58; negative
stereotypes surrounding, 58; in
Tucson, 1900 and 1910, 4–5; in
Tucson, 1990, 5
Mora, Pat (poet), 76
mothers: spending quality time with
children, 79–80; working outside
of home, 29
multilingual: different emotions trig-
gered by use of two languages, 50,
53, 54; versus single language use,
181
music: mariachi, 67–70; songs in
Spanish, children fluent in, 65

nationhood: in borderlands, 182–83;
meaning of, 181–82

native anthropologists, challenges of, 17, 32

newborns: and exposure to human language, 51–52; "failure to thrive" syndrome, 52

nonbarrio, 17; families chosen for study, 20

nursery rhymes, bilingual, children singing, 12

Ortiz, Señora, 114–25, 127–28; personal narrative of poverty-stricken life; in English, 116–18, 120–21, 123–24, 125; in Spanish, 114–16, 119–20, 121–22, 124–25

public schools: complexity of issues facing, 180; embracing diversity, 185; encouraging critical discourse, 186; immigrants perception of, 99; multiculturalism and public policies, 180–88; national identity, formation of, 183

quinceañera (rite of passage for girls), 93

religious influence, on child-rearing, 36, 37–39

rituals and holidays, importance of, 87–91

Robles family, 29–30; Amelia (mother), 29–30; Armando (father), 29–30, 86, 88, 89–91; daughters, 30; grandchildren, 29; son, 30

role models: girls looking to mothers as, 91–92; parents viewed as, 36

Ronstadt, Linda (singer), 9, 67

Salazar family, 28–29, 82–86; daughter; 29, Fernando (father), 28–29; Raquel (mother), 28–29, 37–39, 82–86; sons, 29

school achievement, language use making an impact on, 190–92

Selena (pop star), 95, 138, 153

social capital: defined, 162, 165–66; success in school and, 161–62, 163–64, 165

social class, and household language use, 40–41

socialization of Mexican-origin children, 17

sociolinguistics, and language, 130

Spanish language: enjoying a renaissance with younger Latinos, 177; linguistic insecurity surrounding use of, 176–77; "mock Spanish," 58; telenovelas as source to learn, 151–53; transcript of conversation between mother and child, 104–105

speech habits, 129 30; and everyday household discourse, 132–66

spirituality, impact on lives of study participants, 190

sports activities, 28, 30, 31, 148

students, and culture of academic achievement, 168

study on language socialization, 16–23; confidentiality of data, 22–23; methodology used, 19–22

success in school: culture of Latino students and, 168; high value placed on, 168

Tanner, Deborah (author), on language and gender, 73

teasing, 66–67, 132–33, 148
Teatro Carmen (local Tucson theater), 9
television: as source of Spanish-language input, 151–53; *tele-novelas,* 151–53
traditions, losing, fear on part of older generation, 90
Tucson: ambiguity of being "Mexican," 9–10; Mexicans living in, residential patterns by geographic section, 5

Unz, Ron (chairman of the English for the Children Campaign), 131

violent crime, on Tucson's heavily Hispanic south side, 196–97

women: key roles in raising children, 15; and role in language socialization, 72, 73
women's movement, social history and language, 73–75
words, having power, 174–75

About the Author

Norma González is a Tucson-born and bred applied anthropologist who works in the area of anthropology and education. She received her B.A., M.A., and Ph.D. from the University of Arizona, and she has devoted her research to studying households in the borderlands, language processes, and community and school connections. She is currently an associate professor in the Department of Education, Culture, and Society at the University of Utah.